PowerPoint for Windows 95
VISUAL QUICKSTART GUIDE

VISUAL QUICKSTART GUIDE

PowerPoint
for Windows 95

Rebecca Bridges Altman

Visual QuickStart Guide
PowerPoint for Windows 95
Rebecca Bridges Altman

Peachpit Press
2414 Sixth Street
Berkeley, CA 94710
510/548-4393
510/548-5991 (fax)

Find us on the World Wide Web at: http://www.peachpit.com

Peachpit Press is a division of Addison-Wesley Publishing Company
Copyright © 1995 by Rebecca Bridges Altman

Cover design: The Visual Group

Notice of Rights
All rights reserved. No part of this book may be reproduced or transmitted in any form by any means, electronic, mechanical, photocopying, recording, or otherwise, without the prior written permission of the publisher. For information on getting permission for reprints and excerpts, contact Trish Booth at Peachpit Press.

Notice of Liability
The information in this book is distributed on an "As Is" basis, without warranty. While every precaution has been taken in the preparation of the book, neither the author nor Peachpit Press, shall have any liability to any person or entity with respect to any loss or damage caused or alleged to be caused directly or indirectly by the instructions contained in this book or by the computer software and hardware products described in it.

ISBN 0-201-88431-3

9 8 7 6 5 4 3 2 1

Printed and bound in the United States of America

Printed on recycled paper

Dedication

To my two-year old daughter, Erica, who thought this book was "cute."

Acknowledgments

I'd like to thank the following people for their help with this book:

Jan Altman at Express Train for copy, developmental, and technical editing

Nolan Hester at Peachpit Press for overseeing this book

Roslyn Bullas, also at PeachPit Press

And my husband, **Rick Altman**, for his font and layout expertise.

Table of Contents

Chapter 1   **INTRODUCING POWERPOINT**
Presentation Graphics 2
The PowerPoint Window 4
Key to the PowerPoint Window 5
Mousing Around 6
The Menu, Please 7
Using Shortcut Menus 7
Understanding Drop-Down Menus 8
The File Menu 9
The Edit Menu 10
The View Menu 11
The Insert Menu 11
The Format Menu 12
The Tools Menu 13
The Draw Menu 13
The Window Menu 14
The Help Menu 14
Conversing with Dialog Boxes 15
The Toolbars 16

Chapter 2   **A QUICK TOUR OF POWERPOINT**
About the Tour 17
Launching PowerPoint 17
Choosing a Template 18
Choosing a Layout 19
Creating a Bulleted List 20
Creating a Graph 21
Formatting a Graph 22
Navigating a Presentation 23
Saving, Opening, and Closing Presentations 24
Printing a Presentation 25
Outline View 26
Slide Sorter View 27
Viewing a Slide Show 28

Chapter 3   **CREATING TEXT SLIDES**
About Text Slides 29
Choosing a Text Layout 30

v

TABLE OF CONTENTS

Entering Text into a Placeholder 31
Creating a Text Placeholder 32
Manipulating Text Placeholders 33
Moving Text 34
Using the Spelling Checker 35
Correcting Mistakes Automatically 36
Changing Case 37
Adding Periods 37
Checking for Inconsistent Style 38
Changing Bullets 39
Adjusting Bullet Placement 40
Changing the Font 41
Adding Text Effects and Color 42
Aligning Paragraphs 43
Setting Anchor Points in a Text Placeholder 44
Controlling Line and Paragraph Spacing 45
Copying Formatting Attributes 46

Chapter 4 INSERTING GRAPHS

About Graphs 47
Graph Terminology 48
Inserting a Graph Slide 49
Entering Data 50
Importing Data 51
Linking Data 52
Choosing a Chart Type 53
Inserting Titles 54
Rotating an Axis Title 54
Inserting Data Labels 55
Repositioning Data Labels 55
Revising a Graph 56
Creating Two Graphs on a Slide 57

Chapter 5 FORMATTING GRAPHS

Ways to Format Graphs 59
Formatting the Legend 60
Repositioning the Legend 61
Changing the Color or Pattern of a Data Series 62
Formatting Data Markers 63
Inserting/Removing Gridlines 64
Formatting Gridlines 65
Formatting the Tick Marks 66

	Scaling the Axis	67
	Formatting the Axis Numbers	68
	Formatting Graph Text	69
	Adjusting 3-D Effects	70
	Formatting the Plot Area	71
	Formatting a Graph Automatically	72
	Defining a Custom AutoFormat	73
	Applying a Custom AutoFormat	74

Chapter 6 — CREATING PIE CHARTS

About Pie Charts	75
Inserting a Pie Slide	76
Entering Pie Data	77
Showing Labels, Values, and Percents	78
Formatting Slice Labels	79
Exploding a Slice	80
Coloring the Slices	81
Rotating a Pie	82
Formatting 3-D Effects	83
Resizing and Repositioning a Pie	84
Creating a Doughnut	85
Sizing the Doughnut Hole	85
Creating Two Pies on a Slide	86

Chapter 7 — BUILDING ORGANIZATION CHARTS

About Organization Charts	87
Inserting an Org Chart Slide	88
Entering Text into Boxes	89
Inserting a Box	90
Rearranging Boxes	92
Selecting Boxes	93
Choosing a Style	94
Formatting Box Text	96
Formatting the Boxes	97
Formatting the Lines	98
Zooming In and Out	99
Editing an Existing Org Chart	100

Chapter 8 — CREATING TABLES

About Tables	101
Inserting a Table Slide	102

TABLE OF CONTENTS

Entering Text into a Table 103
Editing an Existing Table 104
Selecting Cells 105
Adjusting Column Widths 106
Adjusting Row Heights 108
Inserting Rows and Columns 109
Deleting Rows and Columns 110
Formatting Text 111
Adding Borders and Shading 112
Aligning Text Within a Cell 114
AutoFormatting a Table 115
Summing Columns 116

Chapter 9 — ADDING GRAPHIC OBJECTS

Types of Graphic Objects 117
Drawing Lines 118
Formatting Lines 119
Drawing Rectangles and Squares 120
Drawing Ellipses and Circles 121
Filling an Object 122
Adding a Drop Shadow 124
Drawing Arcs 125
Creating Polygons and Freehand Drawings 126
Using AutoShapes 127
Inserting Clip Art 128
Searching for Clip Art 129
Using the AutoClipArt Feature 130
Inserting Graphic Files 131
Pasting Graphics 132

Chapter 10 — MANIPULATING GRAPHIC OBJECTS

About Graphic Manipulation 133
Using Rulers and Guides 134
Using Grid Snap 135
Zooming In and Out 136
Displaying a Slide Miniature 137
Aligning Objects 138
Grouping Objects 139
Copying Graphic Attributes 140
Recoloring a Picture 141
Scaling an Object 142
Cropping a Picture 143

TABLE OF CONTENTS

Changing the Stack Order 144
Rotating Objects 145
Flipping Objects 146

Chapter 11 MAKING GLOBAL CHANGES

Formatting a Presentation 147
Changing the Default Colors in a Presentation 148
Creating Color Schemes 149
Creating a Shaded Background 150
Creating a Two-Color Shade 151
Replacing a Font 152
Editing the Slide Master 153
Inserting a Title Master 154
Changing the Default Format for Text 155
Adding Background Items 156
Inserting Footers 157
Applying a Template 158

Chapter 12 WORKING IN OUTLINE VIEW

Introducing Outline View 159
Hiding Text Formatting 160
Collapsing and Expanding the Outline 161
Creating Bulleted Lists 162
Reordering the Slides 163
Outlining a Presentation 165
Importing an Outline 166
Editing an Outline in Word 167

Chapter 13 WORKING IN SLIDE SORTER VIEW

Introducing Slide Sorter View 169
Zooming In and Out 170
Reordering the Slides 171
Copying Slides 172
Moving Slides Between Presentations 173
Copying Slides Between Presentations 174
Inserting an Entire Presentation 175
Deleting Slides 176

ix

TABLE OF CONTENTS

Chapter 14 — **PRODUCING A SLIDE SHOW**
- About Slide Shows 177
- Organizing a Slide Show 178
- Displaying a Slide Show 179
- Using the Slide Navigator 180
- Branching to Other Slides 181
- Annotating a Slide 182
- Hiding a Slide 183
- Adding a Transition Effect to a Slide 184
- Creating a Self-Running Slide Show 186
- Rehearsing the Slide Show 187
- Creating a Build for a Bullet Slide 188
- Animating Objects 190
- Inserting Movie Clips 191
- Adding Sound 192
- Creating Meeting Minutes 194
- Creating an Action Item List 195
- Giving Your Presentation on Another Computer 196
- Giving a Slide Show: The Easy Way 198

Chapter 15 — **PRESENTATION OUTPUT**
- Types of Output 199
- Selecting a Printer 200
- Setting the Slide Size for Printing 200
- Previewing Slides in Black and White 201
- Printing Slides 202
- Stopping a Print Job 203
- Printing the Outline 204
- Adding Notes 206
- Editing the Notes Master 207
- Printing Notes Pages 208
- Formatting Handout Pages 209
- Printing Handouts 210
- Creating Handouts with Notes 211
- Producing 35mm Slides 212
- Sending Slides to Genigraphics 214

INDEX 215

INTRODUCING POWERPOINT

Introduction

Visual QuickStart Guides offer a unique way to learn a software package. For the most part, each page is self-contained with a single topic. Each page has concise step-by-step instructions on how to perform a certain task and is accompanied by illustrations and explanatory captions. This type of organization makes it less overwhelming to learn an extensive program such as PowerPoint, and allows you to master just the features you need to.

At the end of each topic, you'll find a list of helpful tips. These tips provide you with shortcuts, alternate techniques, additional information, and related topics. Some of these tips are undocumented or buried so deep in the documentation that it's unlikely you would ever find them.

Time permitting, you may want to read the book cover-to-cover, but in all likelihood, you will probably just turn to a specific chapter or topic you want to learn. And the way this book is organized, you will be able to do so quickly and efficiently.

For those who are new to the Windows environment, it is especially important to go through Chapter 1 carefully. This chapter covers the basics of using a mouse, as well as working with menus, dialog boxes, and toolbars.

Chapter 2 is a great way to learn the main features of PowerPoint, especially if you have a presentation that needed to be out the door yesterday.

Chapters 3 through 11 explain how to create different types of slides (bulleted lists, graphs, tables, and organization charts) and format your presentations. Chapters 12 and 13 illustrate two additional ways to view and organize presentations: Outline view and Slide Sorter view. Chapters 14 and 15 show you different ways to output your presentation: on screen in a slide show, in printed form, and in 35mm slides.

What's New in PowerPoint for Windows 95

The latest version of PowerPoint works under the new Microsoft operating system, Windows 95. Here are some of the new features that have been added to PowerPoint (and are covered in this book):

- Automatic footers containing the date, customizable text, and/or page numbers.
- A Style Checker that looks for style inconsistencies in a presentation.
- An AutoCorrect feature that corrects mistakes as you type.
- A miniature of the current slide on the screen, so you can see the overall layout no matter what the zoom factor.
- A black-and-white view.
- A Slide Navigator to jump around to different slides during a slide show.
- Slide shows that include movie clips, sound bites, and/or animated objects.
- Branching to other slides during a slide show by clicking on a designated object.
- Handouts that include speaker notes or lines for note-taking.

CHAPTER 1

Presentation Graphics

What exactly can presentation graphics software do? This type of software provides you with tools for creating slides formatted with a variety of different elements, such as: bulleted lists, numerical tables, organization charts, and business graphs (pies, bars, lines, and more).

You also get tools for adding graphic elements to your slides. For example, you can create designs for the background of your slide using the Rectangle, Ellipse, Arc, and Line tools. But don't worry if you aren't artistically inclined—you can always insert a ready-made drawing from the clip art library, or use a professionally designed template (Figure 1).

You might be thinking, "Hey, I can create bulleted lists and tables in my word processor, business graphs in my spreadsheet program, and nice art with my drawing package. Why, then, would I need a presentation graphics package?"

There are three good reasons. First, as its name implies, this type of software *presents graphics*. You can present the graphics in a variety of ways:

- In an onscreen slide show (complete with special transition effects)
- On paper (one per page, or several per page for audience handouts)
- On 35mm slides

Second, a presentation graphics package can bring all the components of a presentation together, into a single file. You can use it to create the slides, or, if you prefer, you can import elements from other programs into slides in the presentation graphics program.

Third, the software offers convenient ways to organize the presentation. Using the Outline (Figure 2) or Slide Sorter views (Figure 3), you can see the structure of the presentation and reorganize the slides, if necessary. Changing the order of the slides is a snap in these two special views.

As you can see, there are quite a few advantages to creating your presentations in a presentation graphics package, and PowerPoint for Windows 95 is an excellent choice for these tasks.

Figure 1. The confetti on this slide was produced by applying a professionally designed template.

INTRODUCING POWERPOINT

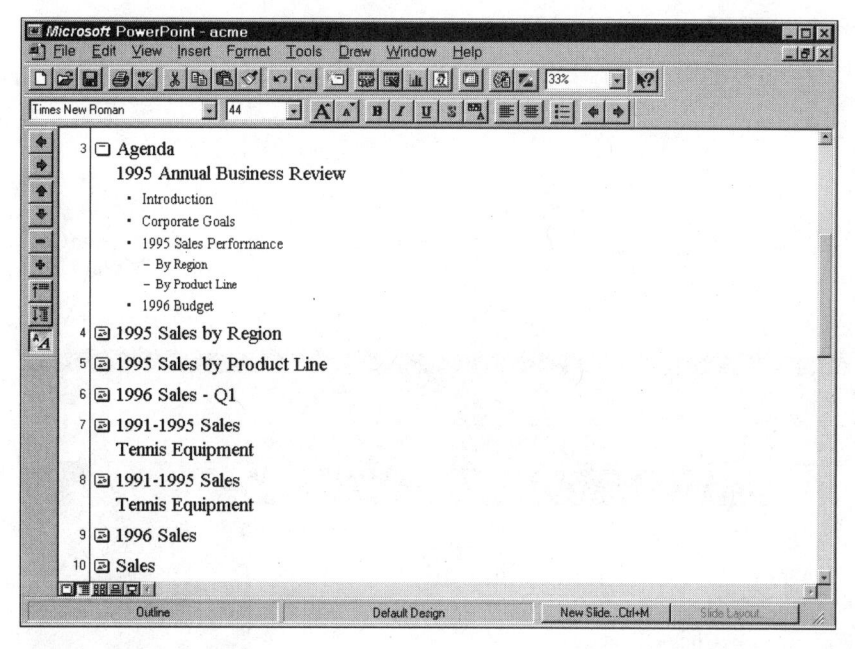

Figure 2. Outline view shows the structure of your presentation, letting you easily reorganize the presentation if necessary.

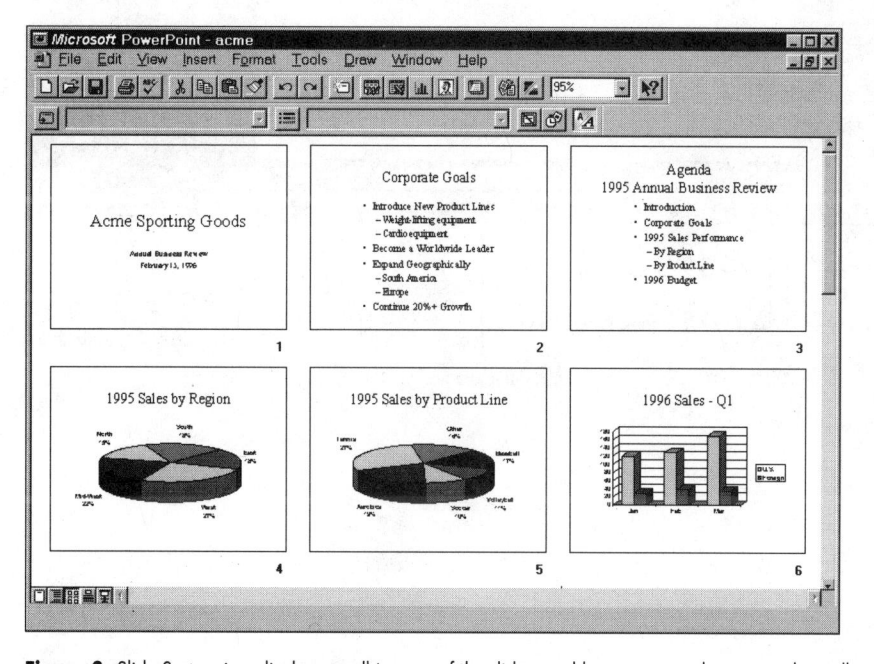

Figure 3. Slide Sorter view displays small images of the slides, and lets you move them around at will.

CHAPTER 1

The PowerPoint Window

Figure 4. Here are the important areas of the PowerPoint window. For further details on any of these areas, refer to the numbered key on the opposite page.

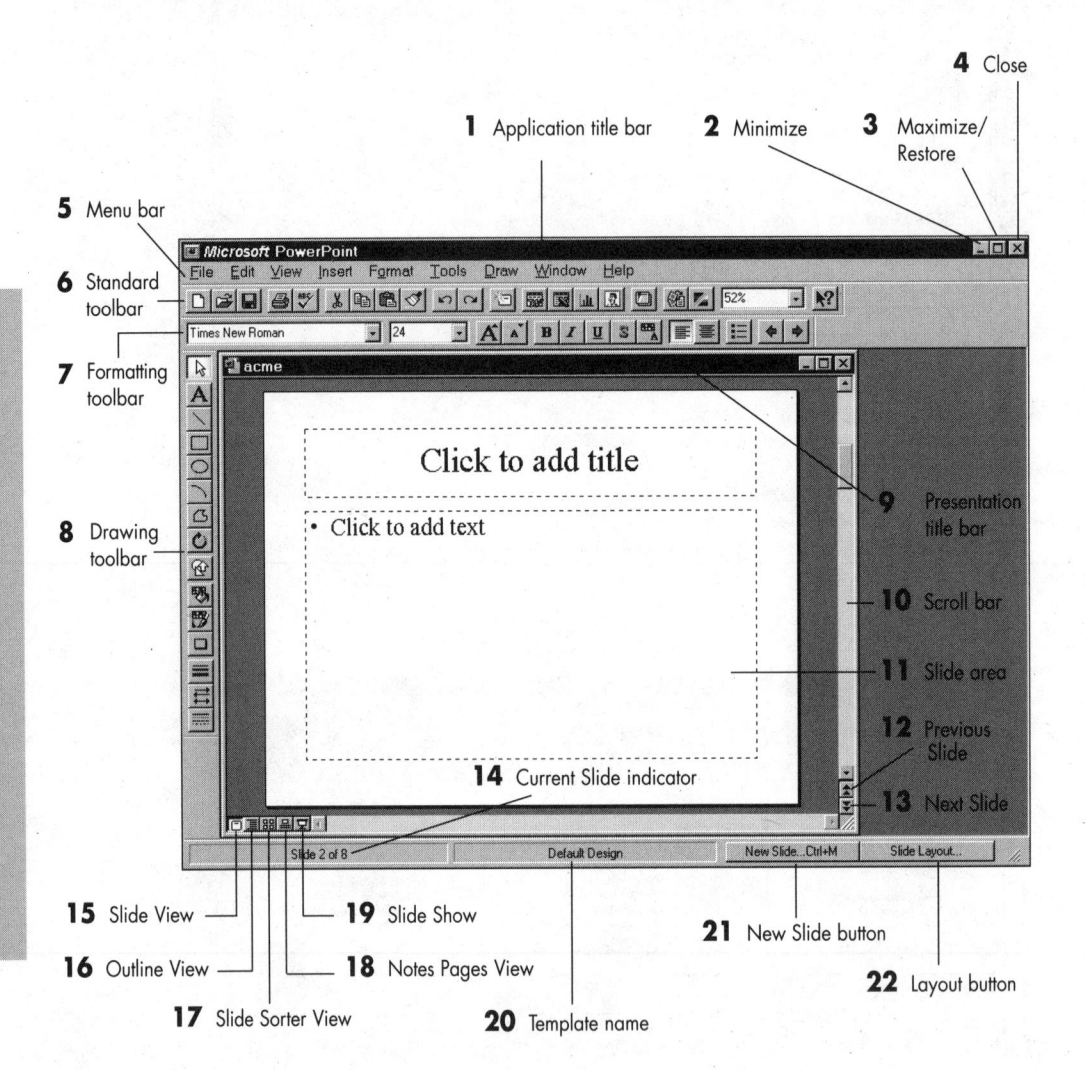

1 Application title bar
2 Minimize
3 Maximize/Restore
4 Close
5 Menu bar
6 Standard toolbar
7 Formatting toolbar
8 Drawing toolbar
9 Presentation title bar
10 Scroll bar
11 Slide area
12 Previous Slide
13 Next Slide
14 Current Slide indicator
15 Slide View
16 Outline View
17 Slide Sorter View
18 Notes Pages View
19 Slide Show
20 Template name
21 New Slide button
22 Layout button

Introducing PowerPoint

Key to the PowerPoint Window

1 Application title bar
Displays the name of the current application (Microsoft PowerPoint).

2 Minimize button
Shrinks the application to a button on the taskbar.

3 Maximize/Restore button
Enlarges the window so that it fills the screen, or restores the window to its previous size.

4 Close button
Closes the window.

5 Menu bar
The main menu of choices. Clicking on a menu item displays a drop-down menu.

6 Standard toolbar
Contains buttons for frequently used tasks, such as opening, saving, and printing.

7 Formatting toolbar
Contains buttons for formatting text.

8 Drawing toolbar
Contains buttons for drawing and formatting objects.

9 Presentation title bar
Shows the name of the current presentation.

10 Scroll bar
Displays other slides in the presentation.

11 Slide area
The work area where you create, format, and modify the slide elements.

12 Previous Slide button
Displays the previous slide in the presentation.

13 Next Slide button
Displays the next slide in the presentation.

14 Current Slide indicator
Indicates the number of the slide currently on the screen.

15 Slide View button
Displays a single slide in the presentation window.

16 Outline View button
Displays an outline of the presentation (slide titles and main text).

17 Slide Sorter View button
Displays miniature versions of each slide, allowing you to see many slides at once.

18 Notes Pages View button
Displays speaker notes pages, allowing you to type notes about the slide. These notes can be printed and referred to during a slide show.

19 Slide Show button
Presents the slides one at a time in an onscreen slide show.

20 Template name
Name of the current template (design). Double-clicking this area lets you apply another template.

21 New Slide button
Inserts a new slide after the current slide.

22 Layout button
Allows you to change the layout of the current slide.

CHAPTER 1

Mousing Around

Until you've used the mouse for a while, you are likely to feel awkward and uncoordinated; that clumsy feeling is perfectly normal. With practice, though, using the mouse will become as natural as using the keyboard. Here are a few techniques that every "mouser" needs to know.

Click

Clicking is used to select menu items, make selections in dialog boxes, and choose toolbar buttons.

Move the mouse until the mouse pointer is on the object you want to click and tap the *left* mouse button. When you click the *right* mouse button, a shortcut menu displays.

See opposite page for more information on the shortcut menu.

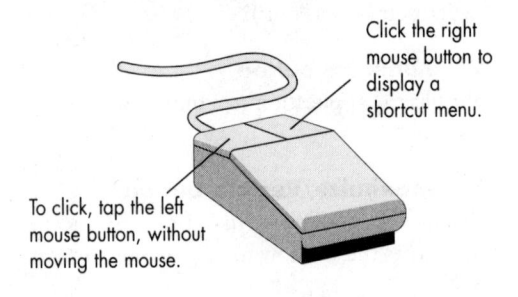

Click the right mouse button to display a shortcut menu.

To click, tap the left mouse button, without moving the mouse.

Double-Click

Double-clicking is used to open folders and run shortcut icons. You can also double-click an item in a dialog box (such as a file name); this action selects the item and closes the dialog box.

Place the mouse pointer on the object and press the left mouse button twice quickly. The proper speed at which you need to make the two clicks depends on your system; you may need to practice double-clicking several times until you get the feel for it.

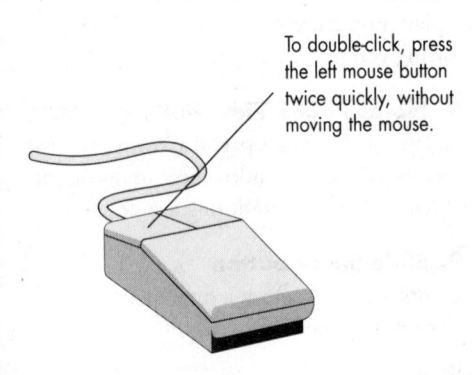

To double-click, press the left mouse button twice quickly, without moving the mouse.

Click and Drag

Dragging is used to move an object from one place to another, or to select a block of text.

Place the mouse pointer on the object you want to move or select. Press and *hold down* the left mouse button as you move the mouse in the direction you want to move the object, or across the passage of text you want to select. Release the mouse button when you are finished.

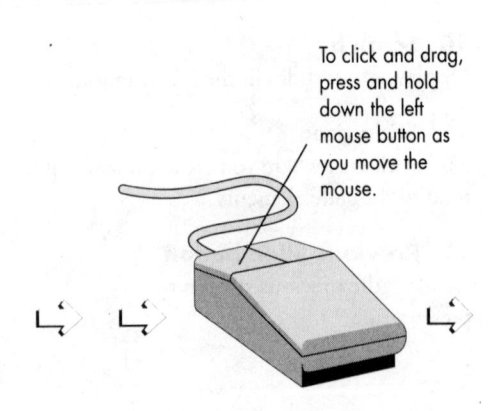

To click and drag, press and hold down the left mouse button as you move the mouse.

Introducing PowerPoint

6

The Menu, Please

PowerPoint uses the standard Windows conventions for accessing menus. Figure 5 describes these conventions.

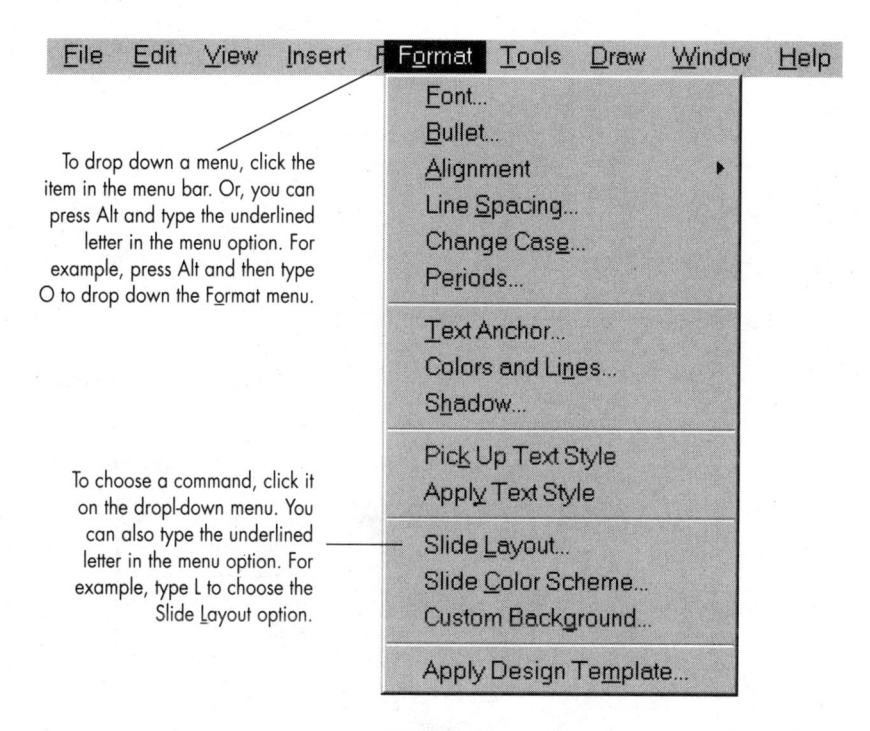

To drop down a menu, click the item in the menu bar. Or, you can press Alt and type the underlined letter in the menu option. For example, press Alt and then type O to drop down the Format menu.

To choose a command, click it on the dropl-down menu. You can also type the underlined letter in the menu option. For example, type L to choose the Slide Layout option.

Figure 5. Ways to access menu commands

Using Shortcut Menus

A shortcut menu lists the most common commands pertaining to a particular object. Options on a shortcut menu vary depending on what you're pointing to. If you're not pointing to anything in particulr, a menu with options for formatting your presentation will appear.

Figure 6 shows the shortcut menu that is displayed when a graphic object (the star) is selected.

First, point to an object.

Then, click the right mouse button to display a shortcut menu.

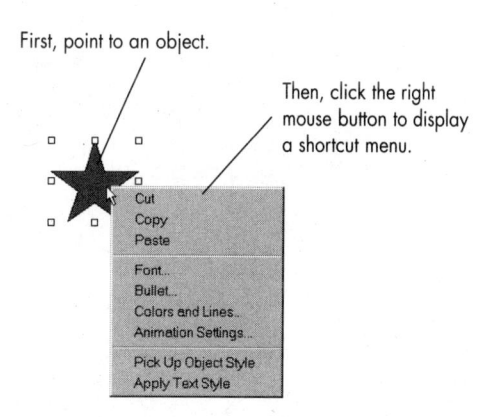

Figure 6. The shortcut menu for a graphic object

CHAPTER 1

Understanding Drop-Down Menus

Figure 7 below explains the different types of commands you'll find on a drop-down menu. In Figures 8 through 16 you'll find descriptions of the commands on all of PowerPoint's menus.

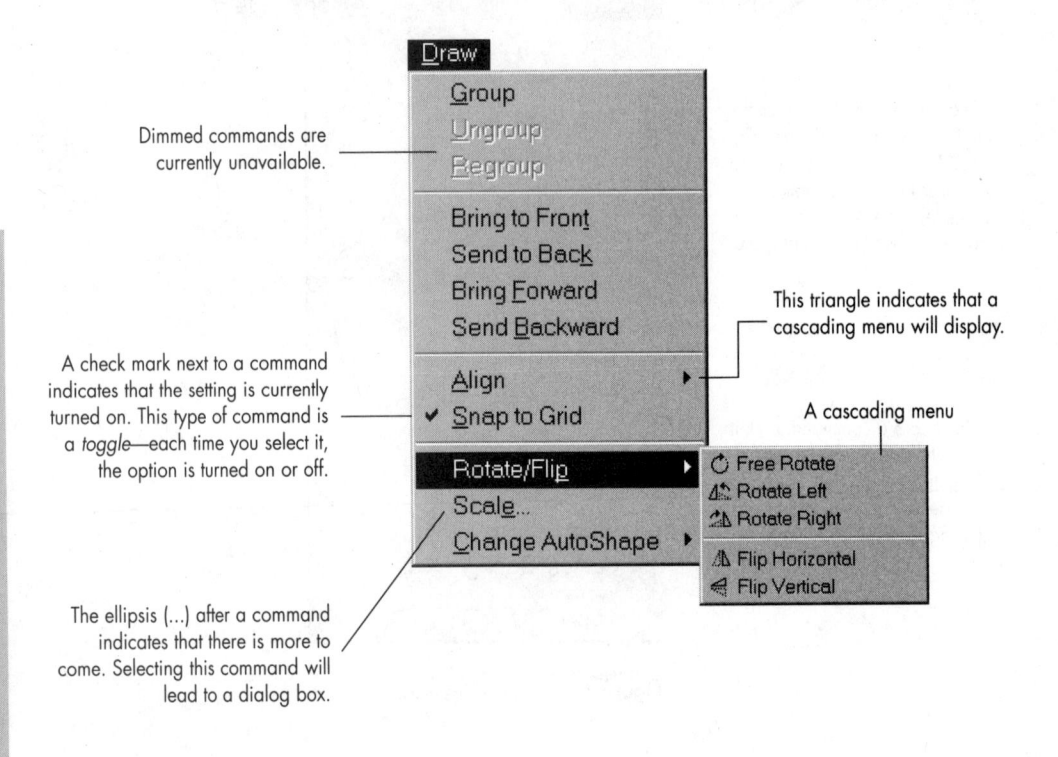

Dimmed commands are currently unavailable.

A check mark next to a command indicates that the setting is currently turned on. This type of command is a *toggle*—each time you select it, the option is turned on or off.

This triangle indicates that a cascading menu will display.

A cascading menu

The ellipsis (...) after a command indicates that there is more to come. Selecting this command will lead to a dialog box.

Figure 7. The elements of a menu

Introducing PowerPoint

8

INTRODUCING POWERPOINT

The File Menu

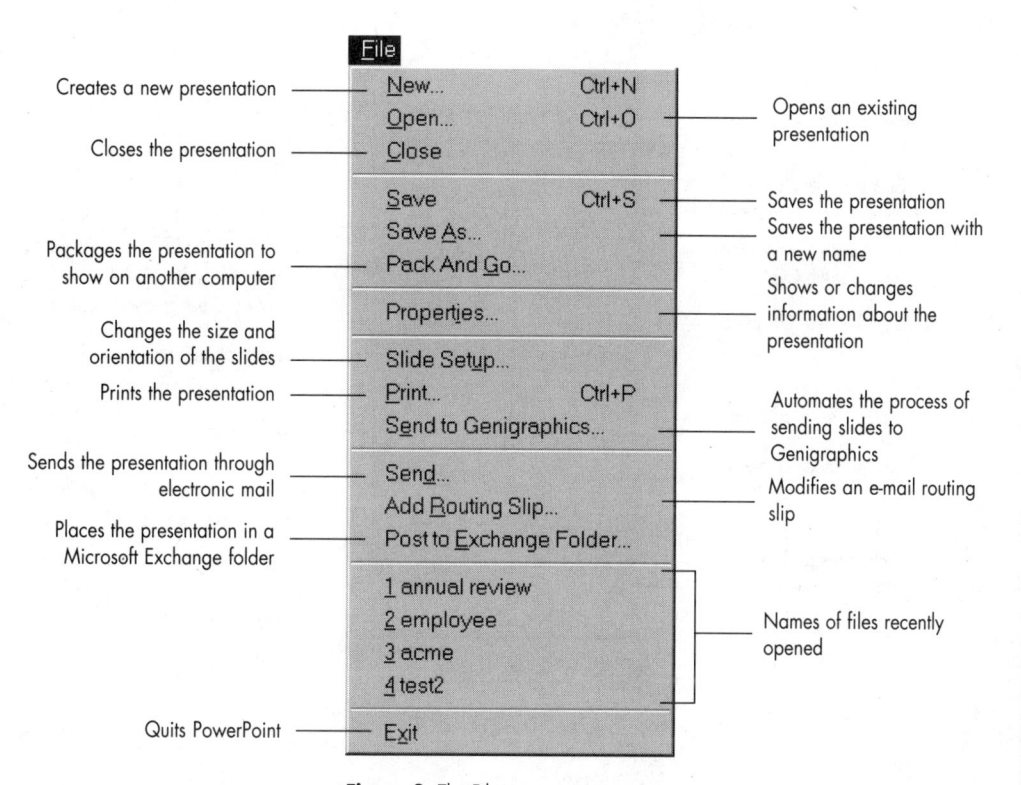

Creates a new presentation — New... Ctrl+N
Opens an existing presentation — Open... Ctrl+O
Closes the presentation — Close

Save Ctrl+S — Saves the presentation
Save As... — Saves the presentation with a new name
Packages the presentation to show on another computer — Pack And Go...

Properties... — Shows or changes information about the presentation
Changes the size and orientation of the slides — Slide Setup...
Prints the presentation — Print... Ctrl+P
Send to Genigraphics... — Automates the process of sending slides to Genigraphics
Sends the presentation through electronic mail — Send...
Add Routing Slip... — Modifies an e-mail routing slip
Places the presentation in a Microsoft Exchange folder — Post to Exchange Folder...

1 annual review
2 employee — Names of files recently opened
3 acme
4 test2

Quits PowerPoint — Exit

Figure 8. The File menu

CHAPTER 1

The Edit Menu

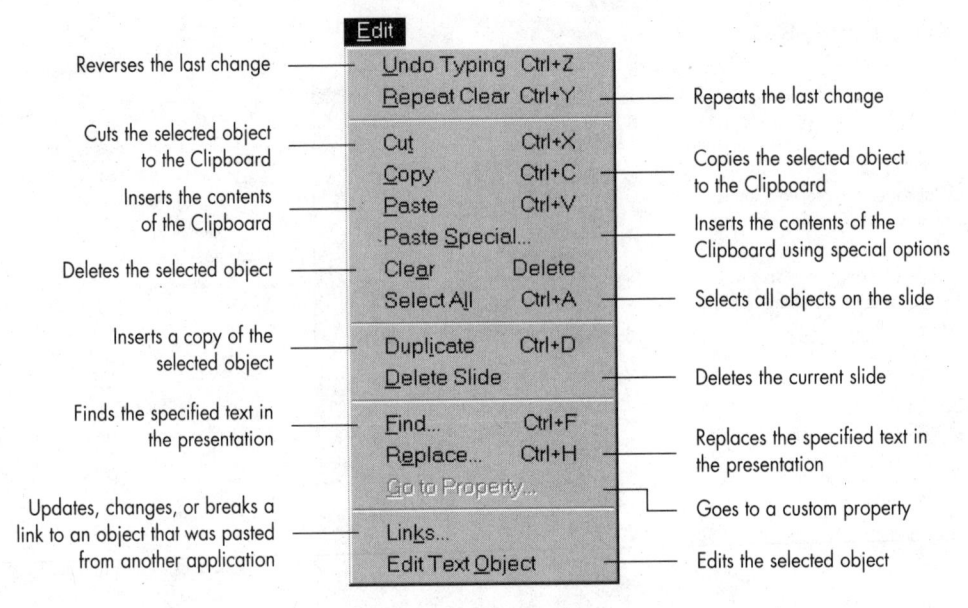

Label (left)	Menu item	Label (right)
Reverses the last change	Undo Typing Ctrl+Z	
	Repeat Clear Ctrl+Y	Repeats the last change
Cuts the selected object to the Clipboard	Cut Ctrl+X	
	Copy Ctrl+C	Copies the selected object to the Clipboard
Inserts the contents of the Clipboard	Paste Ctrl+V	
	Paste Special...	Inserts the contents of the Clipboard using special options
Deletes the selected object	Clear Delete	
	Select All Ctrl+A	Selects all objects on the slide
Inserts a copy of the selected object	Duplicate Ctrl+D	
	Delete Slide	Deletes the current slide
Finds the specified text in the presentation	Find... Ctrl+F	
	Replace... Ctrl+H	Replaces the specified text in the presentation
	Go to Property...	Goes to a custom property
Updates, changes, or breaks a link to an object that was pasted from another application	Links...	
	Edit Text Object	Edits the selected object

Figure 9. The Edit menu

INTRODUCING POWERPOINT

The View Menu

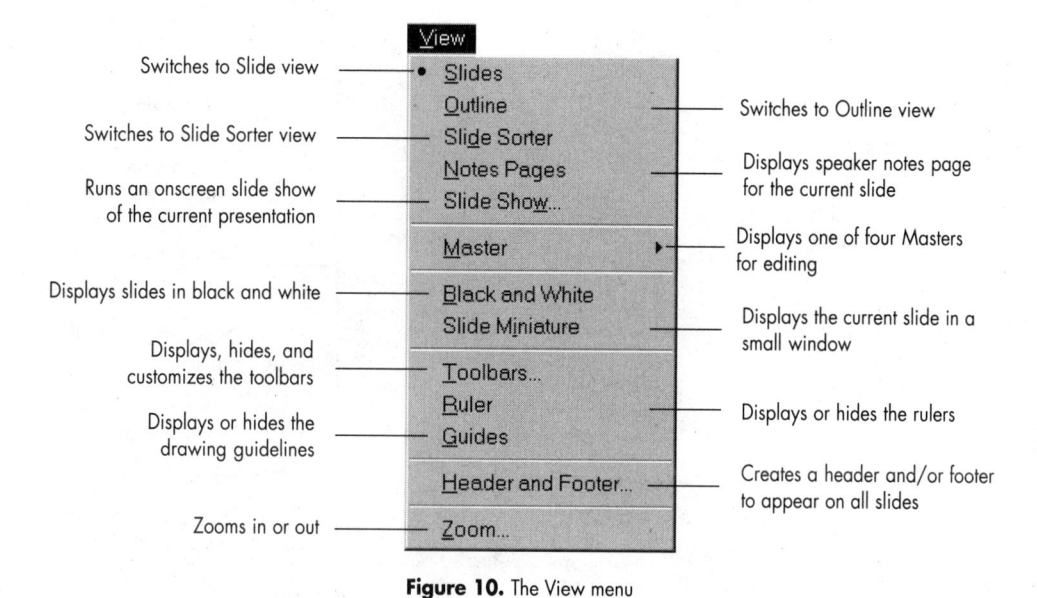

Switches to Slide view — Slides
 — Outline — Switches to Outline view
Switches to Slide Sorter view — Slide Sorter
 — Notes Pages — Displays speaker notes page for the current slide
Runs an onscreen slide show of the current presentation — Slide Show...
 — Master — Displays one of four Masters for editing
Displays slides in black and white — Black and White
 — Slide Miniature — Displays the current slide in a small window
Displays, hides, and customizes the toolbars — Toolbars...
 — Ruler — Displays or hides the rulers
Displays or hides the drawing guidelines — Guides
 — Header and Footer... — Creates a header and/or footer to appear on all slides
Zooms in or out — Zoom...

Figure 10. The View menu

The Insert Menu

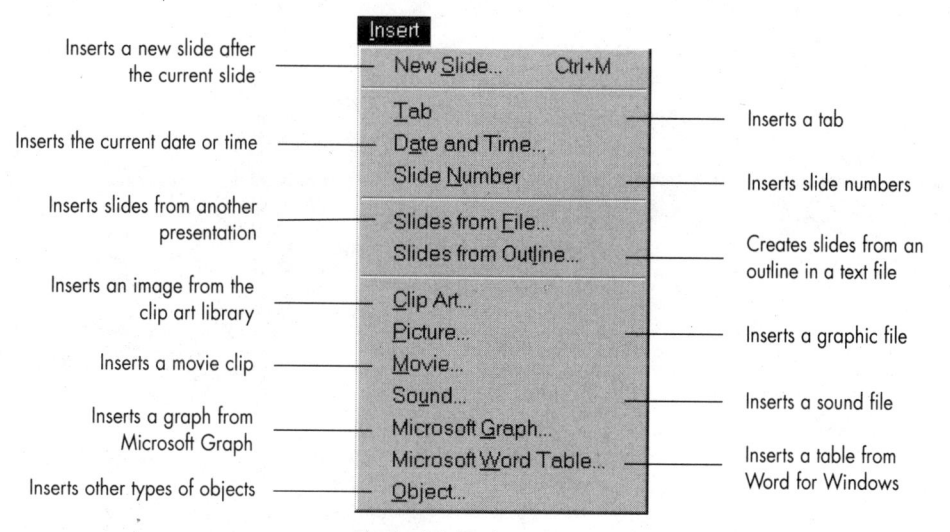

Inserts a new slide after the current slide — New Slide... Ctrl+M
 — Tab — Inserts a tab
Inserts the current date or time — Date and Time...
 — Slide Number — Inserts slide numbers
Inserts slides from another presentation — Slides from File...
 — Slides from Outline... — Creates slides from an outline in a text file
Inserts an image from the clip art library — Clip Art...
 — Picture... — Inserts a graphic file
Inserts a movie clip — Movie...
 — Sound... — Inserts a sound file
Inserts a graph from Microsoft Graph — Microsoft Graph...
 — Microsoft Word Table... — Inserts a table from Word for Windows
Inserts other types of objects — Object...

Figure 11. The Insert menu

11

CHAPTER 1

The Format Menu

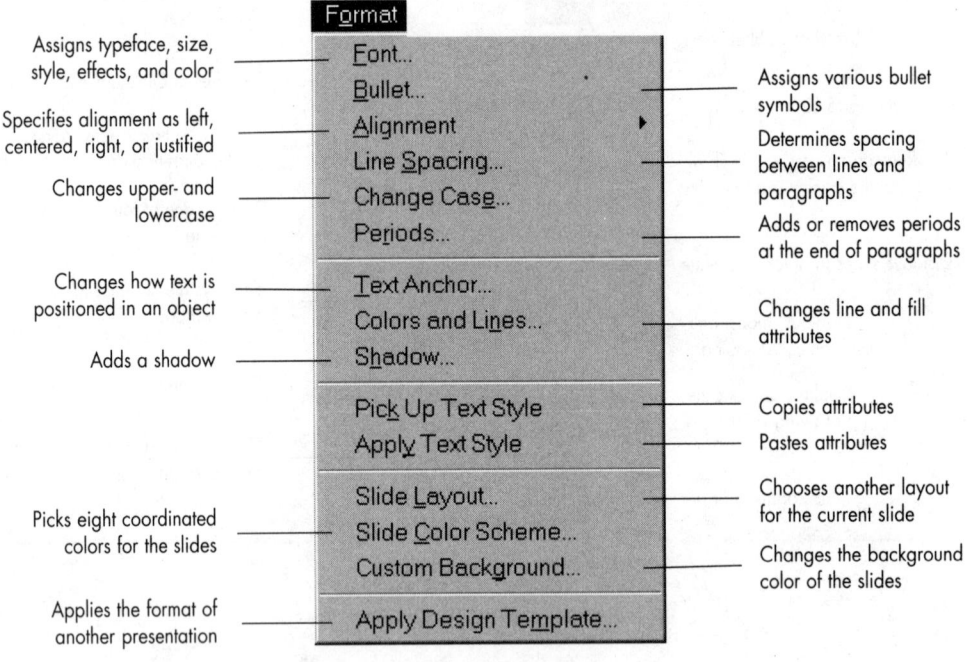

	Format menu item	
Assigns typeface, size, style, effects, and color	Font...	
	Bullet...	Assigns various bullet symbols
Specifies alignment as left, centered, right, or justified	Alignment ▶	
	Line Spacing...	Determines spacing between lines and paragraphs
Changes upper- and lowercase	Change Case...	
	Periods...	Adds or removes periods at the end of paragraphs
Changes how text is positioned in an object	Text Anchor...	
	Colors and Lines...	Changes line and fill attributes
Adds a shadow	Shadow...	
	Pick Up Text Style	Copies attributes
	Apply Text Style	Pastes attributes
	Slide Layout...	Chooses another layout for the current slide
Picks eight coordinated colors for the slides	Slide Color Scheme...	
	Custom Background...	Changes the background color of the slides
Applies the format of another presentation	Apply Design Template...	

Figure 12. The Format menu

INTRODUCING POWERPOINT

The Tools Menu

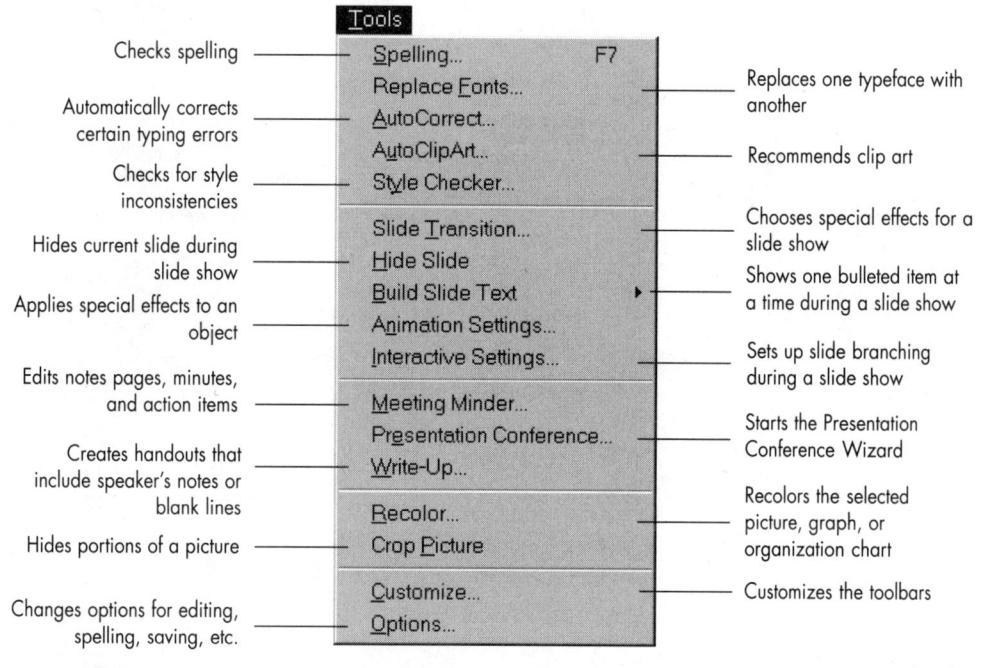

Checks spelling — Spelling... F7
Replace Fonts... — Replaces one typeface with another
Automatically corrects certain typing errors — AutoCorrect...
AutoClipArt... — Recommends clip art
Checks for style inconsistencies — Style Checker...
Slide Transition... — Chooses special effects for a slide show
Hides current slide during slide show — Hide Slide
Build Slide Text — Shows one bulleted item at a time during a slide show
Applies special effects to an object — Animation Settings...
Interactive Settings... — Sets up slide branching during a slide show
Edits notes pages, minutes, and action items — Meeting Minder...
Presentation Conference... — Starts the Presentation Conference Wizard
Creates handouts that include speaker's notes or blank lines — Write-Up...
Recolor... — Recolors the selected picture, graph, or organization chart
Hides portions of a picture — Crop Picture
Customize... — Customizes the toolbars
Changes options for editing, spelling, saving, etc. — Options...

Figure 13. The Tools menu

The Draw Menu

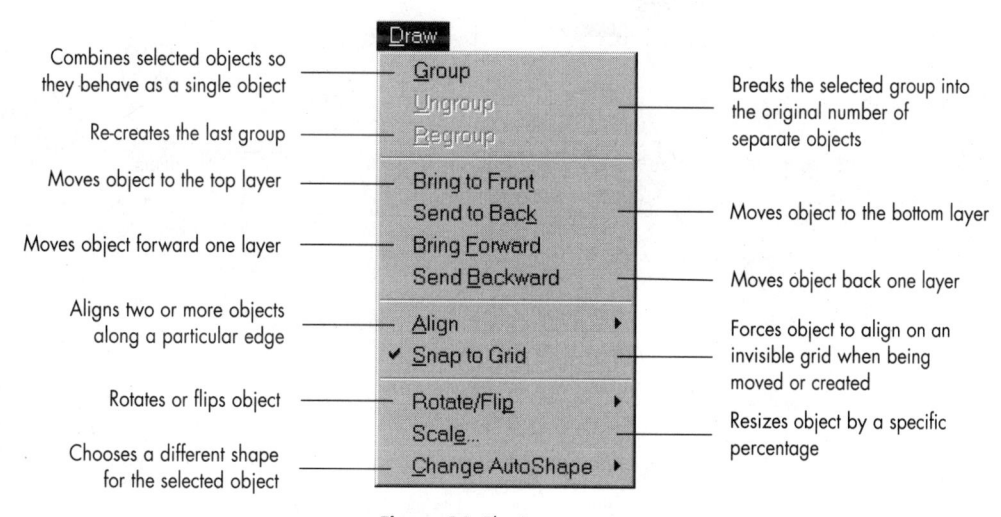

Combines selected objects so they behave as a single object — Group
Ungroup — Breaks the selected group into the original number of separate objects
Re-creates the last group — Regroup
Moves object to the top layer — Bring to Front
Send to Back — Moves object to the bottom layer
Moves object forward one layer — Bring Forward
Send Backward — Moves object back one layer
Aligns two or more objects along a particular edge — Align
Snap to Grid — Forces object to align on an invisible grid when being moved or created
Rotates or flips object — Rotate/Flip
Scale... — Resizes object by a specific percentage
Chooses a different shape for the selected object — Change AutoShape

Figure 14. The Draw menu

13

CHAPTER 1

The Window Menu

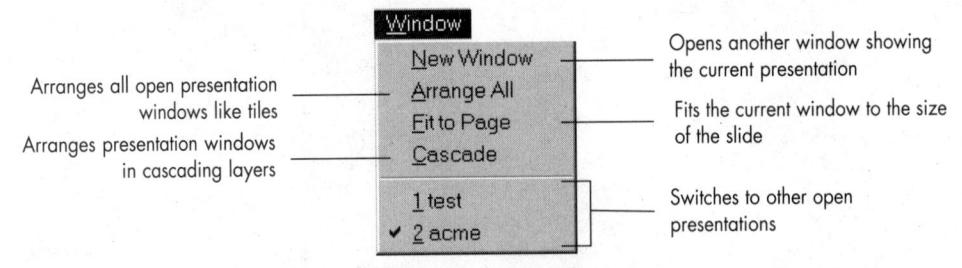

Figure 15. The Window menu

- Arranges all open presentation windows like tiles — Arrange All
- Arranges presentation windows in cascading layers — Cascade
- New Window — Opens another window showing the current presentation
- Fit to Page — Fits the current window to the size of the slide
- 1 test / 2 acme — Switches to other open presentations

The Help Menu

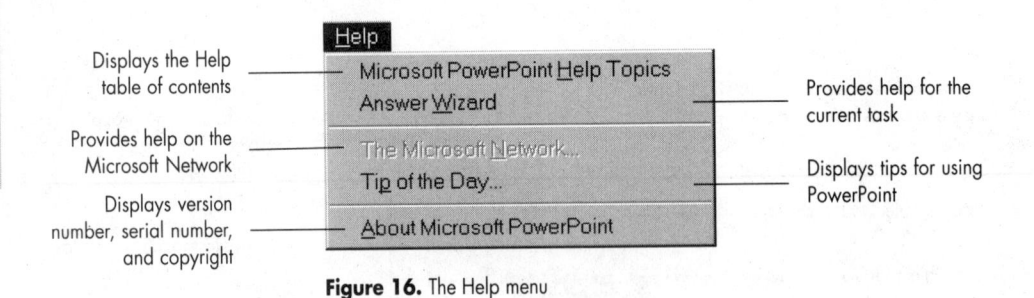

Figure 16. The Help menu

- Displays the Help table of contents — Microsoft PowerPoint Help Topics
- Provides help on the Microsoft Network — The Microsoft Network...
- Displays version number, serial number, and copyright — About Microsoft PowerPoint
- Answer Wizard — Provides help for the current task
- Tip of the Day... — Displays tips for using PowerPoint

INTRODUCING POWERPOINT

Conversing with Dialog Boxes

Figures 17 and 18 point out the various types of options found in dialog boxes.

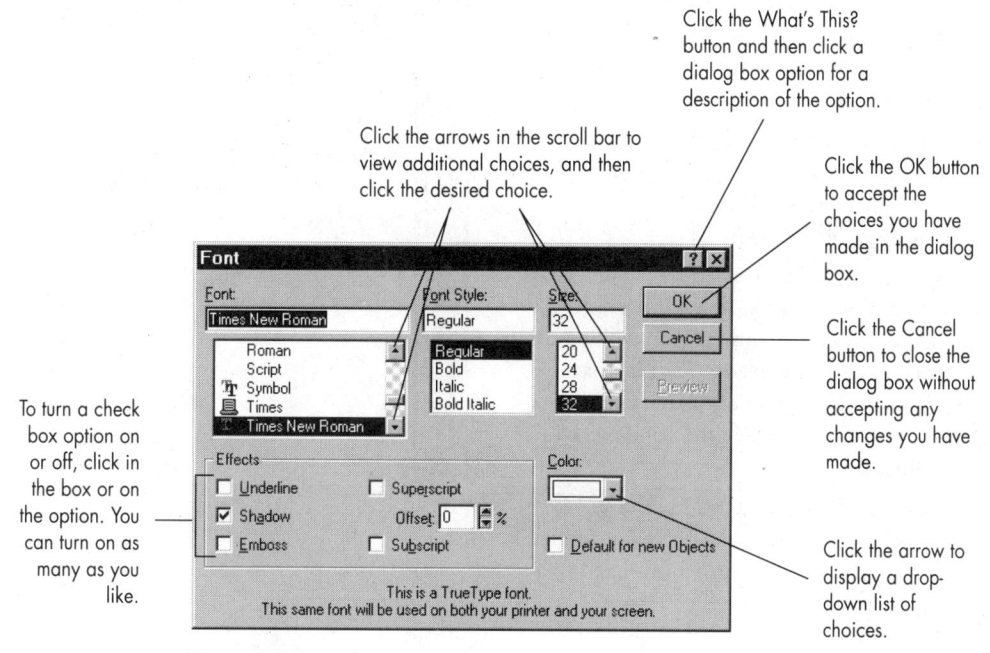

Click the arrows in the scroll bar to view additional choices, and then click the desired choice.

Click the What's This? button and then click a dialog box option for a description of the option.

Click the OK button to accept the choices you have made in the dialog box.

To turn a check box option on or off, click in the box or on the option. You can turn on as many as you like.

Click the Cancel button to close the dialog box without accepting any changes you have made.

Click the arrow to display a drop-down list of choices.

Figure 17. Dialog box options

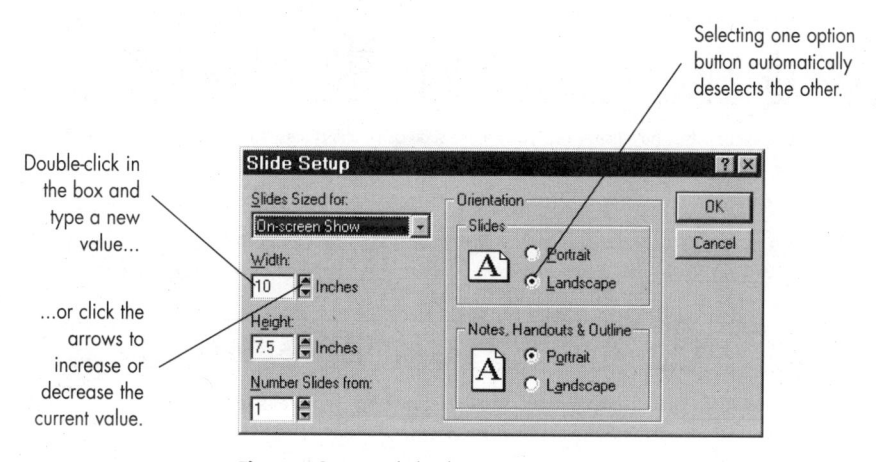

Selecting one option button automatically deselects the other.

Double-click in the box and type a new value...

...or click the arrows to increase or decrease the current value.

Figure 18. More dialog box options

15

CHAPTER 1

The Toolbars

The toolbars contain buttons that offer shortcuts for common PowerPoint commands. Instead of choosing a command from a menu, you can simply click the appropriate button on the toolbar.

By default, three toolbars are displayed in Slide view: the Drawing toolbar (Figure 19), the Standard toolbar (Figure 20), and the Formatting toolbar (Figure 21).

To find out what a particular button does, place the mouse pointer on the button. (Do not actually click the button.) You will see a little yellow bubble (called a *ToolTip*) that gives a short description of the button; the status bar at the bottom of the window gives a lengthier description.

To display and hide toolbars, use the View/Toolbars command. Use the Tools/Customize command to add and remove buttons from a toolbar.

Figure 19. The Drawing toolbar offers buttons for creating, manipulating, and formatting objects (such as lines, boxes, and circles).

Figure 20. The Standard toolbar offers buttons for everyday tasks such as opening files, saving files, printing, editing, and so forth.

Figure 21. The Formatting toolbar makes it easy to format text with a different typeface, size, or style.

A QUICK TOUR OF POWERPOINT

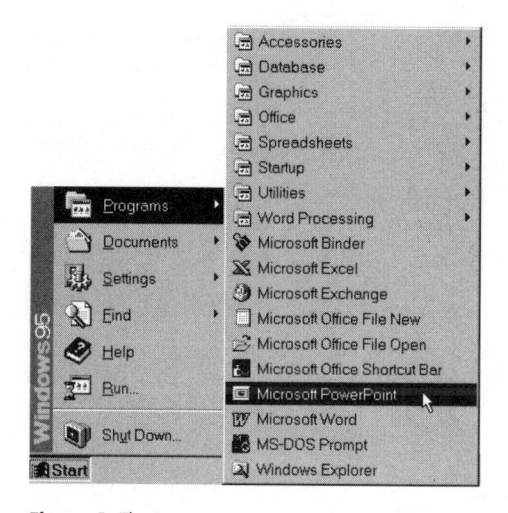

Figure 1. The Programs menu

Figure 2. The Office shortcut bar

About the Tour

Suppose you need to create a set of charts by the end of the day, but you have never used PowerPoint. What will you do? Don't panic—just read this chapter. We understand that in today's busy world, people may not have time to read an entire book before they dive into a real-life project. But by reading this chapter, you'll learn the most important things you need to know about creating a presentation in PowerPoint for Windows.

After reading this chapter, you will be able to create bullet lists and graphs, format the slides, print the slides, view an onscreen slide show, and use Outline and Slide Sorter views to reorganize the presentation. This chapter gives you the bare bones information; for details, turn to the referenced chapters.

Launching PowerPoint

There are a number of ways to launch PowerPoint, depending on how your system is set up. Here are two possible ways:

> Click the Start button, point to Programs, and click Microsoft PowerPoint (Figure 1).
>
> *or*
>
> Click the PowerPoint icon in the Office shortcut bar (Figure 2).

■ Tip

✓ On your system, a shortcut to PowerPoint may be in a folder called *Office*. Look for this folder on your desktop or on your Programs menu.

17

CHAPTER 2

Choosing a Template

A *template* controls the overall look of your presentation—the colors, the format of the text, graphics placed on each slide, and so forth. PowerPoint comes with 60 templates.

1. If the opening dialog box (Figure 3) is displayed, choose Template and click OK.

   or

   If the opening box is not displayed, choose File/New.

2. Click the Presentation Designs tab (Figure 4).

3. Click the List button to see more template names at once.

4. Click a template name and look at the preview box to see what this design looks like.

5. When you find a template you like, click OK.

To learn more about templates, see page 158.

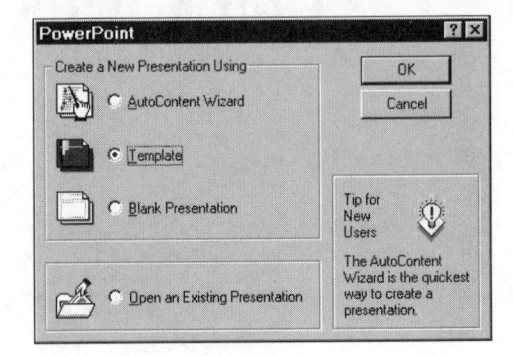

Figure 3. The opening dialog box that displays after launching PowerPoint for Windows

Click the Presentation Designs tab to see the template names.

Click a file name to preview the template.

List button

Preview box

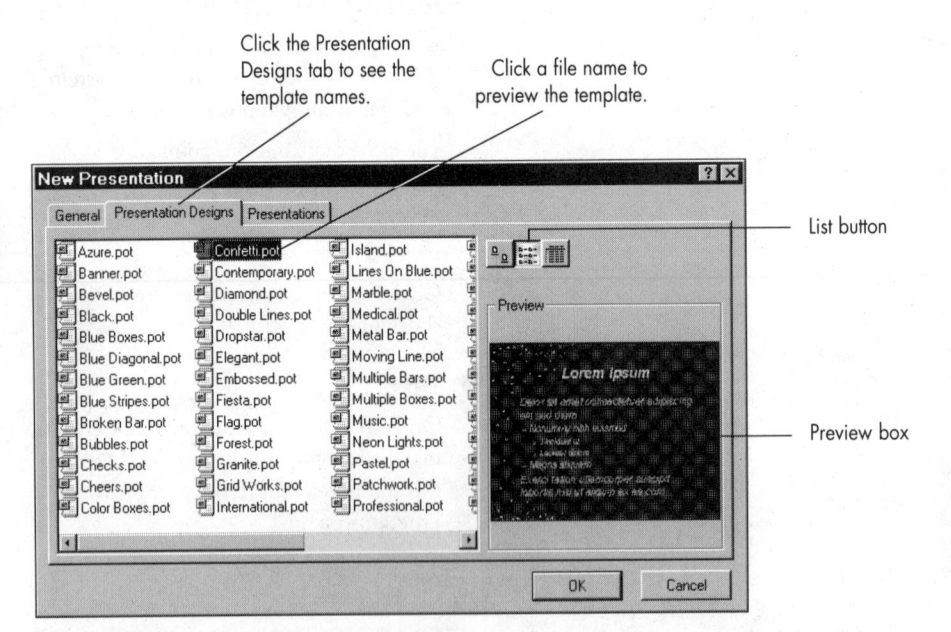

Figure 4. Choosing a template for a new presentation

18

Click a layout... ...to display a description of the layout here.

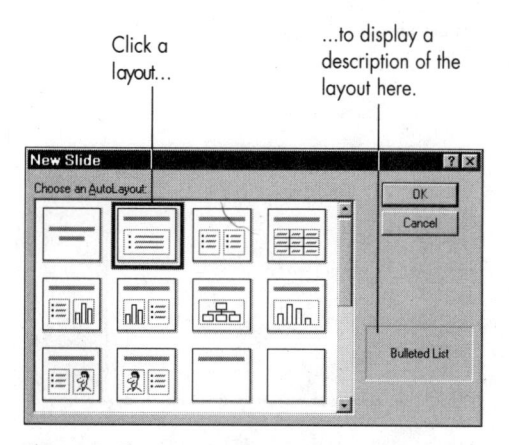

Figure 5. Choose an AutoLayout as you create a new slide.

Scroll bar

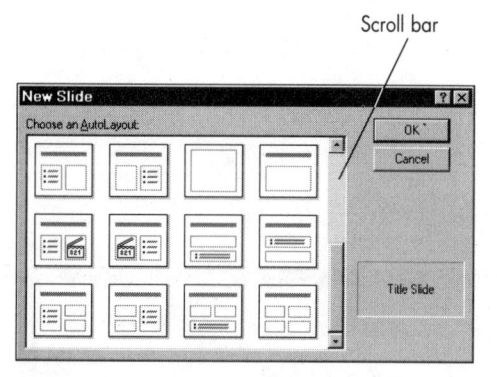

Figure 6. By using the scroll bar, you can see additional layouts.

Choosing a Layout

PowerPoint offers 24 different *AutoLayouts* to help you define the elements you want on a slide: a bulleted list, a graph, a table, an organization chart, and so forth.

You choose a layout from the New Slide dialog box shown in Figure 5. This dialog box automatically displays when you create a new presentation or add a new slide.

1. Click the desired layout (scroll to see more choices). Figure 5 shows the first set of layouts; Figure 6 shows the second set.
2. Click OK.

On the following pages you will see examples of two types of layouts: Bulleted Lists and Graphs.

■ Tips

✓ When you click a layout in the New Slide dialog box, a description of the layout displays in the box (Figure 5).

✓ Instead of clicking on the layout and clicking OK, you can double-click the layout in the New Slide dialog box.

✓ To choose a different layout for an existing slide, click the Slide Layout button at the bottom of the PowerPoint window or right-click the slide background and choose Slide Layout from the shortcut menu.

CHAPTER 2

Creating a Bulleted List

1. If the New Slide dialog box is not displayed, click the New Slide button at the bottom of the PowerPoint window.
2. In the New Slide dialog box, choose the Bulleted List layout.
3. Click the *title placeholder* (Figure 7), and type the title of your bulleted list.
4. Click the *text placeholder* (Figure 7), and type your bulleted text. Follow these simple rules:
   - Press Enter to type another bullet.
   - Press Tab to indent the current line (Figure 8).
   - Press Shift+Tab to unindent the current line.

■ Tip

✓ To change the bullet shape, use the Format/Bullet command.

See Chapter 3, starting on page 29, for additional information on creating text charts.

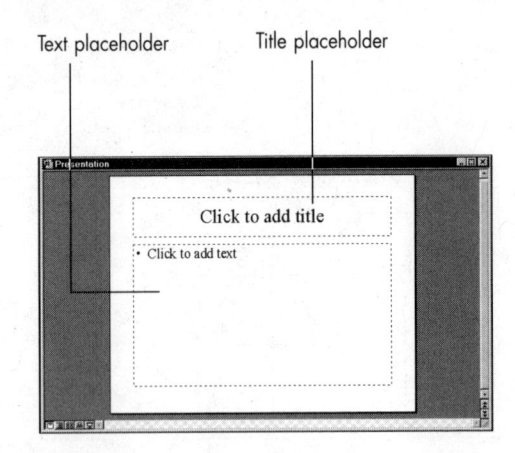

Figure 7. A new Bulleted List slide before any text has been added

Corporate Goals

- Introduce New Product Lines
  - Weight-lifting equipment
  - Cardio equipment
- Become a Worldwide Leader
- Expand Geographically
  - South America
  - Europe
- Continue 20%+ Sales Growth

Press Tab to indent

Press Shift+Tab to unindent

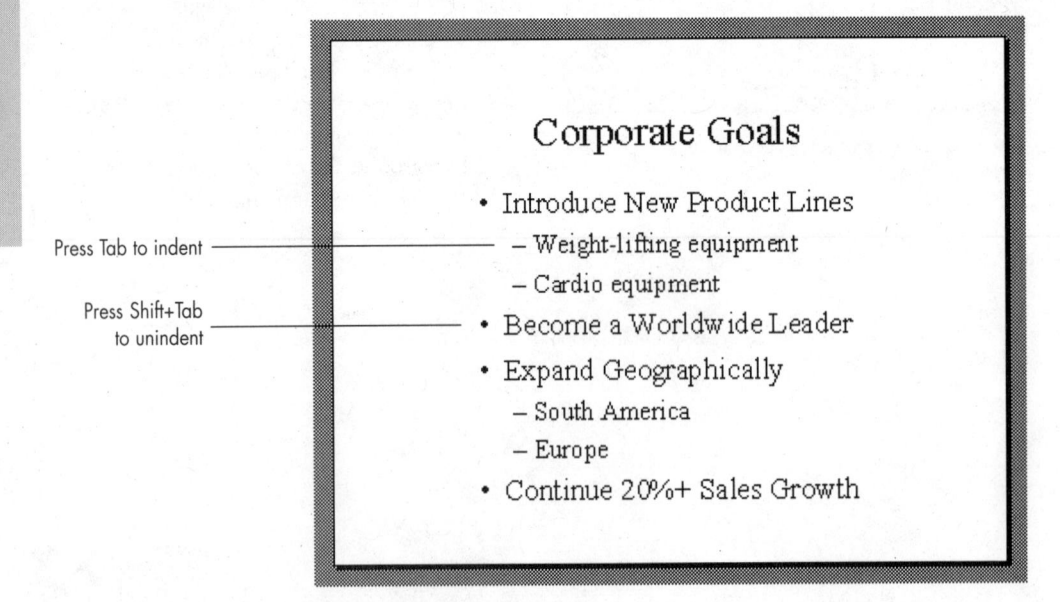

Figure 8. A slide with two levels of bullets

A QUICK TOUR OF POWERPOINT

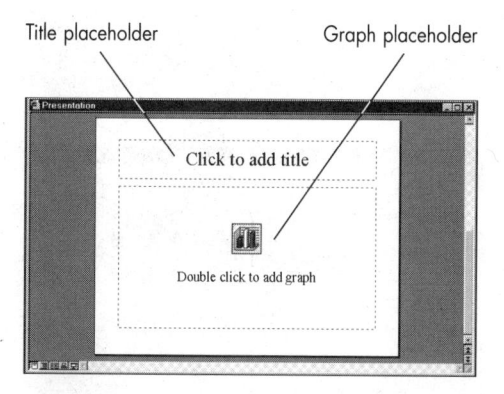

Figure 9. A slide with a graph placeholder.

Figure 10. Enter your chart data in the datasheet.

Figure 11. A column chart

Creating a Graph

1. If the New Slide dialog box is not displayed, click the New Slide button.
2. In the New Slide dialog box, choose the Graph layout.
3. Click the *title placeholder* (Figure 9), and type the title of your graph.
4. Double-click the *graph placeholder* to launch Microsoft Graph. A datasheet with sample data appears.
5. To erase the sample data, click the Select All button (Figure 10) and press Delete.
6. Enter the graph data (Figure 10).
7. To close the datasheet and view the graph, click the datasheet's close button or click outside of the datasheet. Figure 11 shows a column chart of the data in Figure 10.

▪ Tips

✓ To redisplay the datasheet, click the View Datasheet button on the toolbar.

✓ To exit from Microsoft Graph, click the slide, outside of the graph placeholder.

✓ To reload Microsoft Graph, double-click the graph.

See Chapter 4, starting on page 47, for more information on inserting bar, line, and other graphs that have x- and y-axes.

See Chapter 6, starting on page 75, for information on creating pie charts.

CHAPTER 2

Formatting a Graph

To format a graph, you must still be in Microsoft Graph. If the graph has a border around it (like the one in Figure 14), you are still in Graph. If you don't see the border, double-click the graph placeholder to load Microsoft Graph.

1. To change the chart type (3-D column is the default), choose Format/Chart Type (Figure 12).
2. Select 2-D or 3-D.
3. Click the desired chart type and click OK.
4. To format the graph quickly, choose Format/AutoFormat (Figure 13).
5. Select one of the sample graph formats, and click OK. Figure 14 shows a column chart formatted with the sixth AutoFormat option.

■ Tip

✓ The chart type can be selected before you fill in the datasheet.

See Chapter 5, starting on page 59, for additional information on formatting graphs, and Chapter 6, starting on page 75, for information on formatting pie charts.

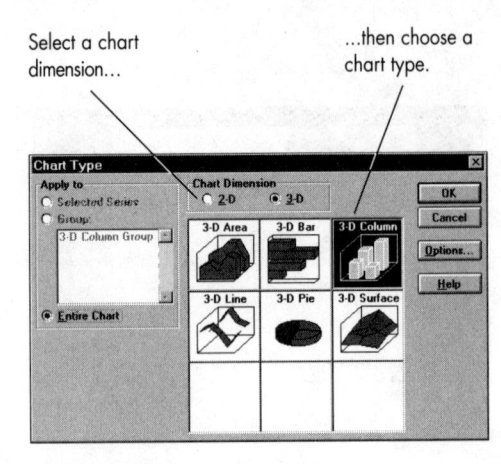

Select a chart dimension... ...then choose a chart type.

Figure 12. Selecting a chart type

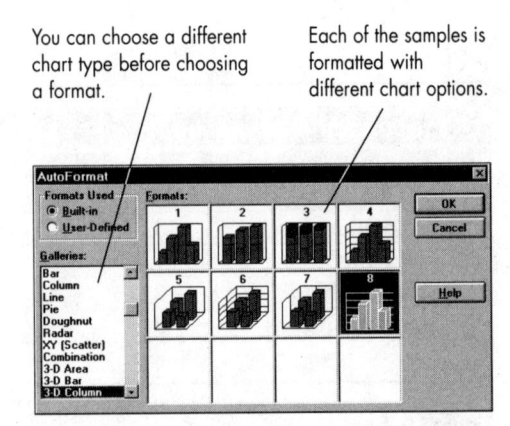

You can choose a different chart type before choosing a format.

Each of the samples is formatted with different chart options.

Figure 13. With the Format/AutoFormat command, you can click one of the sample charts to quickly format your chart.

When a chart has a border around it, you are in Microsoft Graph.

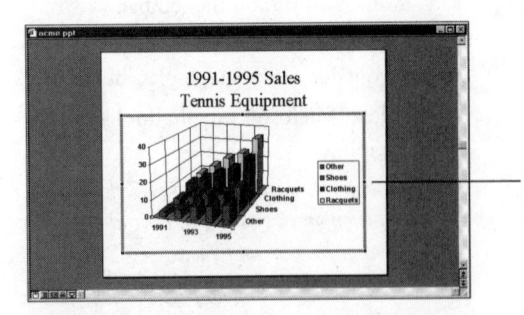

Figure 14. This column chart was formatted using the sixth AutoFormat option.

Navigating a Presentation

The status line at the bottom of the PowerPoint window indicates the current slide number (Figure 15). In Slide view, you can use the following keyboard commands to display other slides in the presentation:

Next Slide	Page Down
Previous Slide	Page Up
First Slide	Ctrl+Home
Last Slide	Ctrl+End

You can also use the Next Slide and Previous Slide buttons in the scroll bar. Use the following guidelines when navigating with the scroll bar:

- Drag the scroll box to the top of the scroll bar to go to the first slide.
- Drag the scroll box to the bottom of the scroll bar to go to the last slide.
- Drag the scroll box up or down to go to a specific slide. (Slide numbers and titles will display to the left of the scroll bar as you drag.)

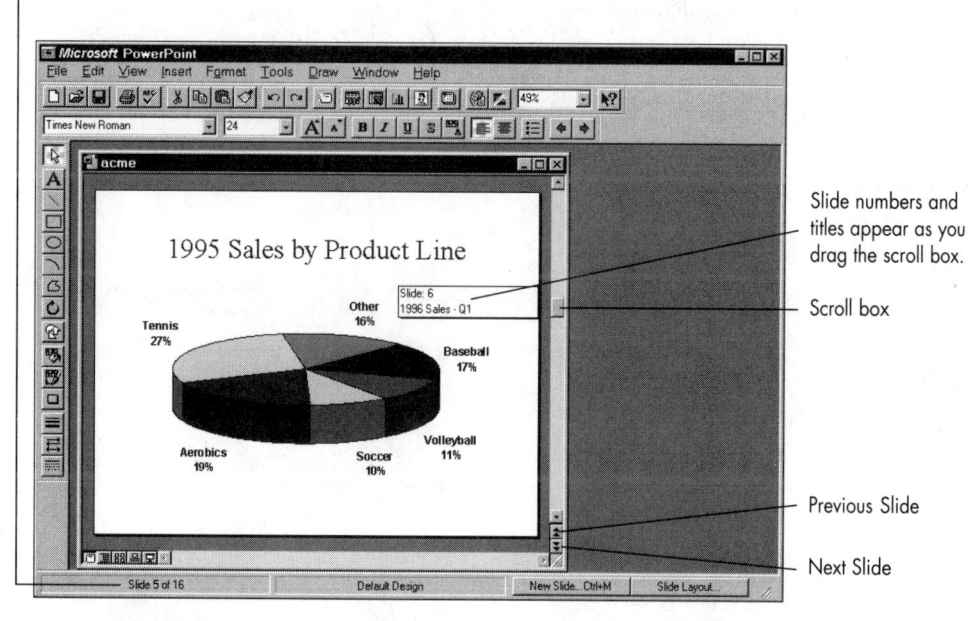

Figure 15. You can use the mouse in the scroll bar to go to other slides in the presentation.

CHAPTER 2

Saving, Opening, and Closing Presentations

The commands for saving, opening, and closing presentations are available on the File menu (Figure 16).

Saving a New Presentation

1. Select File/Save As. The File Save dialog box is shown in Figure 17.
2. In the File Name field, type a descriptive name (up to 255 characters).
3. To save to another folder, double-click the folder or use the Up One Level tool (Figure 17).
4. Click Save.
5. If the Properties dialog box appears, fill in the information (or leave it blank), and then click OK.

PowerPoint presentations are saved with a .PPT extension (for example, ACME.PPT).

Opening an Existing Presentation

1. Select File/Open.
2. To open a file in another folder, double-click the folder or use the Up One Level tool.
3. Click the name in the list and click Open.

Closing the Current Presentation

1. Select File/Close or click the close button on the presentation window.

■ Tips

✓ The shortcuts for saving are Ctrl+S or the Save button (Figure 18). The shortcuts for opening are Ctrl+O or the Open button.

✓ Use the Tools/Options command (the General tab) to control whether the Properties dialog box is displayed.

✓ Another way to open a recently-used presentation is from the Documents menu on the Windows 95 Start menu.

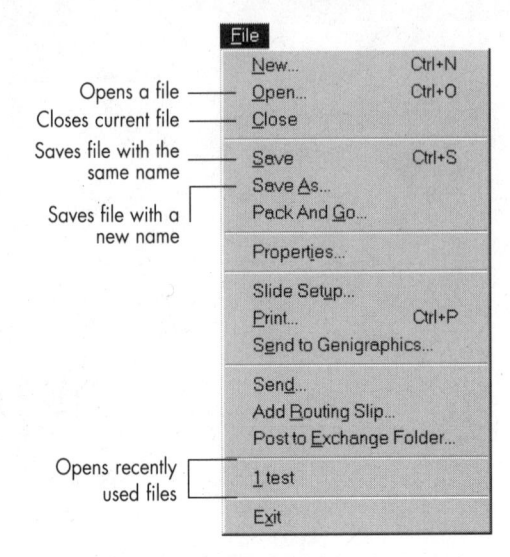

Figure 16. The File menu

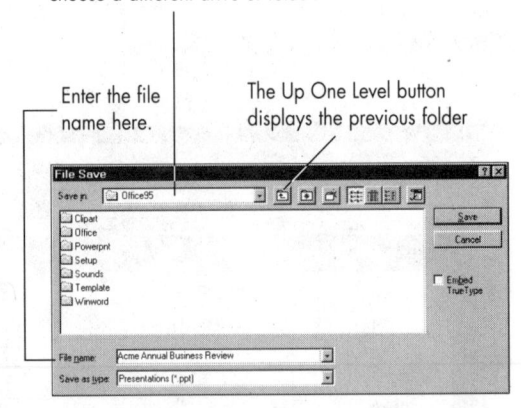

- Opens a file — Open...
- Closes current file — Close
- Saves file with the same name — Save
- Saves file with a new name — Save As...
- Opens recently used files — 1 test

Figure 17. Saving a presentation

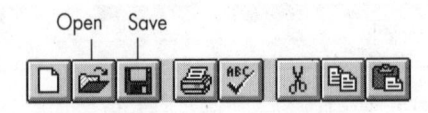

- The current folder. The file will be saved here unless you choose a different drive or folder.
- Enter the file name here.
- The Up One Level button displays the previous folder

Figure 18. The Standard toolbar

- Open
- Save

A Quick Tour of PowerPoint

24

A QUICK TOUR OF POWERPOINT

To print full-page slides, make sure the Print What option says Slides. (The other choices allow you to print an outline, speaker notes, and handouts.)

Be sure to select a print range.

Current printer

Click here to select a different printer.

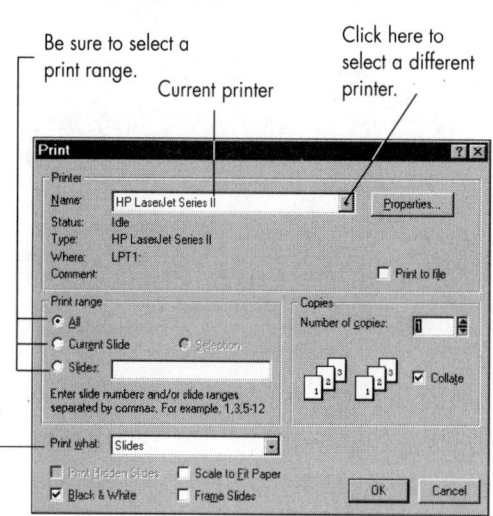

Figure 19. To display the Print dialog box, choose File/Print.

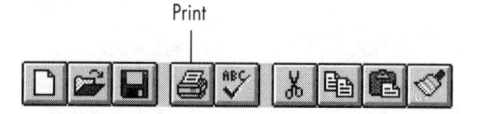

Print

Figure 20. The Standard toolbar

Printing a Presentation

1. Select File/Print. Figure 19 shows the Print dialog box.
2. To print all slides in the presentation, leave All selected for the Print Range.
3. To print specific slides, choose Slides and then enter the range of slides you want to print. Use a dash to specify a range (as in 1-5), and commas between ranges (as in 1-5, 7, 10).
4. In the Print What list box, make sure Slides is selected.
5. Click OK.

■ Tips

✓ The keyboard shortcut for printing is Ctrl+P.

✓ You can also print by choosing the Print button in the toolbar (Figure 20). However, this button does not display the Print dialog box—it prints the range last specified in the Print dialog box. It doesn't give you a chance to specify a print range.

See Chapter 15, starting on page 199, for more information on printing a presentation.

25

CHAPTER 2

Outline View

Outline view (Figure 21) displays an outline of your presentation: the slide titles and any main text, such as bulleted items. Optionally, you can hide or *collapse* part of the outline so that you see only the slide titles. Outline view is ideal for seeing the structure of your presentation and for reordering slides.

1. Click the Outline View button (Figure 22).
2. To display only the slide titles, click the Show Titles button in the Outlining toolbar (Figure 23). To redisplay the entire outline, click the Show All button.
3. To display or hide text formatting, click the Show Formatting button. Compare Figures 21 and 24. Figure 21 displays the formatting; Figure 24 does not.

■ **Tip**

✓ To move a slide, first click the icon in front of the slide title. Then click the Move Up or Move Down button until the slide is in its new position.

See Chapter 12, starting on page 159, for more information about Outline view.

Outlining toolbar

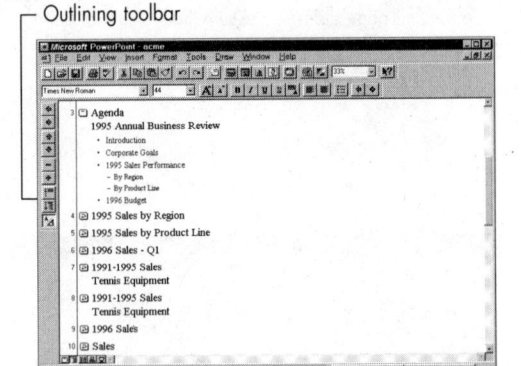

Figure 21. Outline view

Outline View

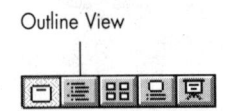

Figure 22. The view buttons

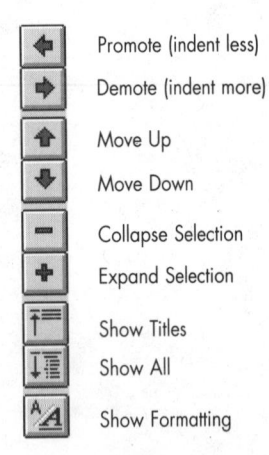

- Promote (indent less)
- Demote (indent more)
- Move Up
- Move Down
- Collapse Selection
- Expand Selection
- Show Titles
- Show All
- Show Formatting

Figure 23. The Outlining toolbar

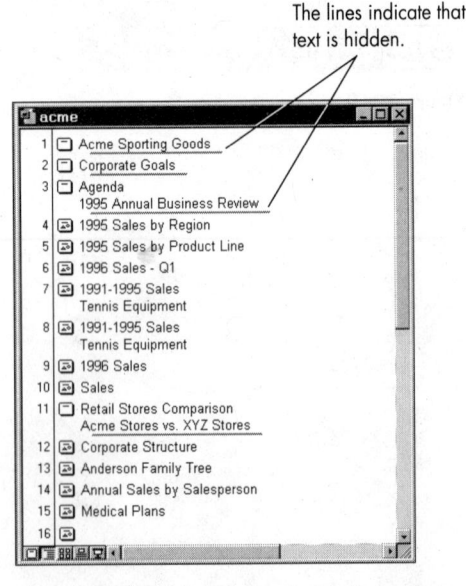

The lines indicate that text is hidden.

Figure 24. This outline shows only the titles (no body text) and does not display the text formatting.

A Quick Tour of PowerPoint

A QUICK TOUR OF POWERPOINT

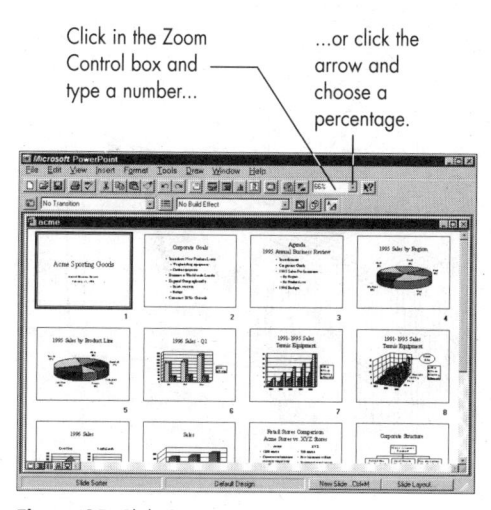

Click in the Zoom Control box and type a number...

...or click the arrow and choose a percentage.

Figure 25. Slide Sorter view

Slide Sorter View

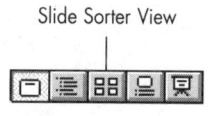

Figure 26. The view buttons

Slide Sorter View

Slide Sorter view (Figure 25) gives you the best of both worlds. As in Outline view, you can see the big picture of your presentation, and you can reorder the slides. As in Slide view, you can actually see the charts on the slides, albeit in miniature form. The size of the slides in Slide Sorter view can be controlled in the Zoom Control field, pointed out in Figure 25.

1. Click the Slide Sorter View button (Figure 26).
2. To see more slides, choose a smaller percentage in the Zoom Control field. (The slides in Figure 27 are zoomed out to 50%.)

   or

   To see fewer slides but more detail, choose a higher zoom percentage in the Zoom Control field. (In Figure 28, the slides are zoomed in to 100%.)

■ Tip

✓ To move a slide, drag it to a new location.

See Chapter 13, starting on page 169, for more information on Slide Sorter view.

Zoom percentage

Zoom percentage

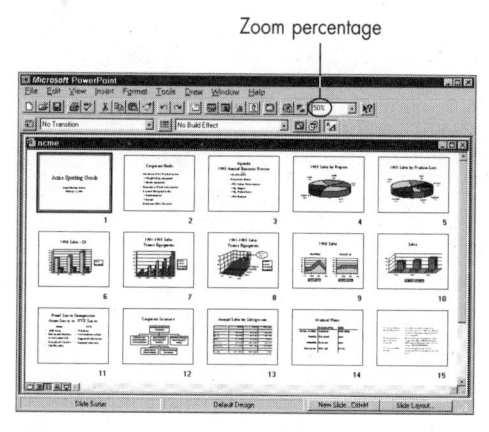

Figure 27. These slides are zoomed out so that more slides are displayed.

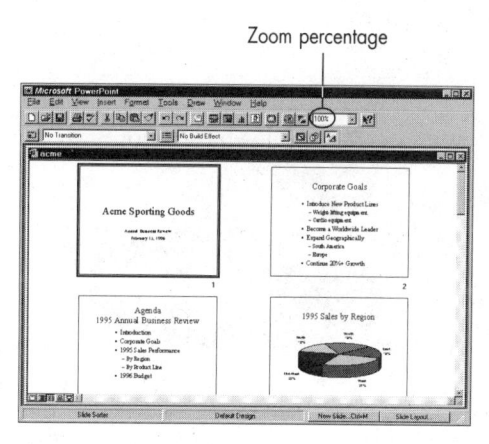

Figure 28. These slides are zoomed in so that more detail is displayed on each slide.

27

CHAPTER 2

Viewing a Slide Show

A *slide show* displays each of the slides in the presentation, one after another, full screen. To show slides to a large audience, you can project the slide show onto a large screen, saving you the time, cost, and trouble of producing 35mm slides.

1. Go to the slide you want to display first in the slide show. (To view the slide show from the beginning of the presentation, press Ctrl+Home to go to the first slide.)
2. Click the Slide Show button (Figure 29). The current slide displays full screen (Figure 30).
3. To view the next slide, click the left mouse button.

See Chapter 14, starting on page 177, for additional information on slide shows.

■ **Tips**

✓ To view the previous slide in a slide show, press PgUp.

✓ To cancel the slide show, press Esc.

✓ You can run a slide show directly from Windows Explorer or My Computer, without having to launch PowerPoint. Just right-click the presentation file name, and choose Show from the shortcut menu.

Figure 29. The view buttons

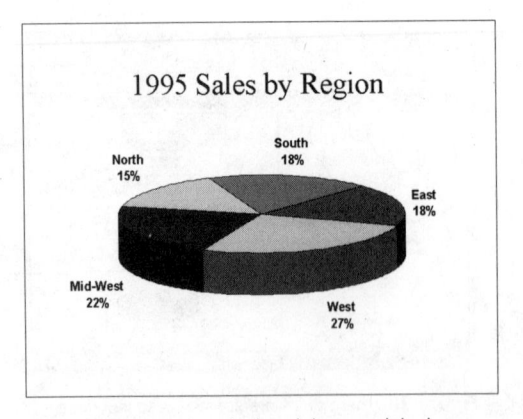

Figure 30. A pie chart displayed during a slide show.

CREATING TEXT SLIDES   3

About Text Slides

In this chapter you'll learn how to create slides that contain text, and how to edit and format the text. The types of slides that consist primarily of text are Title slides (Figure 1), Bulleted Lists (Figure 2), and 2 Column Text (Figure 3).

Slides can also combine text with a graph or with a piece of clip art. The slide in Figure 4 has both text and a graph.

Acme Sporting Goods

Annual Business Review
February 15, 1996

Figure 1. A Title slide

Corporate Goals

- Introduce New Product Lines
  - Weight-lifting equipment
  - Cardio equipment
- Become a Worldwide Leader
- Expand Geographically
  - South America
  - Europe
- Continue 20%+ Sales Growth

Figure 2. A Bulleted List slide

Retail Store Comparison
Acme Stores vs. XYZ Stores

Acme	XYZ
1200 stores	750 stores
Convenient locations in every major city	Few locations in East
Everyday low prices	Suggested retail prices
Monthly sales	Seasonal sales only

Figure 3. A 2 Column Text slide

Text & Graph Layout

- These bullets can give further information about the graph.
- For example, you might explain why 3rd Quarter sales in the East were so high.
- Or, you may want to interpret or summarize the graph.

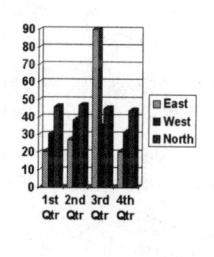

Figure 4. A slide that combines text with a graph

Creating Text Slides

29

CHAPTER 3

Choosing a Text Layout

When you insert a slide into the presentation, you are given the opportunity to choose a layout for the new slide. Of the 24 layouts for new slides, most have a text placeholder. (A *text placeholder* is simply a container for text.) Figure 5 points out the layouts that have body text placeholders.

1. In Slide view, click the New Slide button. The New Slide dialog box (Figure 6) shows the first set of AutoLayouts.
2. Use the scroll bar to see additional layouts, if necessary.
3. Click the desired layout.
4. Click OK.

See also Choosing a Layout on page 19.

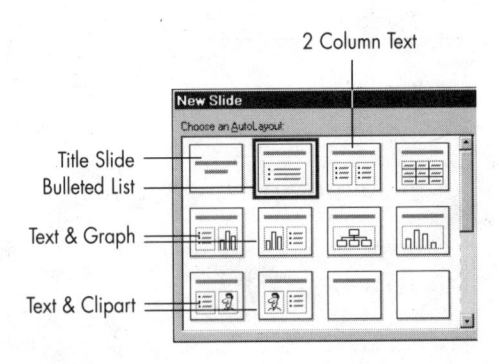

Figure 5. In the first set of layouts, the indicated layouts have body text placeholders.

■ Tips

✓ If you don't find an AutoLayout that fits your needs perfectly, don't despair; you can add, move, or delete placeholders.

See Manipulating Text Placeholders on page 33.

✓ Outline view does not display the New Slide dialog box when you insert a slide. This view automatically inserts a slide with the Bulleted List layout.

See page 162 for information on creating bullet slides in Outline view.

✓ To create a new slide with the same layout as the current slide, hold down Shift as you click the New Slide button. This action bypasses the New Slide dialog box.

✓ To choose a different layout for an existing slide, click the Slide Layout button at the bottom of the PowerPoint window or choose Format/Slide Layout. You can also right-click the slide background and choose Slide Layout from the shortcut menu.

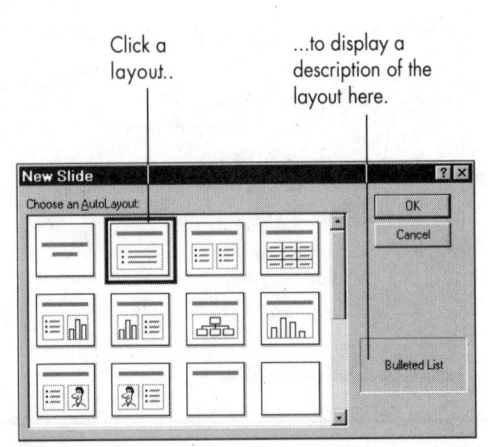

Figure 6. Choose a layout in the New Slide dialog box.

Creating Text Slides

30

CREATING TEXT SLIDES

Dotted lines surround empty AutoLayout text placeholders; these lines disappear as soon as you enter text into the placeholder.

Click to add title

• Click to add text

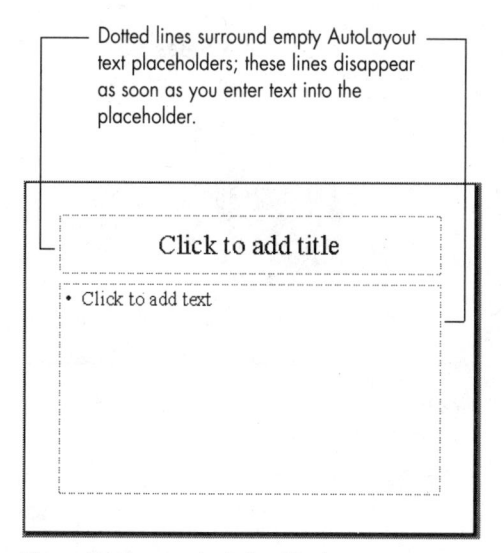

Figure 7. Choosing the Bulleted List layout creates two text placeholders: one for the title and one for the bulleted text.

Entering Text into a Placeholder

Text placeholders created with an AutoLayout have a dotted-line boundary (Figure 7). They tell you exactly what to do to enter text in them: *Click to add title* or *Click to add text*. Thus, entering text into a placeholder is easy:

1. Click inside the placeholder.
2. Start typing. Refer to the table below for ways to edit your text.

■ Tips

✓ To replace existing text with something new, it's not necessary to delete the unwanted text and then insert the new text. Instead, select the unwanted text and start typing—the new text will replace the existing text.

✓ If you start typing on a new slide without clicking a placeholder, the text is placed in the title placeholder.

Moving the Cursor Within a Text Placeholder

To move cursor to...	*Do this...*
Beginning of line	Press Home
End of line	Press End
Next word	Press Ctrl+right arrow
Previous word	Press Ctrl+left arrow

Deleting Text

To delete...	*Do this...*
Character to the right	Press Delete
Character to the left	Press Backspace
Any amount of text	Select the text and press Delete

Selecting Text

To select...	*Do this...*
Word	Double-click word
Paragraph	Triple-click paragraph
All text in placeholder	Click placeholder and press Ctrl+A
Any amount of text	Click and drag

Creating a Text Placeholder

Sometimes you'll need to add your own text placeholders—for example, to annotate a graph (Figure 8) or to insert a footnote on a Title slide (Figure 9).

1. Click the Text tool (Figure 10).
2. Place the pointer on the slide where you want to insert the placeholder.
3. To insert a single line, just click and start typing. Figure 11 shows a placeholder that was inserted this way.
4. To create a word-wrapped text box, drag a box to the desired size. When you type, text will word-wrap inside the box. The placeholder in Figure 12 was created with this technique.

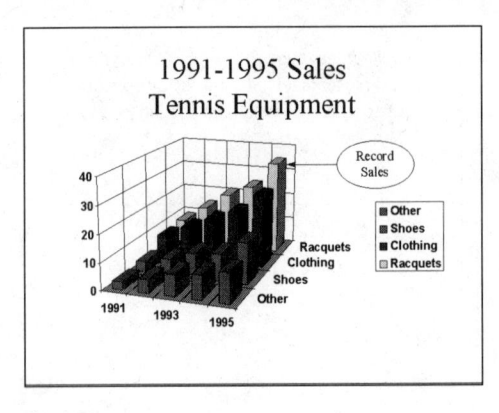

Figure 8. The *Record Sales* annotation is inside an added text placeholder.

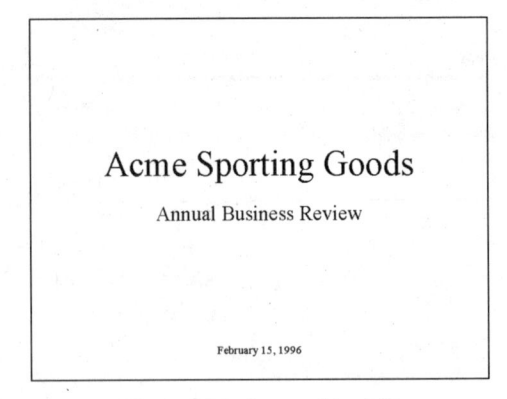

Figure 9. The date at the bottom of the slide is in an added text placeholder.

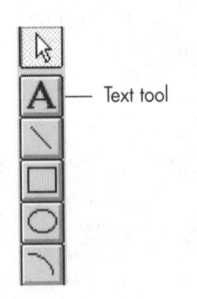

Figure 10. The Drawing toolbar

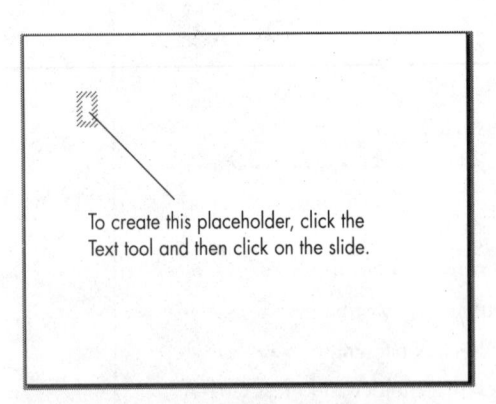

Figure 11. This type of placeholder is ideal for single-line labels. The box grows wider as you type.

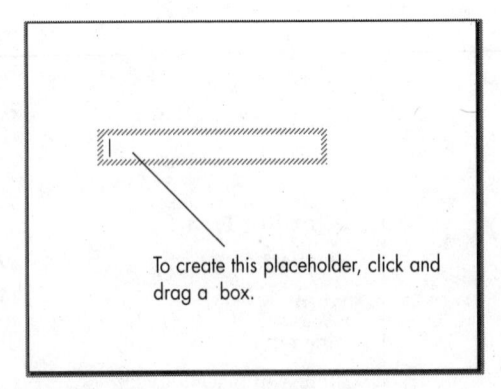

Figure 12. This type of placeholder will word-wrap text within the box.

CREATING TEXT SLIDES

Drag the selection box to move the placeholder. To copy the placeholder, hold down Ctrl as you drag.

Selection box

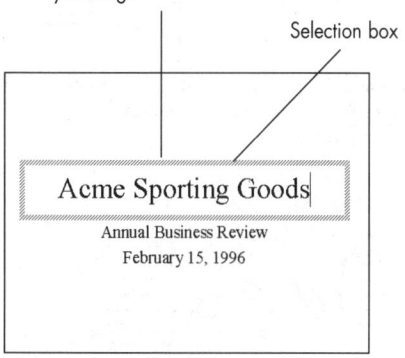

Acme Sporting Goods
Annual Business Review
February 15, 1996

Figure 13. A selection box appears around the text placeholder when you click inside.

Selection handles

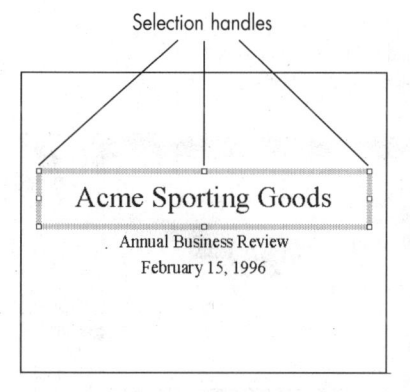

Acme Sporting Goods
Annual Business Review
February 15, 1996

Figure 14. When you Shift-click the placeholder, selection handles appear.

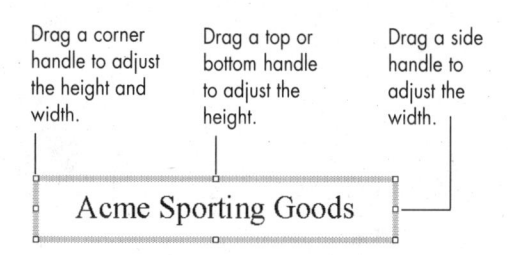

Drag a corner handle to adjust the height and width.

Drag a top or bottom handle to adjust the height.

Drag a side handle to adjust the width.

Acme Sporting Goods

Figure 15. Using selection handles to resize a text block

Manipulating Text Placeholders

Text placeholders can be moved, copied, resized, and deleted.

Moving a Placeholder

1. Click inside the placeholder. You will see a selection box around the placeholder (Figure 13).
2. Place the mouse pointer on the selection box. The mouse pointer becomes an arrow.
3. Drag the placeholder to the desired location on the slide.

Copying a Placeholder

1. Click inside the text placeholder.
2. Place the mouse pointer on the selection box. The mouse pointer becomes an arrow.
3. Hold down Ctrl as you drag to a new location.

Resizing a Placeholder

1. Hold down Shift and click the text placeholder. Selection handles appear (Figure 14).
2. Drag one of the selection handles until the placeholder is the desired size (Figure 15).

Deleting a Placeholder

1. Hold down Shift and click the placeholder. Selection handles appear.
2. Press Delete. If you delete a title or body text placeholder, an empty text placeholder from the AutoLayout will appear.
3. If desired, press Delete again to delete the AutoLayout placeholder.

Creating Text Slides

CHAPTER 3

Moving Text

One way of moving text in a Windows application is using the *cut-and-paste* technique (Figure 16). An alternate method is called *drag and drop* (Figure 17).

Cut-and-Paste

1. Select the text to be moved (Figure 18).
2. Select Edit/Cut.
3. Place the cursor where you want to insert the text.
4. Select Edit/Paste.

Drag-and-Drop

1. Select the text to be moved.
2. Place the pointer in the selection.
3. Hold down the mouse button and begin dragging. You will see a box under the pointer that indicates you are in the middle of moving text, and a vertical line that indicates the insertion point.
4. Release the mouse button when the vertical line is positioned where you want to insert the text. The text will then drop into place.

■ Tips

- ✓ The Standard toolbar contains buttons for cutting, copying, and pasting (Figure 19).
- ✓ To select a bullet item and all its sub-bullets, click the main bullet.
- ✓ When moving bullet items, you can place the cursor at the end of a paragraph (and the text will be inserted after that paragraph) or at the beginning of a paragraph (and the text will be inserted before that paragraph).
- ✓ You can also press Ctrl+X to cut and Ctrl+V to paste.

See page 162 for information on moving bullet items in Outline view.

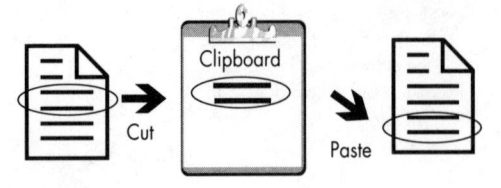

Figure 16. The cut-and-paste technique is a way of moving text. The Clipboard is a temporary storage area for objects that are cut or copied.

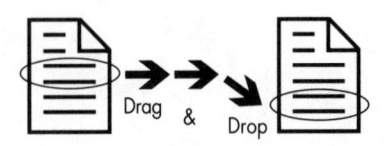

Figure 17. The drag-and-drop technique is another way to move text.

Notice that the bullets themselves are not highlighted (although they will be moved along with the text).

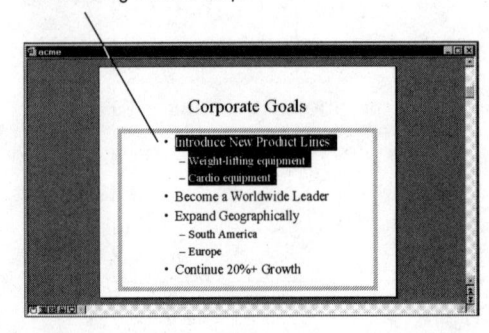

Figure 18. The selected text can be moved by using either cut and paste or drag and drop.

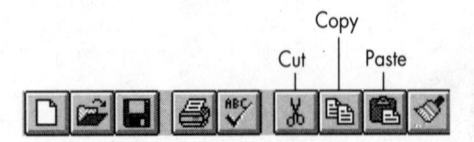

Figure 19. The Standard toolbar

CREATING TEXT SLIDES

Using the Spelling Checker

The spelling checker searches all text placeholders in the presentation and stops at words that aren't in the dictionary.

1. Select Tools/Spelling. The Spelling dialog box appears (Figure 20).
2. If the word is spelled correctly, choose Ignore or Ignore All.

   or

   If you'll use the word frequently, choose Add to add it to the custom dictionary.
3. For misspelled words, choose the correct spelling from the Suggestions list.

   or

   Edit the Change To field and then choose Change or Change All.
4. Repeat steps 2 and 3 for all "suspect" words.

■ Tips

- ✓ The keyboard shortcut for running the spelling checker is F7.
- ✓ The Spelling button is on the Standard toolbar (Figure 21).
- ✓ The spelling checker doesn't find all misspellings. If the mistyped word is an actual word, the spelling checker isn't smart enough to consider the word suspect. Therefore, it's important that you still proofread the text yourself.

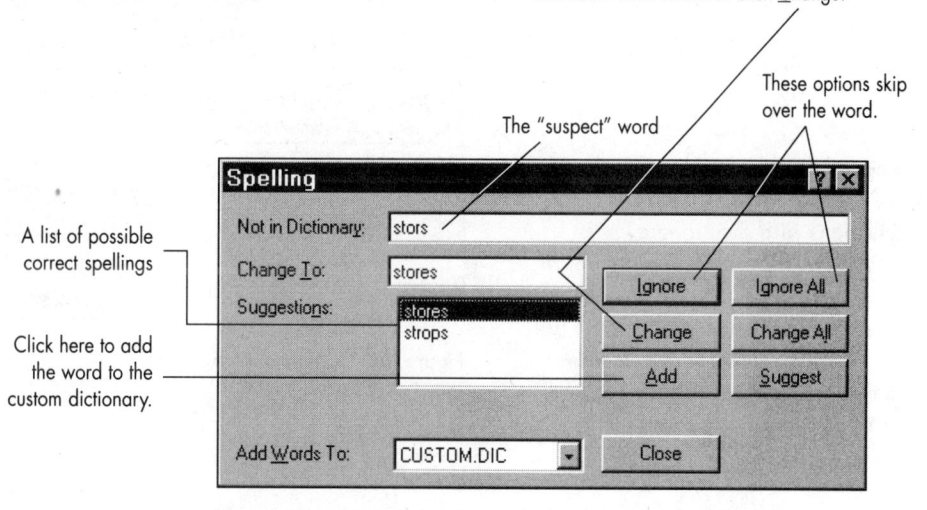

Figure 20. Select Tools/Spelling to display the Spelling dialog box.

Figure 21. The Standard toolbar

35

CHAPTER 3

Correcting Mistakes Automatically

AutoCorrect, a feature new to PowerPoint for Windows 95, automatically corrects mistakes as you type. It will correct capitalization errors, common misspellings, and transpositions (Figure 22). When AutoCorrect is turned on, mistakes are corrected when you press the spacebar after the word.

The AutoCorrect feature is turned on by default when you enter the program. If you want to turn off this feature or customize the replacement list, you will need to go to the AutoCorrect dialog box (Figure 23).

1. Select Tools/AutoCorrect.
2. Turn options on or off, as desired.
3. To add your own replacement item, click the Replace field, and type the word you want replaced. Click the With field, type the replacement word or phrase, then click Add.
4. Click OK when finished.

■ **Tip**

✓ Another way to use the AutoCorrect feature is to automatically replace abbreviations with their longer counterparts. For instance, you can have AutoCorrect replace a code for your company name (such as *asg*) with the full company name (*Acme Sporting Goods*). You'll find this to be a big time saver for words or phrases that you use frequently.

Mistake or Abbreviation	Correction
ANnual	Annual
wednesday	Wednesday
seperate	separate
adn	and
(c)	©
insted	instead

Figure 22. Examples of the types of corrections the AutoCorrect feature makes

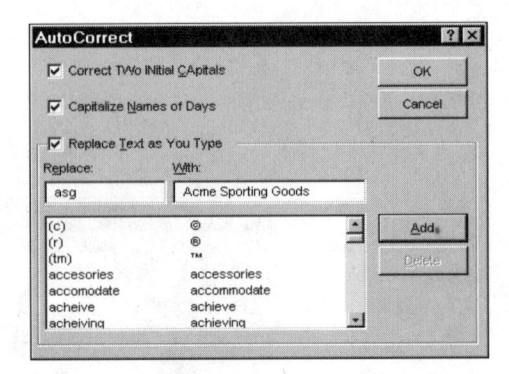

Figure 23. The AutoCorrect dialog box

Creating Text Slides

36

CREATING TEXT SLIDES

Study the upper- and lowercase used in the button names—they show you how that option will format the selected text. For example, the Title Case option capitalizes the first letter of each word in the selected text.

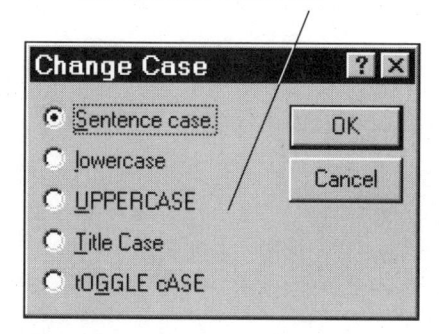

Figure 24. The Change Case dialog box

You can add or remove periods in the main text placeholder.

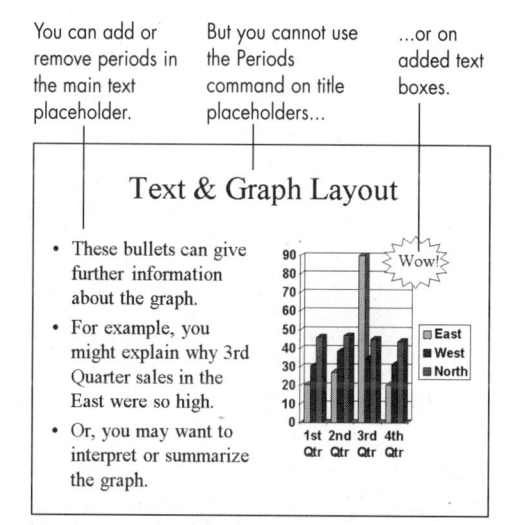

But you cannot use the Periods command on title placeholders...

...or on added text boxes.

Figure 25. All text placeholders are not created equal when it comes to the Periods command.

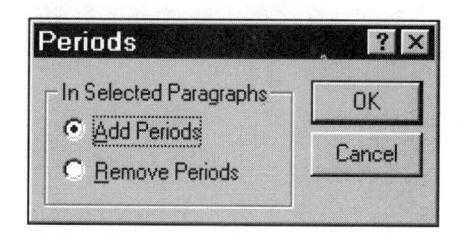

Figure 26. The Periods dialog box

Changing Case

The Change Case command lets you choose different combinations of upper- and lowercase for selected text.

1. Select the text you want to change.
2. Select Format/Change Case.
3. Choose one of the case options (Figure 24).
4. Click OK.

■ Tips

✓ Toggle case is handy when you have mistakenly typed text with Caps Lock on—it turns lowercase letters into uppercase and vice versa.

✓ Title case capitalizes each word in the selected text, except for small words such as *the, and, or, of, at.*

✓ For some reason, you can't go directly from title case to sentence case. Here's a workaround: Go from title case to lowercase and then to sentence case.

Adding Periods

The Periods command lets you add or remove periods from paragraphs. Figure 25 explains the rules about which types of text placeholders are affected by the Periods command.

1. Select the text you want to change.
2. Select Format/Periods. The Periods dialog box is shown in Figure 26.
3. Choose Add Periods or Remove Periods.
4. Click OK.

■ Tip

✓ To check for consistent capitalization and punctuation throughout your presentation, use the Style Checker.

See Checking for Inconsistent Style on the next page.

37

CHAPTER 3

Checking for Inconsistent Style

The Style Checker—a new feature to PowerPoint for Windows 95—makes sure you have consistently capitalized and punctuated your slide titles and body text throughout the presentation. The Style Checker can also check for visual clarity: it makes sure you haven't used too many fonts (or made them too small), placed too many bullet items in a list, or used too many words in a title or bullet item. In addition, you can have the Style Checker spell check the presentation.

1. Select Tools/Style Checker. The Style Checker dialog box appears (Figure 27).
2. If necessary, turn on the options for Spelling, Visual Clarity, and/or Case and End Punctuation.
3. Click the Options button.
4. In the Case and End Punctuation tab (Figure 28), specify the case and end punctuation style for titles and body text.
5. Click the Visual Clarity tab (Figure 29), and change any of the fonts and legibility options.
6. Click OK.
7. Click Start to begin checking.
8. When the Style Checker encounters a style inconsistency or spelling mistake, it may ask you to correct or ignore the error.
9. When checking is complete, a summary dialog box appears (Figure 30).

■ **Tip**

✓ Before running the Style Checker, be sure to adjust the style options to your own personal preferences. (The default settings may not be appropriate.)

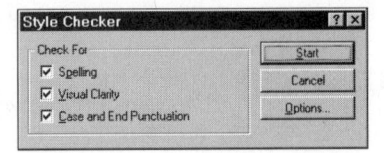

Figure 27. The Style Checker dialog box

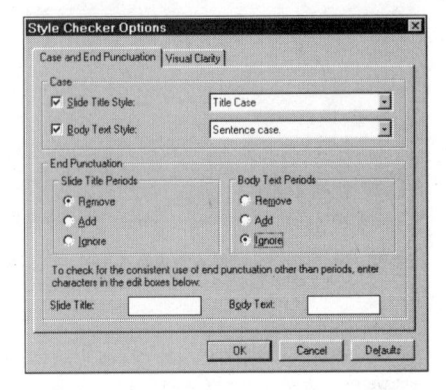

Figure 28. The Case and End Punctuation page

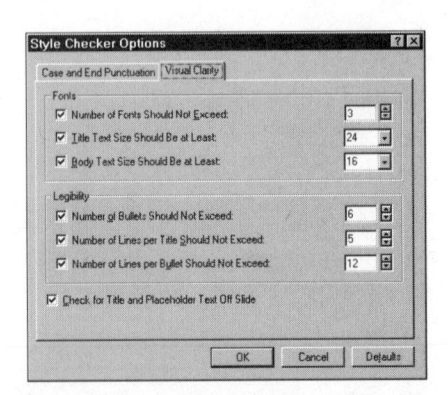

Figure 29. The Visual Clarity page

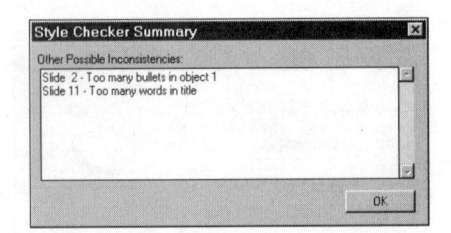

Figure 30. The Style Checker summary

CREATING TEXT SLIDES

Changing Bullets

Figure 31 shows a Bulleted List slide that uses the default bullets. Figure 32 shows this same list with different bullets selected for the two levels.

1. Click anywhere on the line whose bullet you want to change. To change the bullets in several consecutive lines, select them by clicking and dragging.
2. Select F<u>o</u>rmat/<u>B</u>ullet. The Bullet dialog box is shown in Figure 33.

   or

   Right-click the line or selected area, and choose Bullet.
3. In the <u>B</u>ullets From field, click the arrow to display a list of typefaces.
4. Choose the desired typeface. Wingdings and Zapf Dingbats are two typefaces that contain many symbols appropriate for bullets.
5. Click the desired symbol.
6. Change the bullet's color and size, if you like.
7. Click OK.

   See also Creating a Bulleted List on page 20.

■ Tips

✓ To remove a bullet from a line, click the Bullet On/Off button (Figure 34).

✓ To change the bullets for all slides, edit the Slide Master.

   See Changing the Default Format for Text on page 155.

Agenda
1995 Annual Business Review
- Introduction
- Corporate Goals
- 1995 Sales Performance
  - By Region
  - By Product Line
- 1996 Budget

Figure 31. The default bullets

Agenda
1995 Annual Business Review
❑ Introduction
❑ Corporate Goals
❑ 1995 Sales Performance
  ➢ By Region
  ➢ By Product Line
❑ 1996 Budget

Figure 32. Modified bullets

To decrease the size of the bullet, enter a number less than 100. To increase, enter a number greater than 100.

Select a typeface here.

Clicking a symbol zooms in on it.

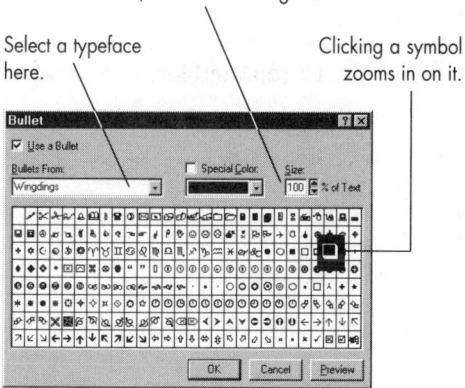

Figure 33. Choose a different bullet in the Bullet dialog box.

Bullet On/Off

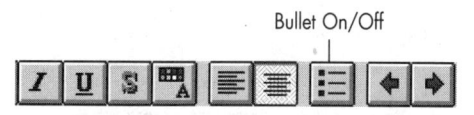

Figure 34. The Formatting toolbar

39

CHAPTER 3

Adjusting Bullet Placement

To change the horizontal spacing between the bullet and the text that follows it, you need to display the rulers (Figure 35) and drag the appropriate markers. Figure 36 shows a Bulleted List slide before any spacing change; Figure 37 shows the same list after a bit of space has been added between the bullet and text.

1. Select <u>V</u>iew/<u>R</u>uler.
2. Click anywhere on the text. For each bullet level, the ruler shows a set of indent markers that can be individually adjusted. For example, if there are two bullet levels, the ruler displays two sets of indent markers.
3. To change the spacing between the bullet and the text, drag the left-indent marker in the ruler (Figure 38).
4. To adjust the position of the bullet, drag the first-line indent marker in the ruler.

   or

   To adjust the position of the bullet *without* changing the spacing between the bullet and the text, drag the square marker in the ruler. (All markers will move together.)

■ Tips

✓ You don't need to select all the text in the placeholder before adjusting the indents—the ruler automatically controls the entire placeholder.

✓ To remove the ruler, choose <u>V</u>iew/<u>R</u>uler again.

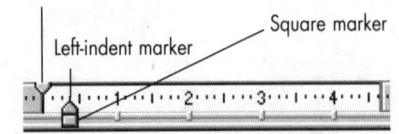

Figure 38. The indent markers in the horizontal ruler

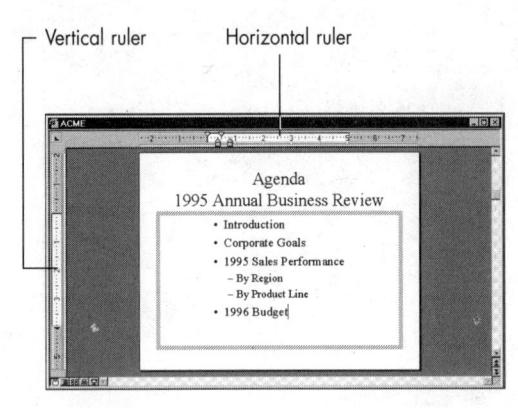

Figure 35. To display the rulers, select View/Ruler.

Figure 36. A Bulleted List slide before any adjustment of indents

Figure 37. The same list after the indents have been increased slightly

Creating Text Slides

40

CREATING TEXT SLIDES

Figure 39. The Formatting toolbar

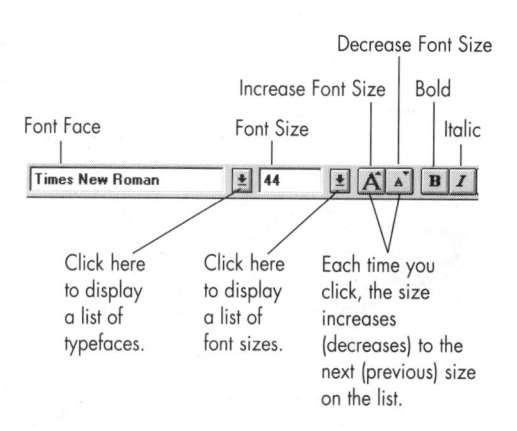

(Formatting toolbar illustration with labels:)
- Font Face — Click here to display a list of typefaces.
- Font Size — Click here to display a list of font sizes.
- Increase Font Size / Decrease Font Size — Each time you click, the size increases (decreases) to the next (previous) size on the list.
- Bold
- Italic

Changing the Font

1. Select the text by clicking and dragging.

   or

   To select an entire text placeholder, hold down Shift and click the text.

2. In the Formatting toolbar, use the Font Face and Font Size fields to change the font. Turn on the Bold or Italic buttons, if desired (Figure 39).

   or

   Select Format/Font. In the Font dialog box (Figure 40), choose a Font, Font Style, and Size and click OK.

   See the next page for more information on the Font dialog box.

■ Tip

✓ Another way to display the Font dialog box is with the shortcut menu: right-click the selected area and choose Font.

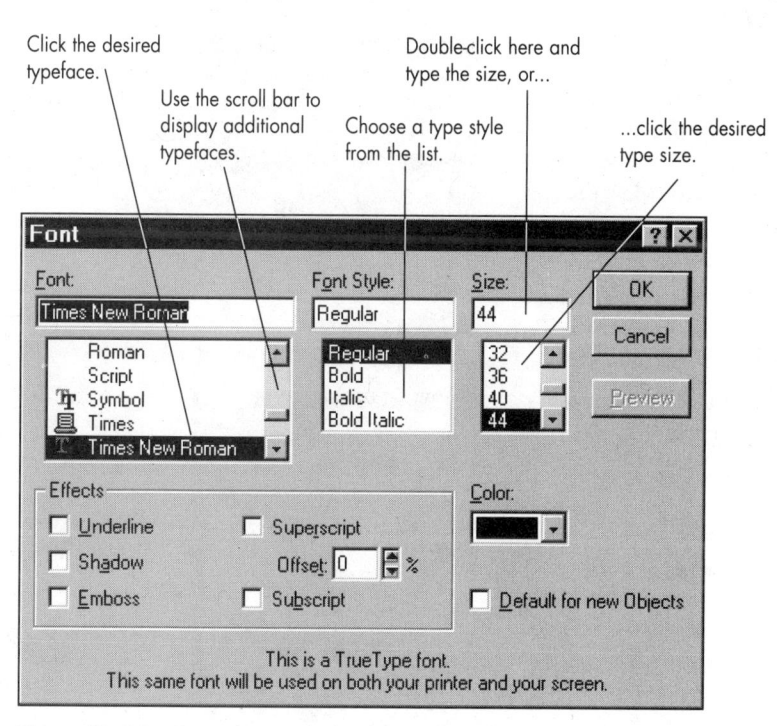

(Font dialog box illustration with labels:)
- Click the desired typeface.
- Use the scroll bar to display additional typefaces.
- Choose a type style from the list.
- Double-click here and type the size, or...
- ...click the desired type size.

Figure 40. Select Format/Font to display the Font dialog box.

CHAPTER 3

Adding Text Effects and Color

In addition to options for typeface, size, and style of text, the Font dialog box has options for special effects (such as Underline, Shadow, and Emboss) and Color. Figure 41 shows examples of these special text effects.

1. Select the text by clicking and dragging.

   or

   To select an entire text placeholder, hold down Shift and click the text.

2. In the Formatting toolbar, turn on the Underline or Text Shadow buttons, if desired (Figure 42).

   or

   Select Format/Font. In the Font dialog box (Figure 43), choose an effect. Figures 43 through 45 explain how to choose a color. Click OK.

■ Tips

✓ Another way to display the Font dialog box is with the shortcut menu: right-click the selected area, and choose Font.

✓ Use the Superscript effect to raise text above the baseline (e.g., x^2). Use the Subscript effect to lower text below the baseline (e.g., H_2O).

✓ Instead of using the Underline effect, you can draw a line with the Line tool. (Do this if you need to control the spacing between the text and the line.)

✓ To control the color and offset of the text shadow effect, select Format/Shadow.

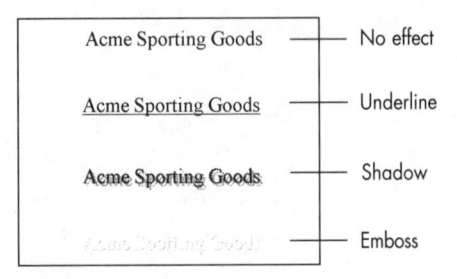

Figure 41. Special text effects

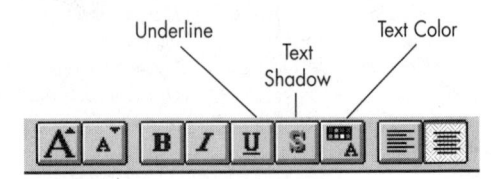

Figure 42. The Formatting toolbar

Figure 43. The Font dialog box

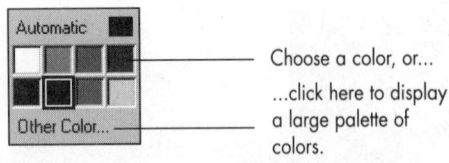

Figure 44. The small color palette that displays when you click the Color field in the Font dialog box or when you click the Text Color button on the toolbar.

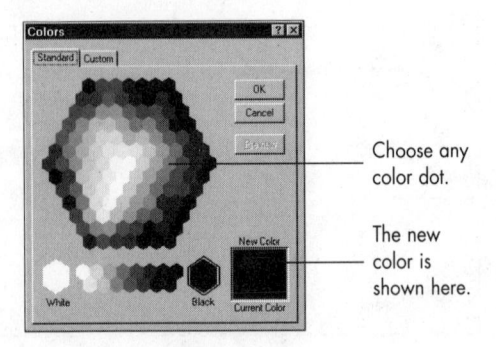

Figure 45. The large color palette

CREATING TEXT SLIDES

This paragraph is **left-aligned** within the text placeholder. This alignment is used for single-line labels, titles, and for bulleted paragraphs.
This paragraph is **justified** within the text placeholder. This alignment is useful for long, wide paragraphs of text.
This paragraph is **centered** within the text placeholder. This alignment is useful for titles and multiple-line labels.
This paragraph is **right-aligned** within the text placeholder. This alignment is useful for special formatting situations.

Figure 46. The four types of paragraph alignment

Aligning Paragraphs

Figure 46 shows examples of the four types of paragraph alignment.

1. Select the paragraphs to be aligned.
2. Select Format/Alignment (Figure 47).
3. Choose Left, Center, Right, or Justify.

■ Tips

- ✓ The Formatting toolbar contains buttons for left-aligning and centering text (Figure 48).
- ✓ To align a single paragraph, just click on it—you don't need to select any text.
- ✓ To select all the text in the placeholder, hold down Shift and click the text. Then, when you give an alignment command, all text will be aligned.
- ✓ Text is aligned within the text placeholder. If the text isn't positioned quite where you want it, try adjusting the size or position of the placeholder.

See the next page to see how to align text on a particular point within a placeholder.

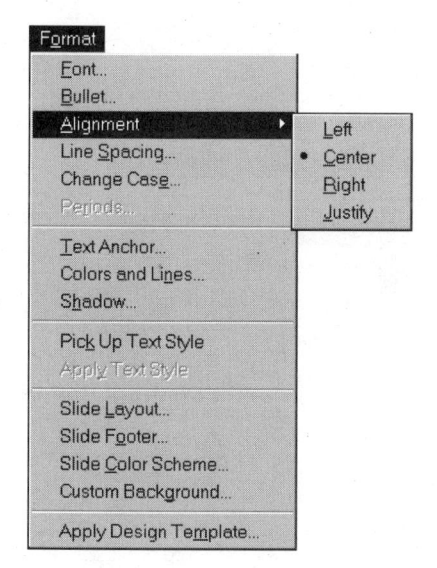

Figure 47. The Alignment submenu

Left Alignment   Center Alignment

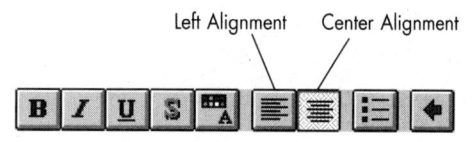

Figure 48. The Formatting toolbar

43

CHAPTER 3

Setting Anchor Points in a Text Placeholder

To control the horizontal and vertical placement of a block of text within a placeholder, you set a *text anchor*. Compare Figures 49 and 50. In Figure 49, the list is anchored on the top left side of the placeholder; in Figure 50, the list is anchored along the top center. While the Format/Alignment command centers each line separately, Format/Text Anchor controls the position of the text as a whole unit. This command also lets you align text vertically.

1. Click anywhere in the text placeholder.
2. Select Format/Text Anchor. The Text Anchor dialog box is shown in Figure 51.
3. Click in the Anchor Point field, and choose where you want the text anchored in the placeholder:
   Top
   Middle
   Bottom
   Top Centered
   Middle Centered
   Bottom Centered
4. Click OK.

■ Tips

✓ If the title has center alignment, bulleted lists often look good when you choose one of the centered text anchor points. This way, the list is centered under the title.

✓ The Top, Middle, and Bottom anchor points are all anchored to the left side of the placeholder.

✓ To add extra space between the placeholder boundary and the text, adjust the Box Margins settings.

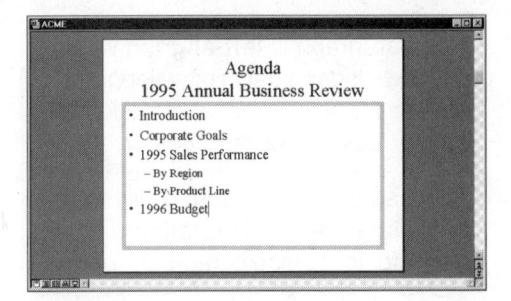

Figure 49. The list is anchored along the top left side of the placeholder.

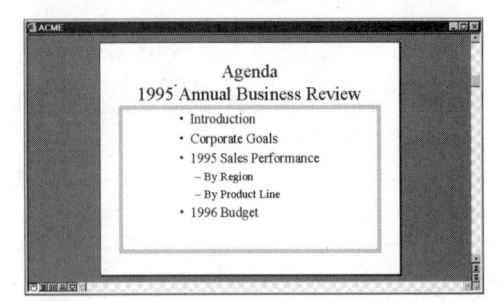

Figure 50. The list is anchored in the top center of the placeholder.

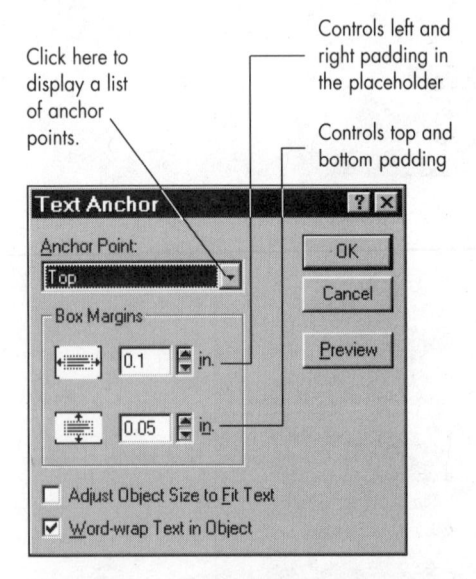

Figure 51. Use the Text Anchor dialog box to control the horizontal and vertical positioning of all the text in a placeholder.

CREATING TEXT SLIDES

Controlling Line and Paragraph Spacing

PowerPoint helps you control spacing between lines in a paragraph as well as between each paragraph. Figure 52 illustrates these two types of spacing.

1. Select the paragraphs to be formatted.
2. Select Format/Line Spacing. Figure 53 shows the Line Spacing dialog box.
3. Enter the new values for Line Spacing, Before Paragraph, and/or After Paragraph.
4. Click OK.

■ Tips

- ✓ You won't usually want to choose both Before Paragraph and After Paragraph spacing. If you choose both, the two spacing values will be added together.
- ✓ Do not use the Enter key to get extra space between paragraphs. The Line Spacing dialog box gives you more precise control over the spacing.
- ✓ To select a single paragraph, just click on it—you don't need to select any text.
- ✓ To select all the text in the placeholder, hold down Shift and click the text. Then, when you give a spacing command, all text will be formatted.
- ✓ If you choose the points measuring system for line or paragraph spacing, it's helpful to know that there are about 72 points to an inch.

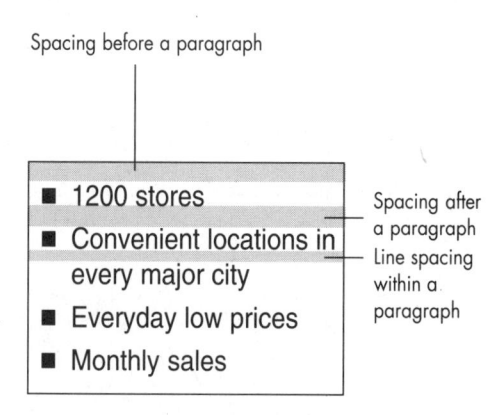

Figure 52. The three types of spacing

- 1200 stores
- Convenient locations in every major city
- Everyday low prices
- Monthly sales

(Spacing before a paragraph; Spacing after a paragraph; Line spacing within a paragraph)

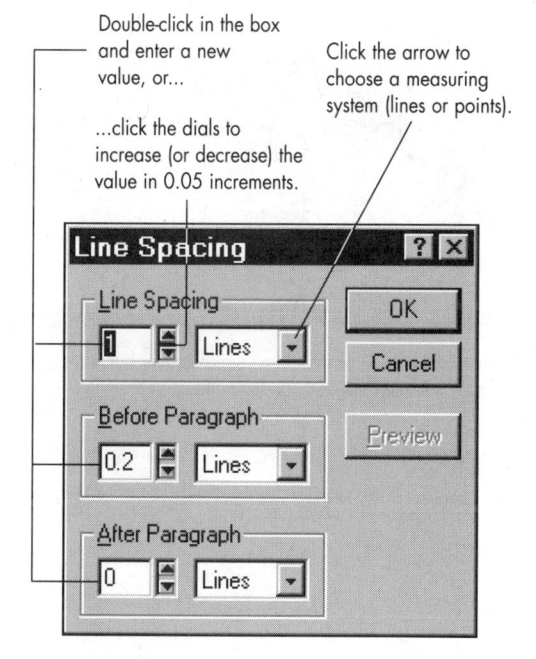

Figure 53. Select Format/Line Spacing to display this dialog box.

(Double-click in the box and enter a new value, or... click the dials to increase (or decrease) the value in 0.05 increments. Click the arrow to choose a measuring system (lines or points).)

Line Spacing: 1 Lines
Before Paragraph: 0.2 Lines
After Paragraph: 0 Lines

45

CHAPTER 3

Copying Formatting Attributes

If you want the text in one placeholder to be formatted exactly like another, you can do so by "painting" the format.

1. Click the text whose format you want to copy, and then click the selection box.
2. Click the Format Painter button (Figure 54).
3. Place the pointer (which now includes a paintbrush) on the text to which you want to apply the format, and drag across the text.

Or, using the Format menu (Figure 55)...

1. Click the text whose format you want to copy.
2. Select Format/Pick Up Object Style.
3. Select the text to which you want to apply the format.
4. Select Format/Apply Object Style.

■ Tips

✓ You can use the Format Painter to "paint" the format of other types of objects (such as boxes, circles, and arrows).

✓ You can also copy formatting attributes using the shortcut menu: right-click the selection, and choose Pick Up Object Style or Apply Object Style.

Figure 54. The Standard toolbar

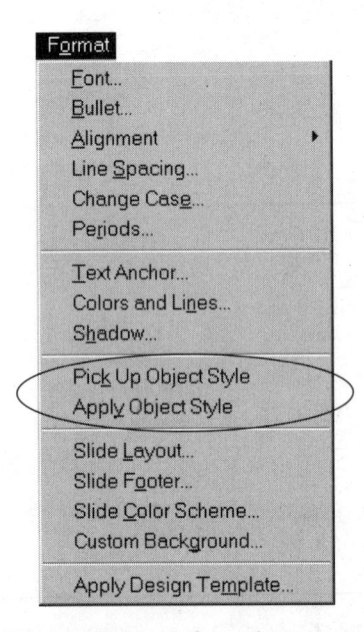

Figure 55. Instead of using the Format Painter button, you can use options on the Format menu.

Types of Formatting You Can "Paint" or Copy

Font
Style
Size
Effects
Color
Alignment
Line spacing
Paragraph spacing
Bullets

INSERTING GRAPHS 4

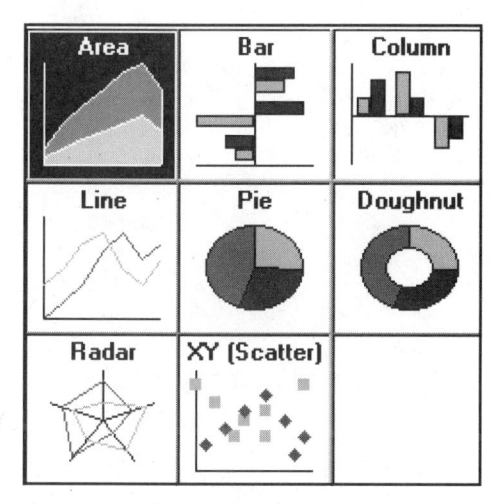

Figure 1. Two-dimensional chart types

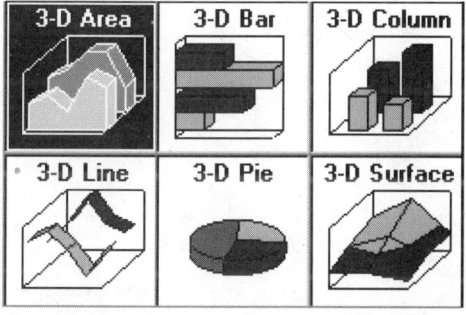

Figure 2. Three-dimensional chart types

About Graphs

You can create a wide variety of two- and three-dimensional graphs in PowerPoint: Area, Bar, Column, Line, Pie, Doughnut, Radar, XY, and Surface (Figures 1 and 2). This chapter concentrates on the types that have axes. Chapter 6 covers pie and doughnut charts.

When you create graphs in PowerPoint, you actually use the *Microsoft Graph* program (Figure 3). When you're in Graph, you'll notice that the toolbar offers tools specific to graphing, and the menu bar contains Data instead of Draw—otherwise, you won't be able to tell that another program is running. (The title bar even says PowerPoint.)

To launch Graph, double-click a graph placeholder or an embedded graph; you'll see a thick border around the graph (Figure 3) when you're in Graph. To return to PowerPoint, click anywhere on the slide outside of this border.

Graph offers its own toolbar.

This border around the graph indicates you're in Graph.

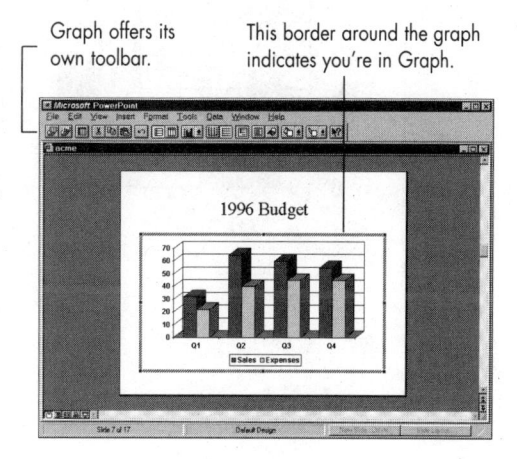

Figure 3. Working in Microsoft Graph

Inserting Graphs

47

CHAPTER 4

Graph Terminology

Figure 4 points out the key areas of a column chart; many chart types have these same areas.

The *y-axis* is known as the value axis since it always displays numbers on its scale. The *x-axis* is known as the category axis because it displays categories of data (quarters, months, years, names, and so forth).

Tick marks appear next to each value on the y-axis and between categories on the x-axis. *Gridlines* may extend from the tickmarks to help you interpret the values at each *data point*. A set of data points makes up a *data series*.

When a graph has more than one data series (Figure 3 has two—Sales and Expenses), a *legend* identifies each series.

■ Tip

✓ On a 3-D chart, the value axis is called the *z-axis*.

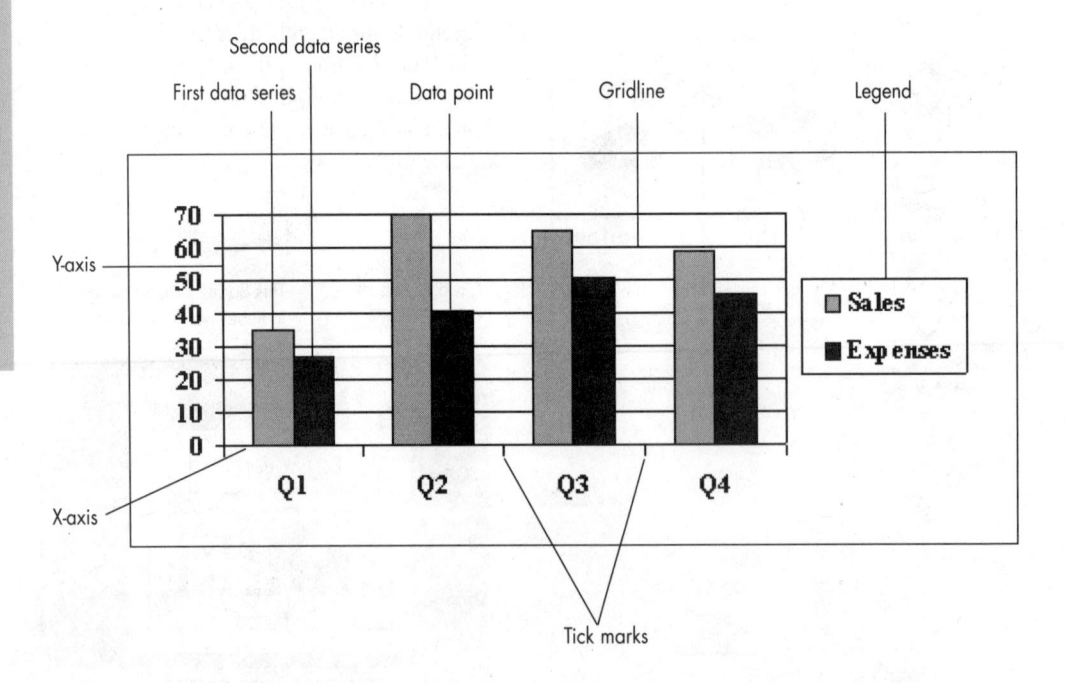

Figure 4. Key areas of a column chart

48

INSERTING GRAPHS

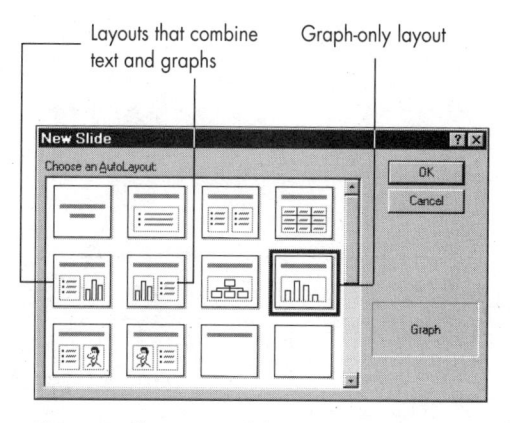

Figure 5. Choose a graph layout in the New Slide dialog box.

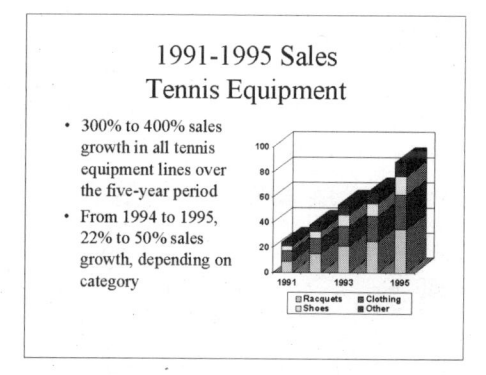

Figure 6. The Text & Graph AutoLayout

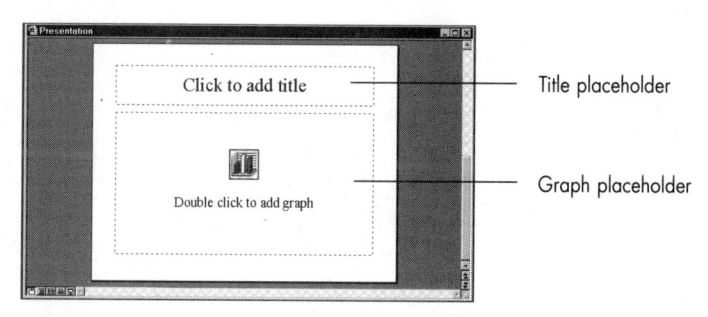

Figure 7. A new slide with title and graph placeholders in the Graph layout

Inserting a Graph Slide

PowerPoint offers three AutoLayouts that include graphs (Figure 5). An example of a slide that combines a bulleted list with a graph is shown in Figure 6.

1. Click the New Slide button at the bottom of the PowerPoint window.
2. In the New Slide dialog box, choose one of the graph layouts (Figure 5).
3. Click OK. The slide appears with title, graph, and perhaps text placeholders (Figure 7).
4. Click the title placeholder and type the title of your graph.
5. If the slide has a text placeholder, click it and type the text.
6. Double-click the graph placeholder to create your graph.

■ Tip

✓ In the text placeholder of a Text & Graph or Graph & Text layout, you can provide details about the graph, such as an interpretation of the data or a conclusion that can be drawn from the data.

For information on creating multiple graphs on a slide, see Creating Two Graphs on a Slide on page 57.

Inserting Graphs

49

CHAPTER 4

Entering Data

You enter your chart data in the datasheet window (Figure 8). The datasheet initially appears with sample data. Be sure to erase it before entering your own data. Each box in the datasheet is called a *cell*.

1. If you haven't already done so, double-click the graph placeholder to launch Microsoft Graph.
2. If the datasheet window isn't displayed, click the View Datasheet button (Figure 9).
3. To erase the sample data, click the Select All button (Figure 8) and press Delete.
4. Enter your graph data (Figure 10).
5. To view the graph, move the datasheet aside (by dragging the window's title bar) or close the datasheet window (by clicking the Close button).

■ Tips

✓ Be sure to use the Select All button when deleting the sample data. If you don't and your data consumes fewer rows and columns than the sample data, Microsoft Graph still reserves space for this data on the graph (Figure 11). To fix this problem, use the Exclude Row/Col command on the Data menu.

✓ If you accidentally enter data in a row or column and then erase it, Graph reserves space for this erased data, anyway. Again, you can fix this problem by using the Exclude Row/Col command.

✓ Figure 10 shows the default layout for entering data. However, feel free to enter legend labels in the top row and x-axis labels in the leftmost column. But if you do this, you must let Graph know that the data series are entered into columns instead of rows. Use the Series in Columns command on the Data menu, or click the By Column button on the Graph toolbar (Figure 9).

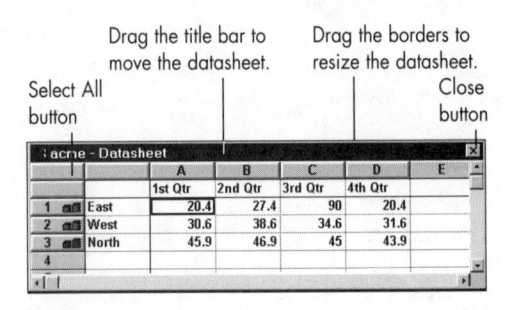

Figure 8. The sample data in the datasheet

Figure 9. When you see the Graph toolbar, you know you're in Microsoft Graph.

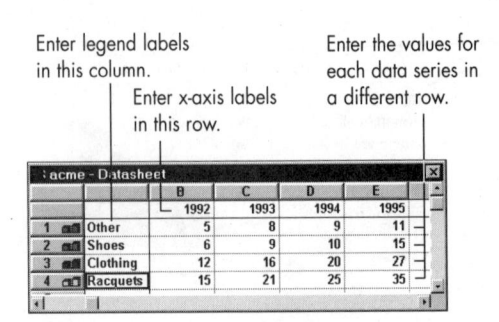

Figure 10. How to enter data in the datasheet

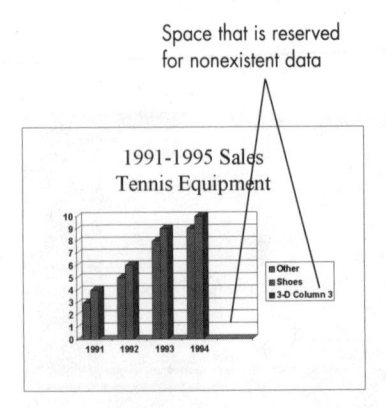

Figure 11. The Exclude Row/Col command on the Data menu will fix the problems on this graph.

Inserting Graphs

50

INSERTING GRAPHS

Choose the file type first.

Don't forget to specify to import the entire file or a range.

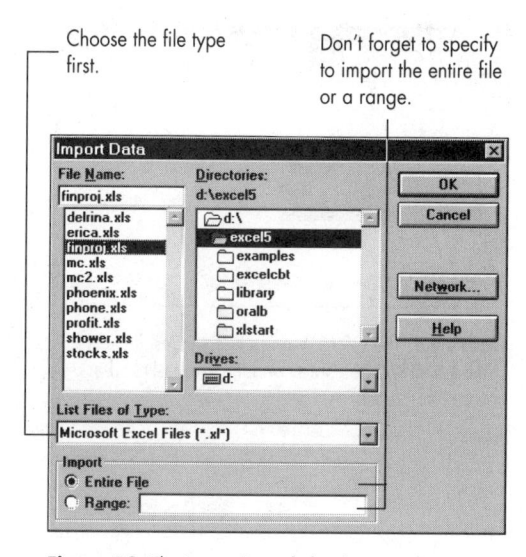

Figure 12. The Import Data dialog box

Import Data

Figure 13. The Graph toolbar

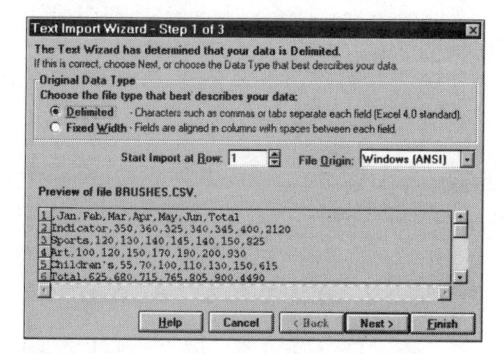

Figure 14. The Text Import Wizard steps you through the process of importing a text file.

Importing Data

If the chart data already exists in Microsoft Excel, Lotus 1-2-3, or in a text file, you don't need to retype it in the datasheet—you can *import* the data.

1. Delete the sample data in the datasheet (see previous page).
2. Click the first cell of the datasheet.
3. Select Edit/Import Data. The Import Data dialog box appears (Figure 12).
4. Click the List Files of Type field to display a list of file types, and choose the desired type (such as Microsoft Excel or Lotus 1-2-3).
5. Choose Entire File.

   or

   Choose Range and then type the range of cells to be imported.
6. Choose the appropriate drive and directory where the file is located.
7. In the File Name list, click the file name.
8. Click OK.

■ Tips

✓ You can also import data by clicking the Import Data button (Figure 13).

✓ The range can be specified with either cell coordinates (such as A5:H10) or a range name.

✓ If you aren't sure of the range, import the entire file and then use Edit/Delete (not the Delete key) to remove rows and columns you don't need.

✓ When importing a text file, you are prompted for information on how the file is delimited. *Delimiters* are the characters between fields, such as commas, spaces, and tabs. Figure 14 shows one of the Text Import Wizard dialog boxes.

Inserting Graphs

51

Linking Data

Another way to import data is to *link* it from an existing spreadsheet file. When data is linked, changes made to the source file are automatically reflected in the PowerPoint datasheet and graph.

1. Launch the application that created the source file, and open the file (Figure 15).
2. Select the data to be linked, and select Edit/Copy.
3. Switch back to PowerPoint.
4. Create a new graph slide, double-click the graph placeholder, and then delete the sample data in the datasheet.
5. Click the first cell of the datasheet.
6. Select Edit/Paste Link, and click OK to continue.
7. Look at the sample chart in the ChartWizard dialog box (Figure 16), and change any options if necessary.
8. Click OK.
9. Move or close the datasheet to see your new slide.

■ Tips

✓ As long as the chart is open in Graph, changes to the source file are instantly reflected in the datasheet and graph. If you change the spreadsheet when the chart is not open in Graph, the chart is not updated until you reopen it in Graph (that is, until you double-click the embedded graph on the slide).

✓ If you forget the name or location of the source file, select Edit/Link to display the Link dialog box (Figure 17).

✓ A fast way to open your source file is to click the Open Source button in the Link dialog box.

✓ Use the Change Source button in the Link dialog box if you have moved or renamed the source file.

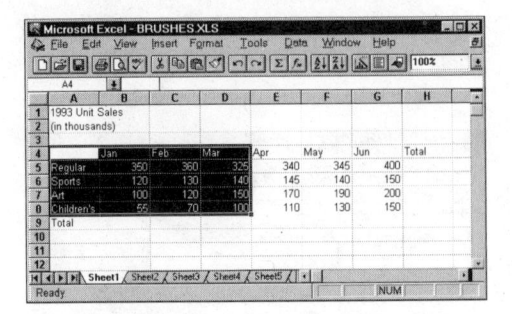

Figure 15. The selected range in a Microsoft Excel spreadsheet will be copied and then paste-linked in a PowerPoint datasheet.

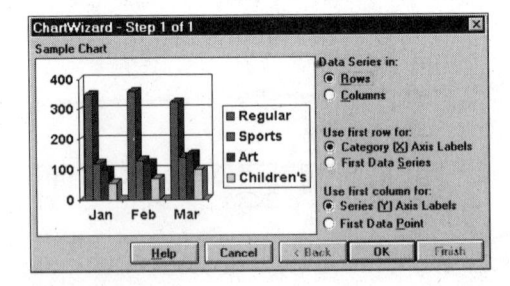

Figure 16. The ChartWizard dialog box. Feel free to change any options if the sample graph is not laid out properly.

The source application, file name, sheet name, and imported cell range

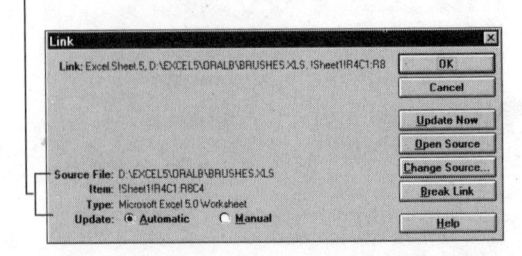

Figure 17. While in the datasheet, select Edit/Link to display the Link dialog box.

INSERTING GRAPHS

Choose a chart dimension first. Then, click a chart type. Finally, click here to choose a subtype.

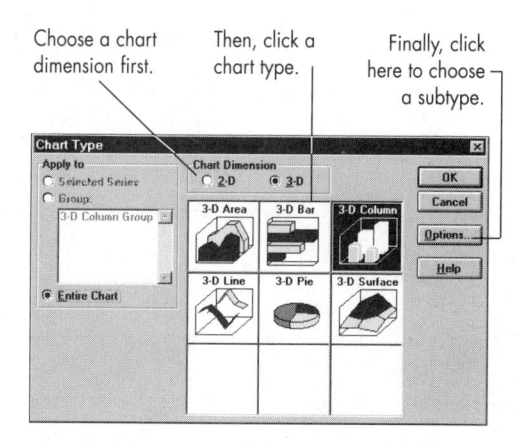

Figure 18. The Chart Type dialog box

A preview of the selected subtype

Subtype tab

Subtypes

Redisplays Chart Type dialog box

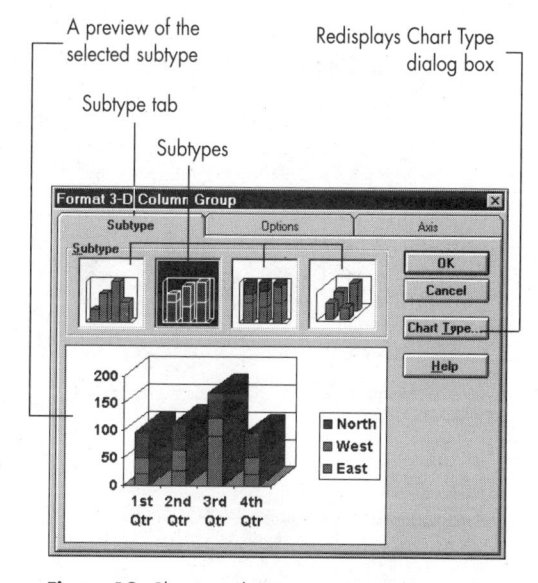

Figure 19. Choose a chart type variation.

Chart Type

Click here to display a palette of chart types.

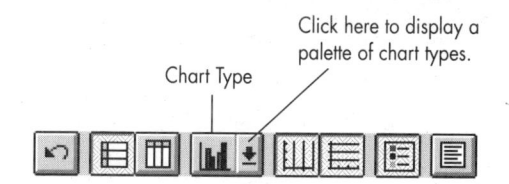

Figure 20. The Graph toolbar

Choosing a Chart Type

The default chart type is 3-D column. You can choose a different chart type before or after you enter data in the datasheet. In addition to choosing a chart type, you can choose a *subtype*. Subtypes are variations of the selected chart type. For example, a 3-D column graph has subtypes for clustered bars, stacked bars, 100% bars, and so forth.

1. If necessary, double-click the embedded graph to go into Microsoft Graph.
2. Select Format/Chart Type. The Chart Type dialog box appears (Figure 18).
3. For the Chart Dimension, choose 2-D or 3-D.
4. Click one of the chart types.
5. Click Options (Figure 19).
6. In the Subtype page, click the desired subtype. Watch the preview box to see how your graph looks.
7. Click OK.

■ Tip

✓ Another way to change the chart type is with the Chart Type button (Figure 20). By clicking the arrow next to the button, you will see a palette of 14 chart types. However, you cannot choose subtypes here.

Inserting Graphs

53

CHAPTER 4

Inserting Titles

You can insert titles at the top of the chart or on any of the axes.

1. Select Insert/Titles. The Titles dialog box appears (Figure 21).
2. Select one or more of the titles.
3. Click OK. For each title, a placeholder containing dummy text is inserted (Figure 22).
4. With the placeholder selected, type the title text. (The dummy text automatically disappears .)

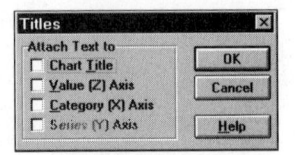

Figure 21. Choose one or more titles.

Rotating an Axis Title

Frequently, you will want the value axis title rotated 90 degrees (Figure 23).

1. Select the axis title—make sure the placeholder has selection handles around it. (If you see the text cursor, click elsewhere on the graph and then again on the title.)
2. Select Format/Selected Axis Title.
   or
   Press the right mouse button to display the shortcut menu, and choose Format Axis Title.
3. Click the Alignment tab (Figure 24).
4. Choose one of the Orientation options.
5. Click OK.

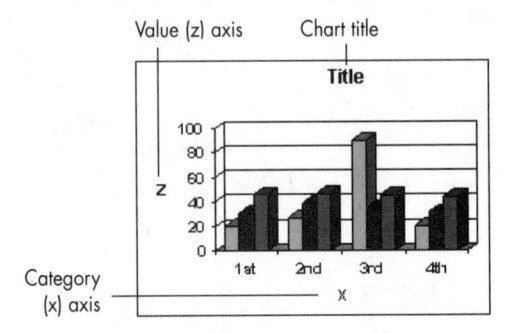

Figure 22. Chart and axis title placeholders

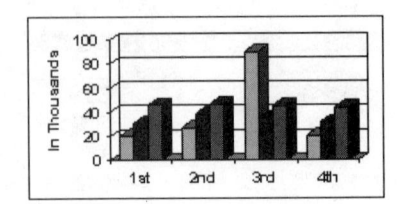

Figure 23. The value axis title is rotated 90 degrees.

■ Tip

✓ The Titles command is not available when the datasheet is open. Just click the close button on the datasheet window to close the datasheet.

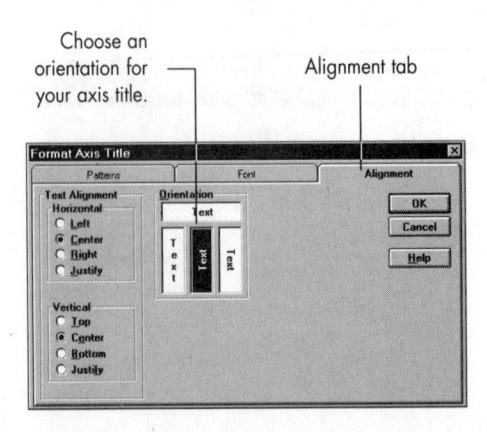

Figure 24. Use this dialog to rotate an axis title.

Inserting Graphs

54

INSERTING GRAPHS

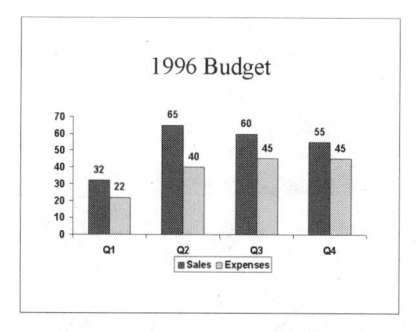

Figure 25. Data labels appear above each data point.

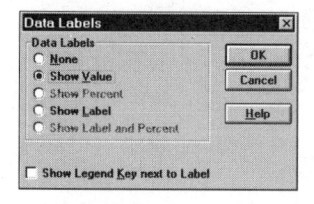

Figure 26. Select Insert/Data Labels to display the Data Labels dialog box.

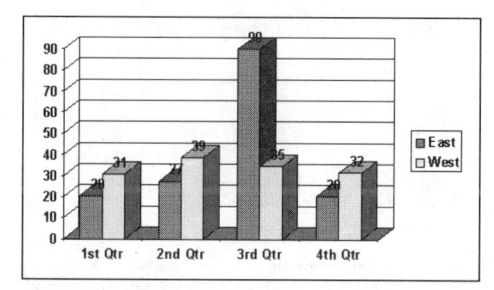

Figure 27. With the data labels in the default positions, the values are difficult to read.

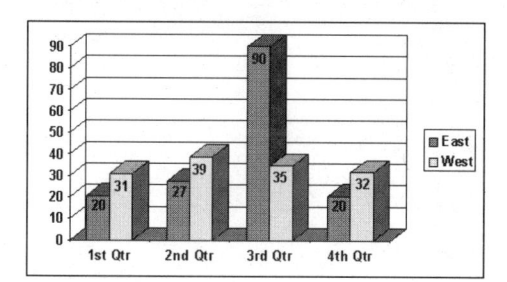

Figure 28. After the data labels are moved inside the columns, the values become easier to see.

Inserting Data Labels

You can place *data labels* on data points to show their exact values (Figure 25).

1. Press Esc to make sure nothing is selected.
2. Select Insert/Data Labels. The Data Labels dialog box appears (Figure 26).
3. Choose Show Value and click OK.

Repositioning Data Labels

Graph inserts the data labels near the data point but sometimes the labels from one series will overlap the labels from another, or the label may be unreadable in its current position (Figure 27). Fortunately, you can position the data labels exactly where you want them (Figure 28).

1. Click the data label you want to move.
2. Drag the label to the desired positon.
3. Repeat the above steps for each label to be repositioned.

■ Tips

- ✓ The Data Labels command is not available when the datasheet is open. Just click the close button on the datasheet window to close the datasheet.
- ✓ Data labels are not appropriate for all graphs. If the graph has many data points or many data series, the graph may look too busy with data labels.
- ✓ If a label appears above the plot area, you can either move the label or change the upper value on the y-axis scale.

  See Scaling the Axis on page 67.
- ✓ You can change the size and color of data labels with the Format/Selected Data Labels command, on the Font page.

Inserting Graphs

55

CHAPTER 4

Revising a Graph

To revise a previously-created graph, you need to reopen it in Microsoft Graph.

1. Double-click the embedded graph (Figures 29 and 30).
2. If you need to update the data and the datasheet is not currently displayed, click the View Datasheet button (Figure 31). If you don't need to change the data, go to step 6.
3. To replace the contents of a cell, click the cell and type the new value. The graph instantly reflects the change to the datasheet.
4. To edit the contents of a cell, double-click the cell. A text cursor appears. Position the cursor where you want to make the change, and then insert or delete characters. Press Enter when you are finished.
5. Click the graph to close the datasheet.
6. Make any desired changes to the graph (insert titles, insert data labels, change the chart type, and so forth).
7. When you are finished making changes, click the slide outside of the graph to return to PowerPoint.

■ Tip

✓ If you're unsure whether or not you're in Microsoft Graph or PowerPoint, display the Help menu. The bottom menu choice will be either "About Microsoft Graph" or "About Microsoft PowerPoint."

Figure 29. Opening the embedded graph in Microsoft Graph

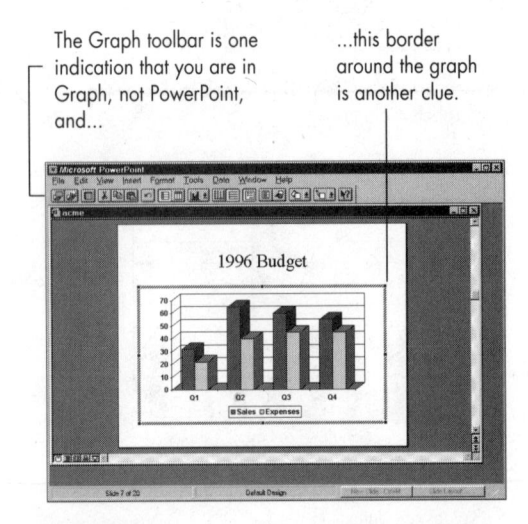

Figure 30. The graph after it is opened in Microsoft Graph

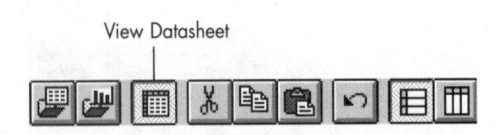

Figure 31. The Graph toolbar

INSERTING GRAPHS

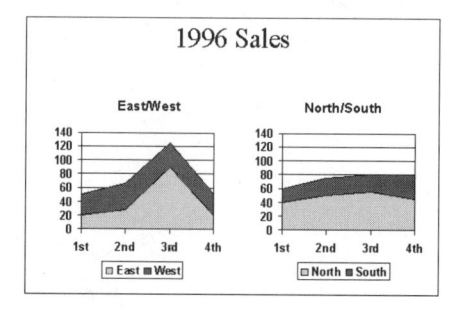

Figure 32. Two graphs on one slide

Figure 33. A slide with the Graph & Text layout

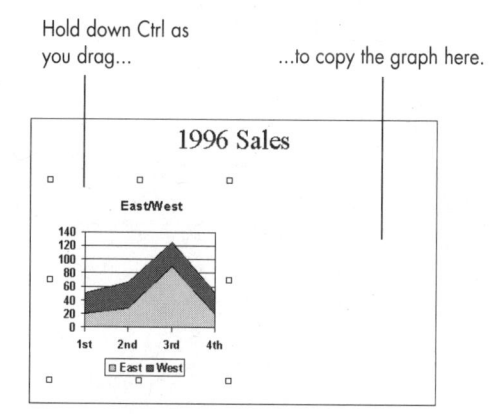

Figure 34. Creating a second graph on a slide

Creating Two Graphs on a Slide

Although PowerPoint doesn't offer a layout for two graphs, you can easily create such a slide (Figure 32).

1. Use the New Slide button to insert a new slide with the Graph & Text or Text & Graph layout.
2. To delete the text placeholder, hold down Shift as you click the placeholder and press Delete (Figure 33).
3. Create the first graph: Double-click the graph placeholder, enter data, choose a chart type, and so forth.
4. Exit Graph by clicking the slide outside the graph.
5. To copy the graph, place the mouse pointer on the embedded graph, and hold down Ctrl as you drag to the other side of the slide (Figure 34).
6. Revise the second graph by double-clicking it, entering data, choosing the chart type, and so on.
7. Exit Graph.

■ Tips

✓ To make sure the two graphs are aligned with one another, use the Draw/Align command.

See Aligning Objects on page 138.

✓ It's easier to compare data in the two graphs when the axes use the same scale.

See Scaling the Axis on page 67.

✓ Each graph should have its own title. You can either use the Insert/Titles command in Microsoft Graph or use the Text tool in PowerPoint.

See Inserting Titles on page 54 and Creating a Text Placeholder on page 32.

57

FORMATTING GRAPHS 5

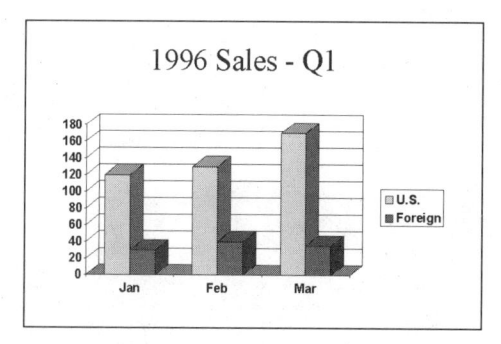

Figure 1. A 3-D column graph with the default settings

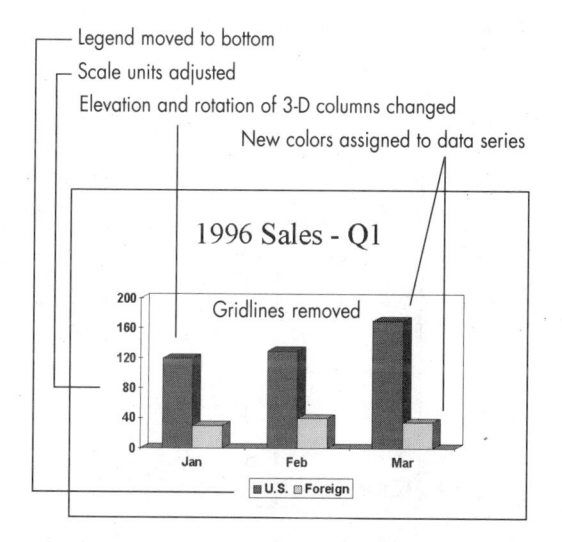

Legend moved to bottom
Scale units adjusted
Elevation and rotation of 3-D columns changed
New colors assigned to data series
Gridlines removed

Figure 2. The same 3-D column graph after formatting

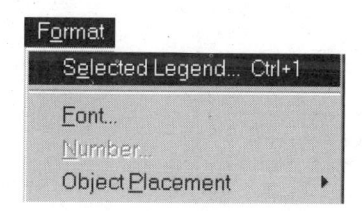

Figure 3. When the legend is selected, the Format menu offers the command S<u>e</u>lected Legend.

Ways to Format Graphs

Microsoft Graph offers an abundance of ways to format your graphs. You can reposition the legend, add and remove gridlines, change the color of the data series, change the upper and lower limits on the value axis, and so forth. Figure 1 shows a graph with the default settings, and Figure 2 shows the same graph after formatting.

See Graph Terminology on page 48.

Here is the basic procedure for formatting a graph:

1. If you're not already in Microsoft Graph, double-click your embedded graph.
2. Select the area of the graph you want to format—you may need to click more than once. For example, to format the legend, click the legend until you see selection handles around it.
3. Select Format/Selected *xxx*, where *xxx* is the name of the selected area. For example, if the legend is selected, the command will be Selected Legend (Figure 3).

Another way to display the appropriate Format dialog box is to double-click the area you want to format. Alternatively, you can point to the area you want to format and press the right mouse button to display the shortcut menu. Then click Format *xxx*, where *xxx* is the name of the selected area.

■ **Tip**

✓ Sometimes you'll think you have selected a certain area, but in fact have selected a different area. A clue that you have done this is when the Format menu shows Selected *xxx* and *xxx* is not the area you want to format. If this happens, cancel the menu and reselect the area.

Formatting Graphs

59

CHAPTER 5

Formatting the Legend

By default, the legend has a thin border around it. If you like, you can thicken the border, add a drop shadow, shdade the background, or remove it altogether. Figure 4 shows a legend with the default border. In Figure 5 the legend is formatted with a drop shadow.

1. Select the legend.
2. Select Format/Selected Legend. The Format Legend dialog box appears.

   or

   Right-click the legend and choose Format Legend from the shortcut menu.
3. Click the Patterns tab (Figure 6).
4. To choose a different border style (such as dashed lines), display the Style list (Figure 7) and choose one of the styles.
5. To choose a different line thickness, display the Weight list (Figure 8) and choose one of the weights.
6. To add a drop shadow, turn on the Shadow check box.
7. To shade the background of the legend, click one of the colors in the palette under Area (Figure 6).
8. To remove the border, choose None under Border.
9. Click OK.

■ Tip

✓ To enlarge the legend, drag the selection handles.

To format the legend text, see Formatting Graph Text on page 69.

To reposition the legend, see the opposite page.

Figure 4. The default legend border

Figure 5. A shadowed legend border

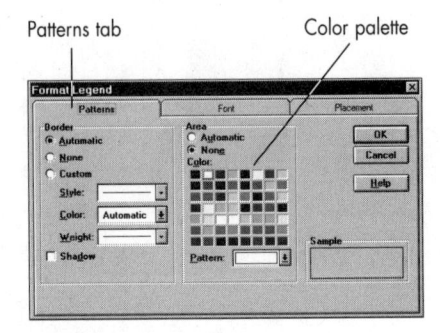

Figure 6. Formatting the legend

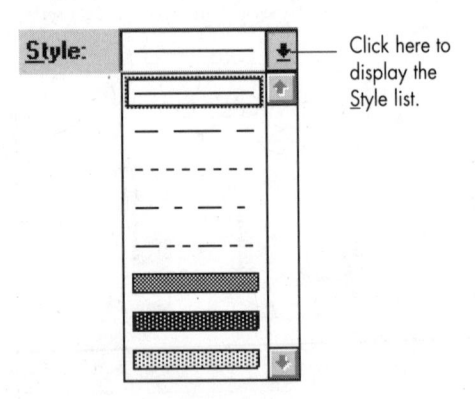

Figure 7. The Style list

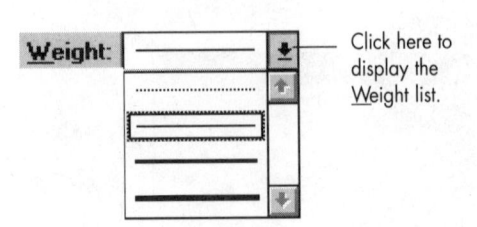

Figure 8. The Weight list

FORMATTING GRAPHS

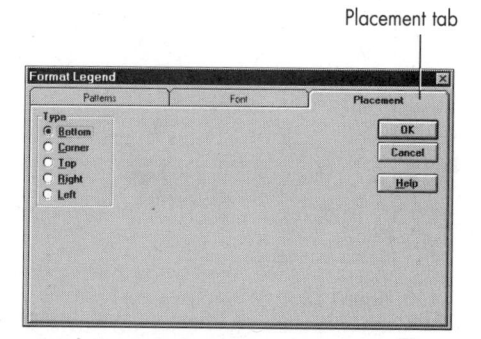

Figure 9. Choosing a legend position

Placement tab

Repositioning the Legend

You can place the legend in a variety of standard positions on the graph.

1. Select the legend.
2. Select Format/Selected Legend.

   or

   Right-click the legend and choose Format Legend from the shortcut menu.
3. Click the Placement tab (Figure 9).
4. Choose one of the placement positions illustrated in Figure 10.
5. Click OK.

■ Tips

✓ When you reposition a legend using the Format Legend dialog box, the plot area resizes to allow room for the legend in its new location. However, Microsoft Graph still allows room for the legend in its former location, as well (Figure 11). To solve this problem, resize the plot area yourself: Select the plot area and drag the selection handles.

For more information on selecting the plot area, see page 71.

✓ Another way to reposition the legend is to drag it to the desired location (Figure 12). Unfortunately the plot area does not adjust automatically, so you may need to resize or move the plot area yourself.

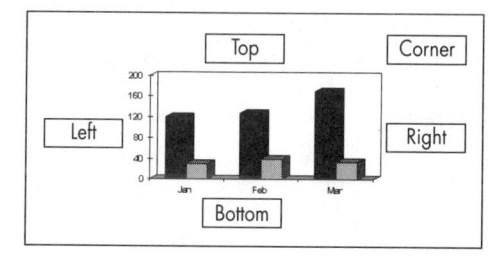

Figure 10. Legend placements

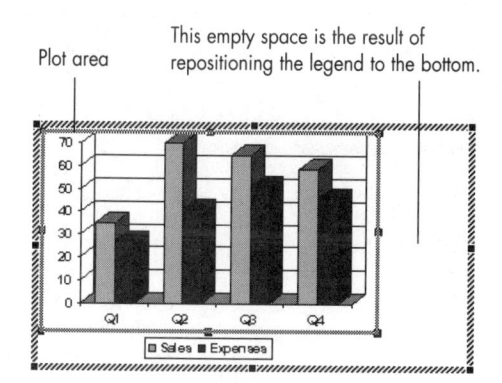

Figure 11. You may want to resize the plot area after repositioning the legend.

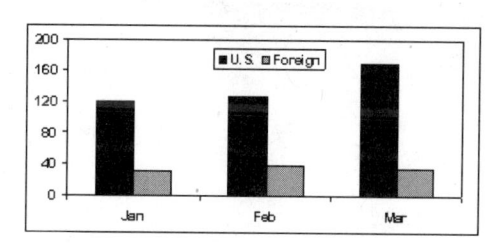

Figure 12. The legend was positioned inside the plot area by dragging it manually.

Formatting Graphs

61

CHAPTER 5

Changing the Color or Pattern of a Data Series

Figure 13 shows an area graph with a pattern assigned to one of its data series.

1. Click one of the data series (a line, bar, column, area, and so forth). There should be selection handles around the series as shown in Figures 14 and 15.
2. Select Format/Selected Data Series.

   or

   Right-click a data point in the series and choose Format Data Series from the shortcut menu.
3. Click the Patterns tab (Figures 16 and 17). Note that the Format Data Series dialog box has different options depending upon the chart type.
4. Choose a color in the Color palette.
5. Choose a pattern in the Pattern palette.
6. Click OK.

■ Tip

✓ Patterns have two colors: one for the pattern itself (dots, lines, etc) and one for the background. Select the pattern color in the pattern palette and choose the background color in the color palette.

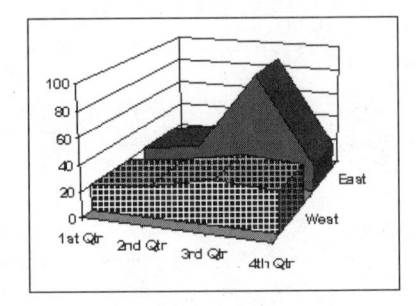

Figure 13. The West data series has a criss-cross pattern.

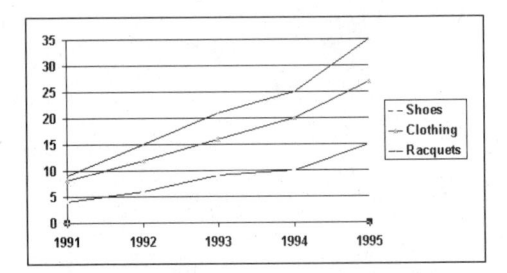

Figure 14. The first data series is selected in this column graph.

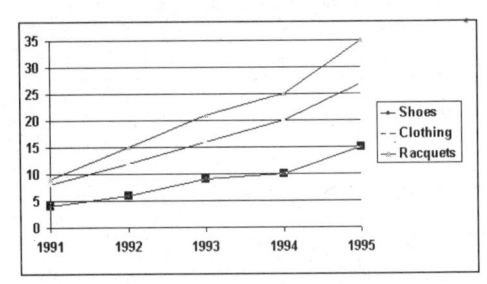

Figure 15. The last data series is selected in this line graph.

Patterns tab

Click here to display the color palette.

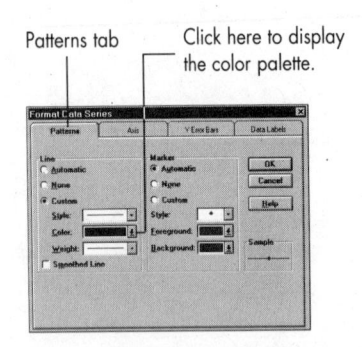

Figure 17. The Patterns page for line graphs offers options specific to this graph type.

Patterns tab

Choose a color in the color palette.

Click here to display the pattern palette.

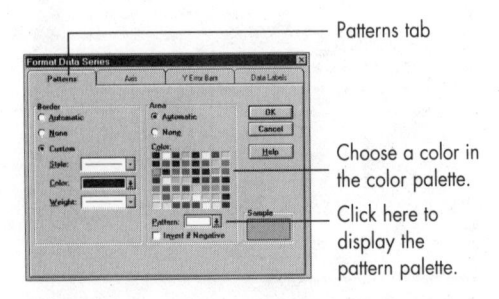

Figure 16. The Patterns page for bar, column, area, and surface graphs (for a 2-D graph)

Formatting Graphs

FORMATTING GRAPHS

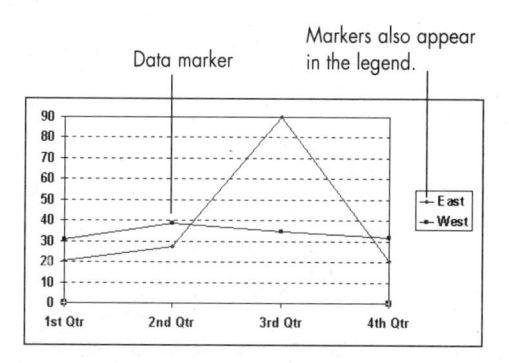

Figure 18. A line graph with data markers

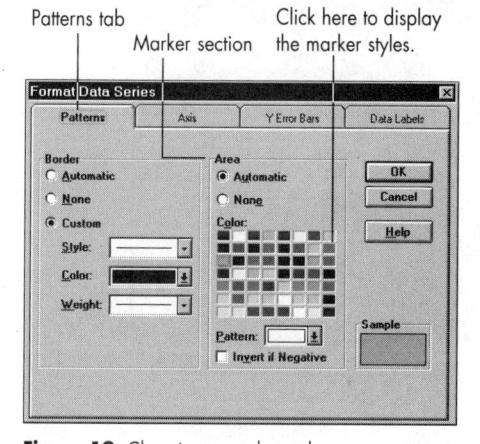

Figure 19. Choosing a marker style

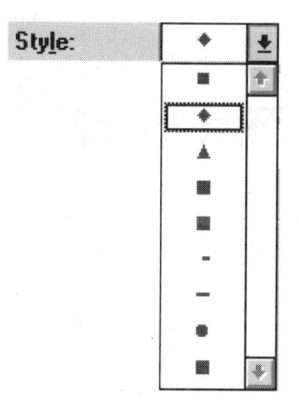

Figure 20. The list of marker styles

Formatting Data Markers

Data markers are symbols, such as circles or squares, that appear at data points on line, XY, and radar graphs. The markers also appear in the legend to help you identify each data series (Figure 18).

1. Click one of the data series. There should be selection handles at each data point.
2. Select Format/Selected Data Series.

   or

   Right-click a data point in the series and choose Format Data Series from the shortcut menu.
3. Click the Patterns tab (Figure 19).
4. In the Marker section, display the Style list and choose a marker style (Figure 20).
5. Click OK.
6. Repeat steps 1–5 for other data series, if desired.

■ Tips

✓ In the Marker section, choose None if you don't want any markers on the line. Make sure, though, that each line is a different color so you have some way of differentiating the series.

✓ The markers appear quite small in Microsoft Graph and in PowerPoint (Figure 18). However, the markers will be easily discernable when you print the slide or show it in a Slide Show.

Formatting Graphs

63

CHAPTER 5

Inserting/Removing Gridlines

Gridlines are the lines that extend from the tick marks on the axes (Figure 21). They are useful for interpreting the actual values of the data points. A graph can have horizontal and/or vertical gridlines.

1. Select Insert/Gridlines. The Gridlines dialog box appears (Figure 22).
2. To insert/remove vertical gridlines, turn on/off the Major Gridlines check box under the Category Axis heading.
3. To insert/remove horizontal gridlines, turn on/off the Major Gridlines check box under the Value Axis heading.
4. Click OK.

■ **Tips**

✓ You can also insert and remove gridlines with the Vertical Gridlines and Horizontal Gridlines buttons (Figure 23). These buttons are toggles—they will insert or remove gridlines each time you click them.

✓ *Minor gridlines* extend from the minor tick marks (ticks between the scale increments). You will not usually want minor gridlines because the graph would then contain too many lines (Figure 24).

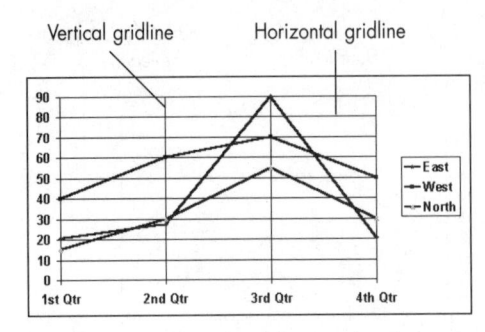

Figure 21. A line graph with horizontal and vertical gridlines

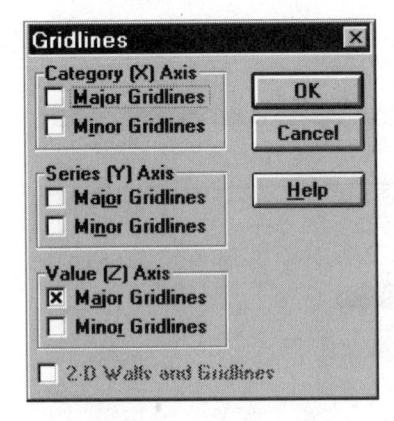

Figure 22. The Gridlines dialog box (for a 3-D graph)

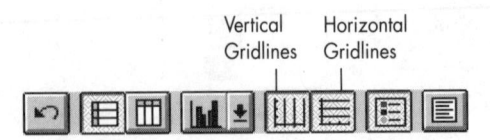

Figure 23. The Graph toolbar

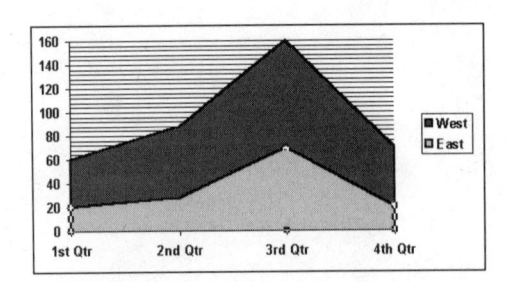

Figure 24. Minor gridlines

Formatting Graphs

64

FORMATTING GRAPHS

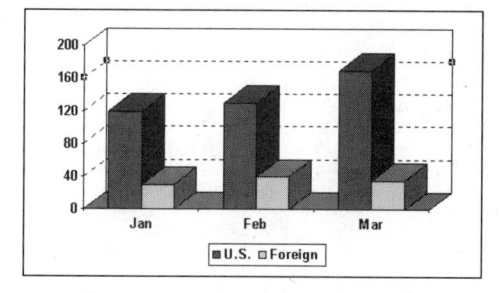

Figure 25. Gridlines with a dotted style

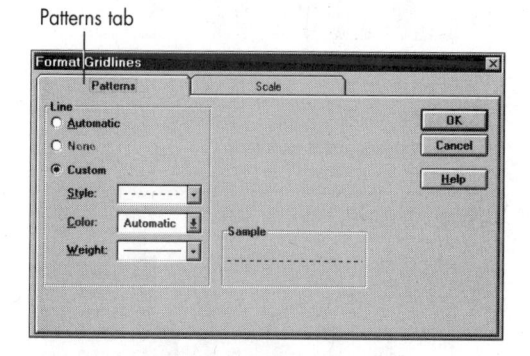

Figure 26. Choosing a different format for the gridlines

Formatting Gridlines

You can change both the thickness and the style of the gridlines (Figure 25).

1. Select one of the gridlines.
2. Select Format/Selected Gridlines.

    or

    Right-click a gridline and choose Format Gridlines from the shortcut menu.
3. Choose the Patterns tab (Figure 26).
4. To choose a different line style (such as dashed lines), display the Style list and choose one of the styles.
5. To choose a different color, display the Color palette and choose a color.
6. To choose a different line thickness, display the Weight list and choose one of the weights.
7. Click OK.

Formatting Graphs

65

CHAPTER 5

Formatting the Tick Marks

A *tick mark* is a tiny line next to each label on an axis. You can place tick marks inside, outside, or crossing the axis (Figures 27 and 28). You can also choose to have *minor tick-marks* between the major marks (Figure 29).

1. Select the axis whose tick marks you want to format.
2. Select Format/Selected Axis.

   or

   Right-click the axis and choose Format Axis from the shortcut menu.
3. Click the Patterns tab (Figure 30).
4. In the Tick Mark Type section, select the type of Major mark: None, Inside, Outside, or Cross.
5. Select the type of Minor mark: None, Inside, Outside, or Cross.
6. Click OK.

■ Tip

✓ The frequency of the tick marks depends on the major and minor units.

See Scaling the Axis on the opposite page for information on specifying the major and minor units.

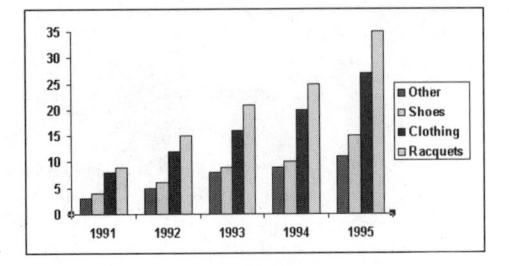

Figure 27. The x- and y-axes have outside tick-marks.

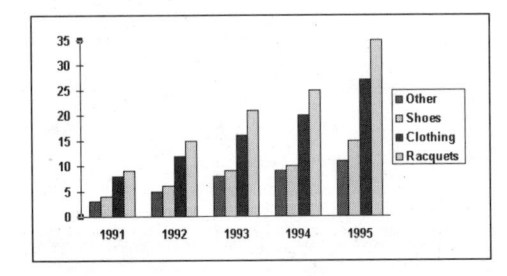

Figure 28. On this graph, the tick marks cross the y-axis; no marks appear on the x-axis.

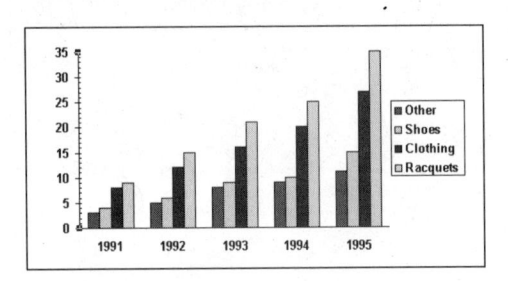

Figure 29. The y-axis has major tick marks on the outside, and minor tick marks on the inside.

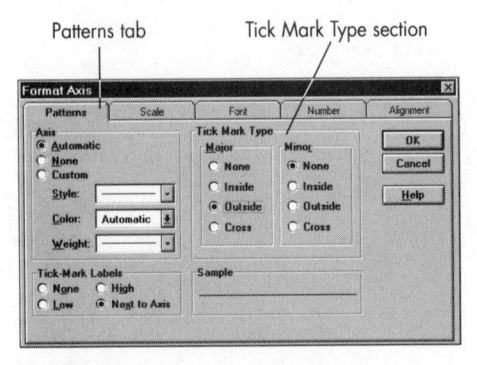

Figure 30. Choosing types of tick marks

FORMATTING GRAPHS

- Minimum value is 0.
- Major Unit is 10.
- Maximum value is 90.
- Number of categories between tick-mark labels is 1.

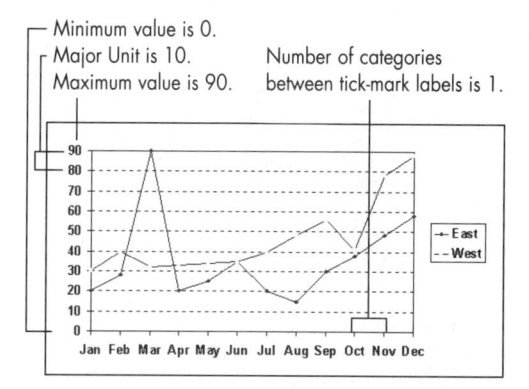

Figure 31. The default y-axis and x-axis scales

- Minimum value is 0.
- Major Unit is 20.
- Maximum value is 100.
- Number of categories between tick-mark labels is 2.

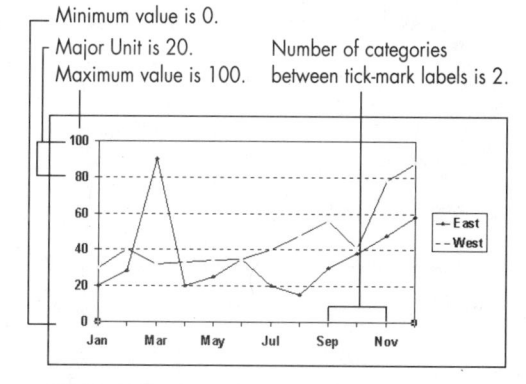

Figure 32. Scaling has been adjusted on this line graph.

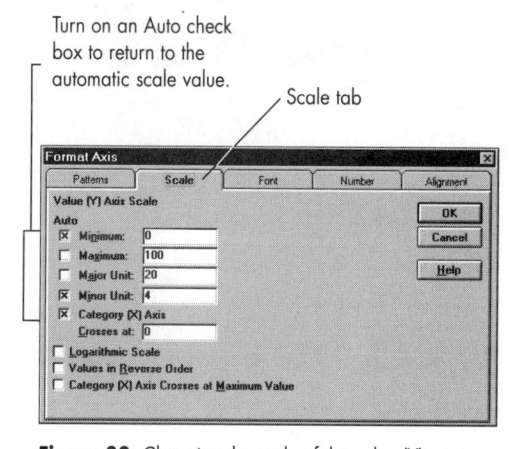

Turn on an Auto check box to return to the automatic scale value.

Scale tab

Figure 33. Changing the scale of the value (Y) axis

Scaling the Axis

On the *value axis* (such as the y-axis in Figure 31), Microsoft Graph lets you adjust the maximum value, minimum value, and major unit (increments between labels). On the *category axis* (such as the x-axis in Figure 31), you can adjust the number of categories between labels and tick marks. Figure 32 shows the line graph after adjusting the scales.

1. Select the axis to be scaled. Selection handles appear at both ends of the axis.
2. Select Format/Selected Axis.

   or

   Right-click the axis and choose Format Axis from the shortcut menu.
3. Click the Scale tab (Figures 33 and 34).
4. For the value axis, enter new values for the Minimum, Maximum, Major Unit, and/or Minor Unit. (The X disappears in the Auto column when you change a value.)

   or

   For the category axis, enter new values for Number of Categories between Tick-Mark Labels and/or Number of Categories between Tick Marks.
5. Click OK.

■ **Tip**

✓ To return to the default scale values, turn on the check box in the Auto column, next to the appropriate item (Figure 33).

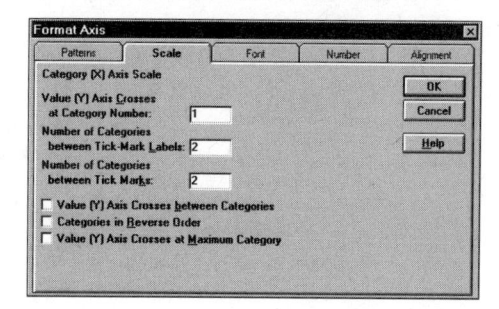

Figure 34. Changing the scale of the category (X) axis

67

CHAPTER 5

Formatting the Axis Numbers

Figure 35 shows a value axis in which the numbers have been formatted to display dollar signs.

1. Select the axis whose numbers you want to format.
2. Select F<u>o</u>rmat/S<u>e</u>lected Axis.

   or

   Right-click the axis and choose Format Axis from the shortcut menu.
3. Choose the Number tab (Figure 36).
4. From the <u>C</u>ategory list, choose the appropriate formatting category (such as Number, Percentage, or Currency).
5. In the list of <u>F</u>ormat Codes, choose the code with the appropriate formatting.
6. Click OK.

■ Tips

✓ After clicking a format code, look at the Sample (circled in Figure 36) to preview what the number will look like.

✓ Instead of formatting all the numbers to currency, you can insert an axis title that explains that the values are in dollars (Figure 37).

   See Inserting Titles on page 54.

✓ Data label values can also be formatted. Suppose some of the numbers in the datasheet have 1 decimal place and others have none. For a consistent appearance, you may want to format all the data labels on the graph to 0 decimal places.

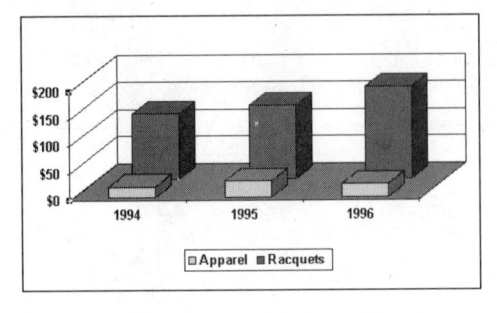

Figure 35. The numbers on the value axis have been given a Currency format.

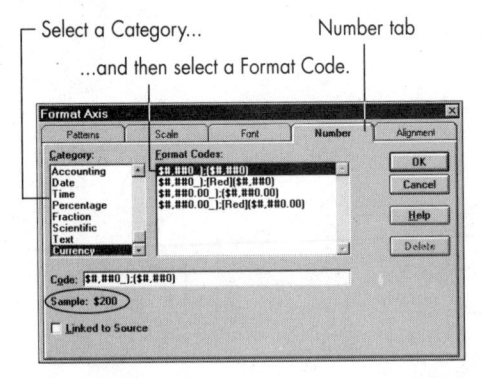

Figure 36. Formatting axis numbers

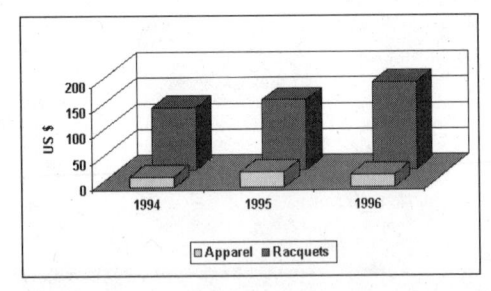

Figure 37. In this 3-D column graph, the value axis has a title that explains the scale is in U.S. dollars.

FORMATTING GRAPHS

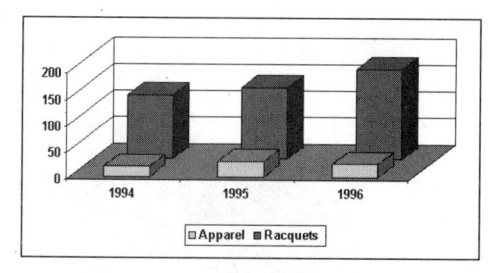

Figure 38. The text in this graph uses the default typeface (Arial) and size (18 points).

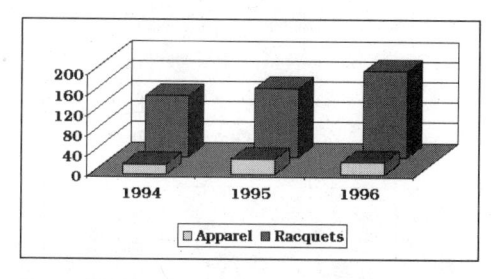

Figure 39. The text in this graph has been formatted to 22-point Bookman.

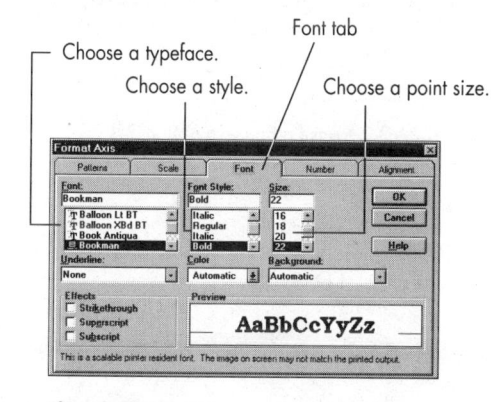

Figure 40. Formatting graph text

- Choose a typeface.
- Choose a style.
- Font tab
- Choose a point size.

Formatting Graph Text

You can format the text in each graph area (legend, titles, and so forth) with a particular typeface, size, and style (Figures 38 and 39).

1. Select the area whose text you want to format.

   or

   Within a selected title, drag across the individual characters you want to format.

2. Select Format/Selected *xxx* where *xxx* is the area you selected.

   or

   Right-click the text and choose Format *xxx* from the shortcut menu.

3. Click the Font tab (Figure 40).

4. In the Font list, choose the desired typeface (use the scroll bar if necessary).

5. Select the desired Font Style (Regular, Italic, Bold, Bold Italic).

6. In the Size list, choose the desired point size (use the scroll bar if necessary).

7. Click OK.

■ Tips

✓ To format all the chart text to the same font, select the entire chart area (Figure 41).

✓ To avoid the "ransom note" look, use only one typeface on a graph.

Click just inside this border to select the chart area.

Selection handles here indicate the chart area is selected.

Figure 41. Select the chart area to format all the text at once.

Formatting Graphs

69

CHAPTER 5

Adjusting 3-D Effects

You can adjust the three-dimensionality of your 3-D graphs—their chart depth, gap depth, and gap width. Figure 42 shows a 3-D column graph with the default 3-D settings and Figure 43 shows the same graph after formatting.

You can see in Figures 42 and 43 that the *chart depth* is the depth of the graph's base, the *gap depth* is the vertical distance between each data point, and the *gap width* is the horizontal distance between each data point.

1. Select Format/1 3-D *xxx* Group where *xxx* is the type of graph, such as Column or Line.
2. Click the Options tab (Figure 44).
3. Click the arrows to adjust each 3-D setting. Watch the preview in the dialog box to see how the new values affect the three-dimensionality of the graph.
4. Click OK.

■ Tip

✓ You can also adjust the 3-D view of a graph. Figure 45 shows a graph after adjusting the elevation, rotation, and perspective, using the Format/3-D View command.

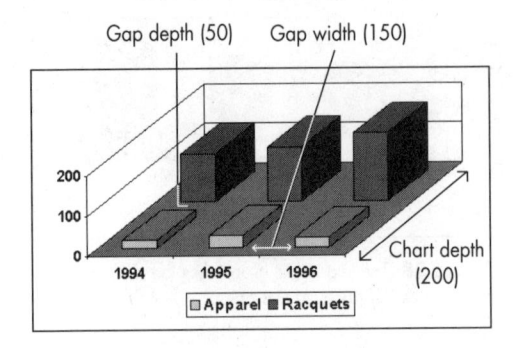

Figure 42. A 3-D column graph with the default 3-D settings

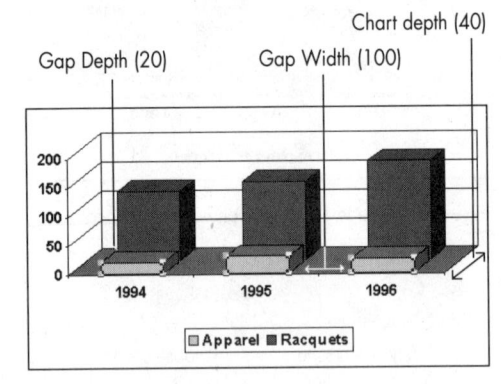

Figure 43. A 3-D column graph with altered 3-D settings

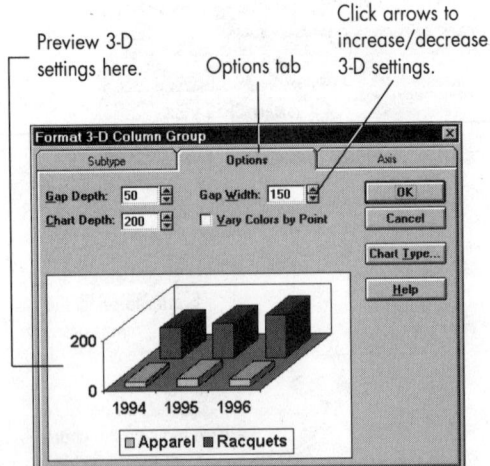

Figure 44. Adjusting 3-D settings for a 3-D column graph.

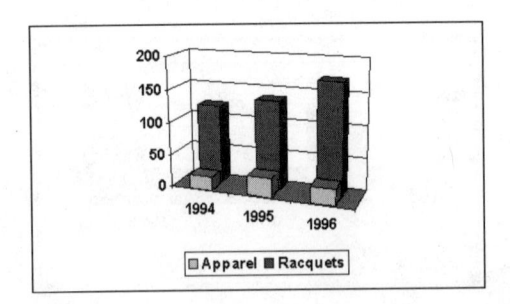

Figure 45. This 3-D column graph has a different perspective.

FORMATTING GRAPHS

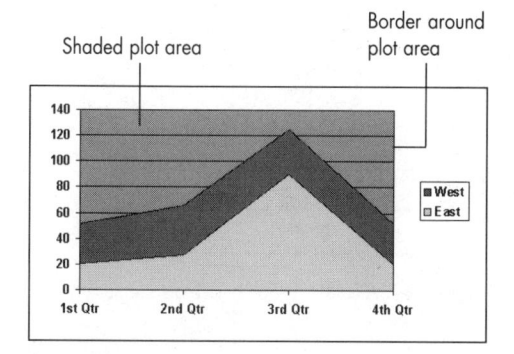

Figure 46. An area graph with a formatted plot area

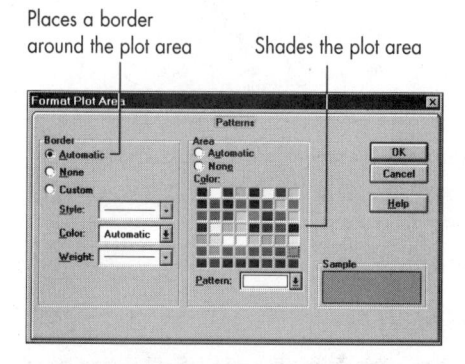

Figure 47. Formatting the plot area

Formatting the Plot Area

The *plot area* is the box formed by the horizontal and vertical axes. Figure 46 shows a graph with a formatted plot area.

1. Select the plot area (see first tip below).
2. Select Format/Selected Plot Area. The Format Plot Area dialog box appears (Figure 47).

   or

   Right-click the plot area and choose Format Plot Area from the shortcut menu.
3. To place a border around the plot area, turn on Automatic in the Border section.
4. To shade the plot area, choose a color from the palette in the Area section.
5. Click OK.

■ Tips

✓ The plot area can be tricky to select because there are so many other items inside or near this area. On 2-D graphs, either click inside the plot area in an area not occupied by any other item (Figure 48). On 3-D graphs, click between numbers on the value axis.

✓ In the Format Plot Area dialog box, you can also adjust the line style, weight, and color of the border.

For information on resizing the plot area, see page 61.

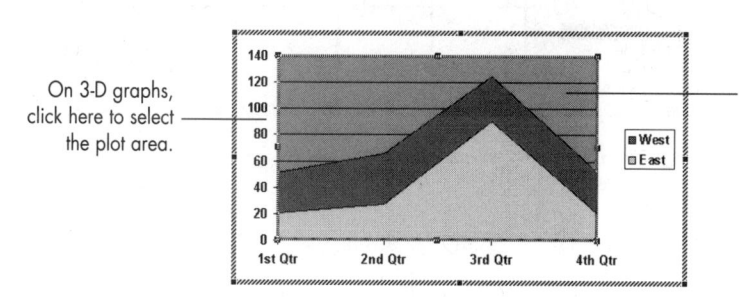

Figure 48. Selecting the plot area

71

CHAPTER 5

Formatting a Graph Automatically

With Microsoft Graph's *autoformatting* feature, you can quickly choose a chart type and apply formatting. Figures 49 and 50 show a graph before and after autoformatting.

1. Select Format/AutoFormat. The AutoFormat dialog box appears (Figure 51).
2. In the Galleries list, choose a chart type. The Formats area then displays subtypes with different formatting options.
3. Click one of the formats.
4. Click OK.

See opposite page for information on creating your own custom formats.

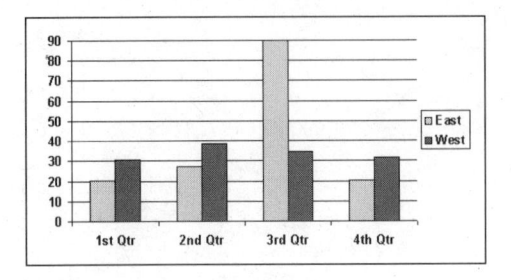

Figure 49. A column graph before autoformatting

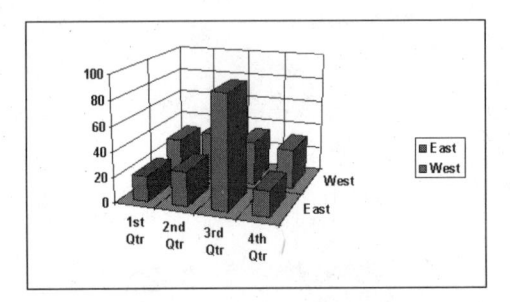

Figure 50. The same graph after autoformatting

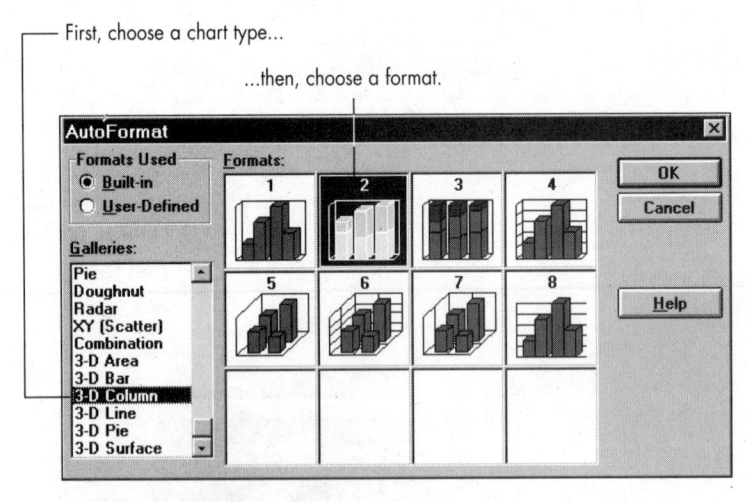

Figure 51. Choosing an AutoFormat

FORMATTING GRAPHS

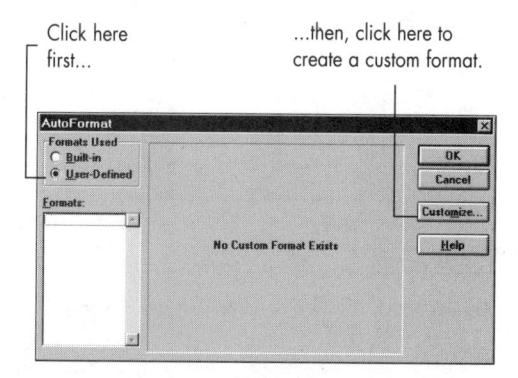

Figure 52. Creating a custom format

Click here first...

...then, click here to create a custom format.

Figure 53. This dialog box lists the custom formats that have already been defined and lets you add and delete formats.

Click here to add a custom format.

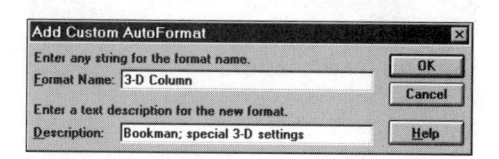

Figure 54. Enter the name and description for the custom format.

Defining a Custom AutoFormat

Suppose you want to format a series of graphs with the same settings. You can create your own AutoFormat and then apply it to any graph; these are called *user-defined* AutoFormats (as opposed to *built-in* AutoFormats).

1. Format a graph with the exact settings you want to duplicate in other graphs. This graph should be the active graph.
2. Select Format/AutoFormat.
3. In the Formats Used section, select User-Defined (Figure 52).
4. Click the Customize button. The User-Defined AutoFormats dialog box appears (Figure 53).
5. Click the Add button. The Add Custom AutoFormat dialog box appears (Figure 54).
6. In the Format Name field, type a name for the format (up to 31 characters).
7. In the Description field, describe the format in more detail (up to 32 characters).
8. Click OK.
9. Click Close.
10. Click OK.

■ Tip

✓ It's best to keep the format name under 15 characters. (Although the name can be up to 31 characters long, only the first 15 characters or so will show in the Formats list.)

CHAPTER 5

Applying a Custom AutoFormat

Figures 55 and 56 show a graph before and after applying a custom format.

1. Display the graph you want to format.
2. Select F*o*rmat/*A*utoFormat.
3. In the Formats Used section, select *U*ser-Defined (Figure 57).
4. In the *F*ormats list, click the name you want to use.
5. Click OK.

■ **Tip**

✓ The preview box (Figure 57) shows you how the active graph looks with the selected custom format. Because the preview box is so small in comparison to the actual graph, the labels may wrap or overlap. For example, in Figure 57, the x-axis labels (1991, 1992, etc.) wrap onto two lines. This does not mean that the labels will wrap on the actual graph.

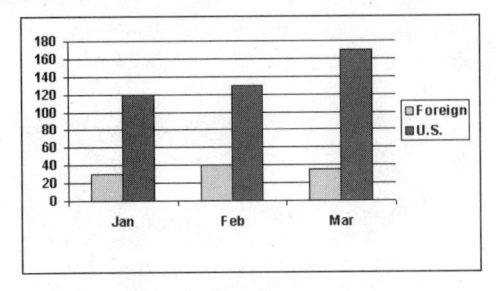

Figure 55. A chart before applying a custom format

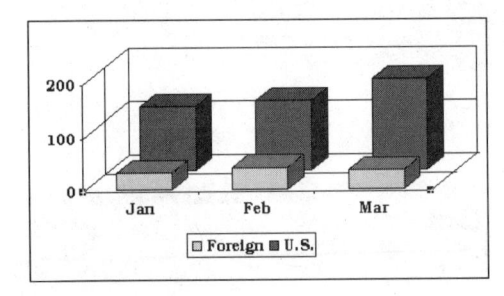

Figure 56. The same chart after applying a custom format

To apply a custom format, click here first...

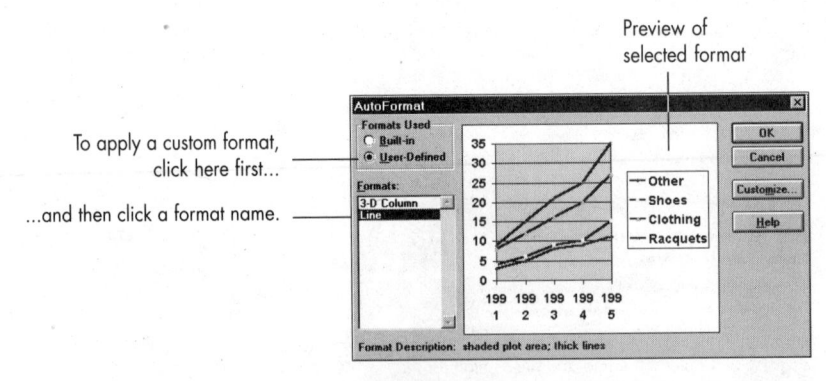

...and then click a format name.

Preview of selected format

Figure 57. Use F*o*rmat/*A*utoFormat to apply a custom format.

CREATING PIE CHARTS 6

1995 Sales by Product Line

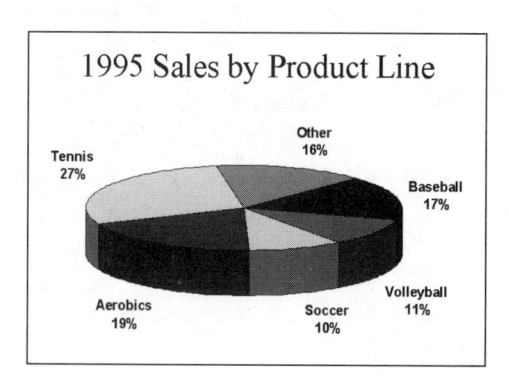

Other 16%
Tennis 27%
Baseball 17%
Aerobics 19%
Soccer 10%
Volleyball 11%

Figure 1. A 3-D pie chart

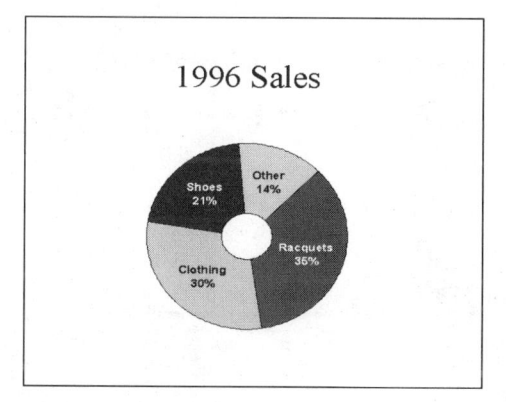

1996 Sales

Other 14%
Shoes 21%
Racquets 35%
Clothing 30%

Figure 2. A doughnut chart

1995 Sales by Product Line

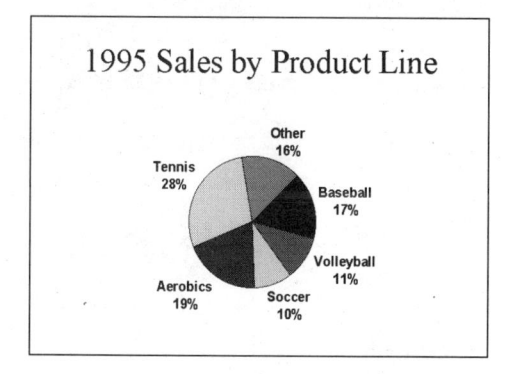

Other 16%
Tennis 28%
Baseball 17%
Volleyball 11%
Soccer 10%
Aerobics 19%

Figure 3. A 2-D pie chart

About Pie Charts

A pie chart shows the relative proportions of several items. By looking at the relative size of the pie slices and their accompanying percentage figures, you can clearly see the relationship between the items (Figure 1).

Unlike column and line graphs, which typically show different values over time, pie charts show values at a particular point in time (such as 1995 sales). Pie charts are one of the simplest types of graphs to create because they have only one data series.

Microsoft Graph offers a number of ways to enhance your pie charts. For instance, you can explode a slice, assign new colors or patterns to the slices, and rotate the pie.

■ Tips

✓ Another chart type similar to a pie is a doughnut (Figure 2). Like pie charts, doughnut charts show the breakdown of a total at a certain point in time.

✓ Microsoft Graph offers pie chart types in 2-D (Figure 3) and 3-D (Figure 1).

Creating Pie Charts

75

CHAPTER 6

Inserting a Pie Slide

Pie charts use the graph AutoLayouts, just as the other types of graphs do.

1. Click the New Slide button at the bottom of the PowerPoint window.
2. In the New Slide dialog box, choose one of the graph AutoLayouts (Figure 4).
3. Click OK. The slide appears with title and graph placeholders (Figure 5).
4. Click the title placeholder and type the title of your graph.
5. Double-click the graph placeholder to create your graph.
6. Select Format/Chart Type. The Chart Type dialog box appears (Figure 6).
7. For the Chart Dimension, choose 2-D or 3-D.
8. Click the pie chart type.
9. Click OK. You are now ready to fill in the datasheet.

See Entering Pie Data on the next page.

■ Tips

✓ Another way to choose the pie chart type is with the Format/AutoFormat command (Figure 7).

See Formatting a Graph Automatically on page 72.

✓ Later in this chapter (page 86) you'll learn how to create two pie graphs on a slide.

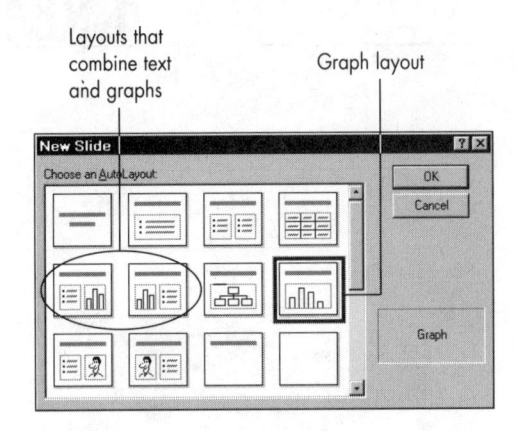

Figure 4. Choose a graph layout in the New Slide dialog box.

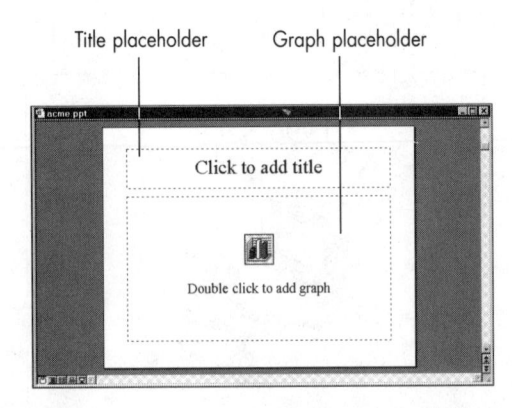

Figure 5. A new slide with title and graph placeholders

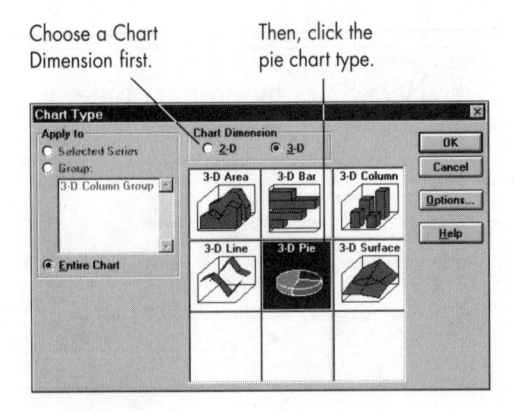

Figure 6. Choosing the pie chart type

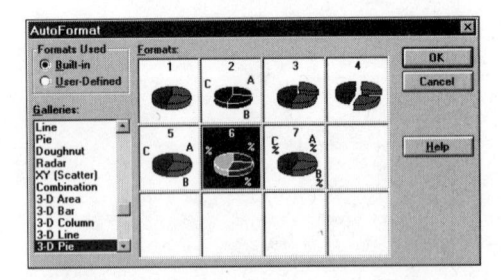

Figure 7. Choosing an AutoFormat for a pie chart

CREATING PIE CHARTS

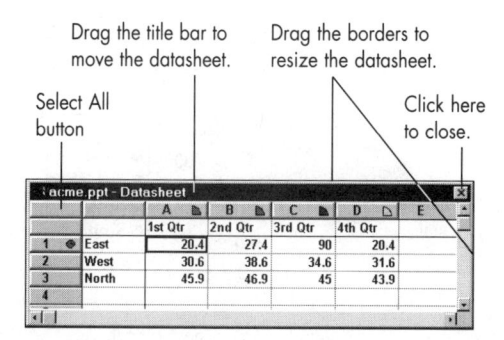

Drag the title bar to move the datasheet.
Drag the borders to resize the datasheet.
Select All button
Click here to close.

Figure 8. The sample data in the datasheet

View Datasheet
By Column
By Row

Figure 9. The Graph toolbar

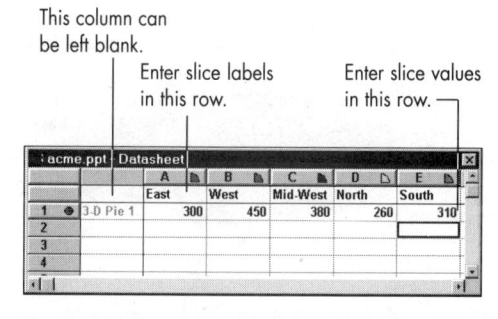

This column can be left blank.
Enter slice labels in this row.
Enter slice values in this row.

Figure 10. How to enter pie data in the datasheet

Figure 11. Another way to enter pie data

Entering Pie Data

You enter your chart data in the datasheet window (Figure 8). The datasheet contains sample data that you erase before entering your own data.

1. If you haven't already done so, double-click the graph placeholder to launch Microsoft Graph.
2. If the datasheet window isn't already displayed, click the View Datasheet button (Figure 9).
3. To erase the sample data, click the Select All button (Figure 8) and press Delete.
4. Enter the graph data (Figure 10).
5. To view the graph, move or close the datasheet.

■ Tips

✓ Be sure to use the Select All button when deleting the sample data. If you delete a range of cells and your data consumes fewer columns than the sample data, Microsoft Graph will still insert a slice label for this data on the chart. To fix this problem, use the Exclude Row/Col command on the Data menu or the Delete command on the Edit menu.

✓ If you accidentally enter data in a column and then erase it, Graph will still reserve space for this data. Again, you can fix this problem by using the Exclude Row/Col command on the Data menu or the Delete command on the Edit menu.

✓ Feel free to enter slice labels in the first column and values in the second column (Figure 11). If you do this, you must let Graph know that the data series are entered into columns instead of rows. Use the Series in Columns command on the Data menu or click the By Column button on the Graph toolbar (Figure 9).

77

CHAPTER 6

Showing Labels, Values, and Percents

By default, a pie chart doesn't have any identifying labels next to its slices—there is only a legend. Figures 12 through 15 show the different types of data (slice) labels you can place on a pie chart.

1. Select Insert/Data Labels.
2. Choose one of the options in the Data Labels dialog box (Figure 16).
3. Click OK.

■ Tips

✓ The Data Labels command is not available if the datasheet is open.

✓ When you display only values or percents, you will need a legend to identify the slices, like the one in Figures 12 and 13.

✓ To remove the legend, select it and press Delete. You will then need to resize the graph.

See Resizing and Repositioning a Pie on page 84.

✓ Another way to insert data labels is with the Format/AutoFormat command.

See Formatting a Graph Automatically on page 72.

✓ You can position the data labels exactly where you want them.

See Repositioning Data Labels on page 55.

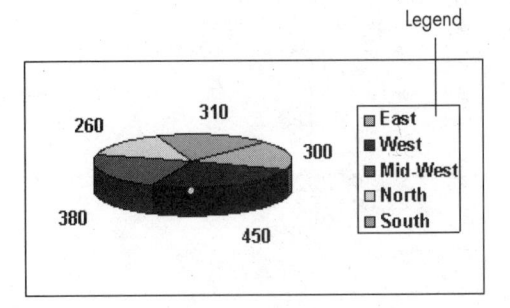

Figure 12. This chart has values next to each slice.

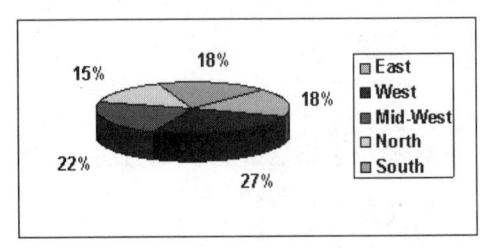

Figure 13. This chart has percentages next to each slice.

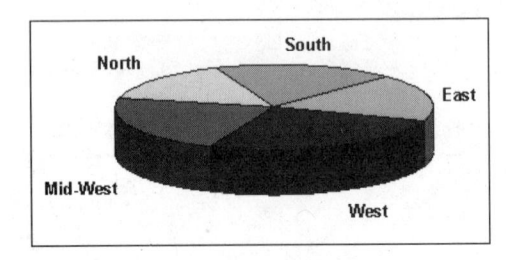

Figure 14. This chart has labels next to each slice.

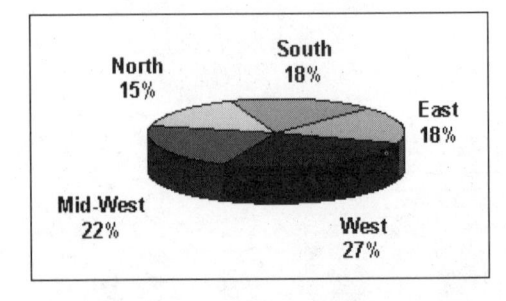

Figure 15. This chart has labels and percentages next to each slice.

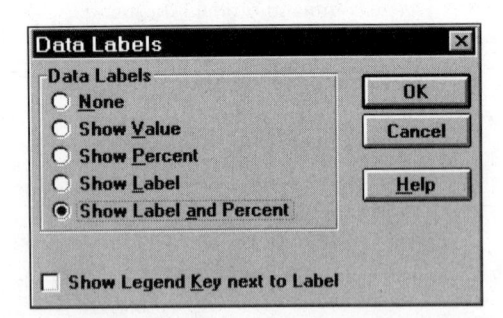

Figure 16. Inserting data labels on a pie chart

CREATING PIE CHARTS

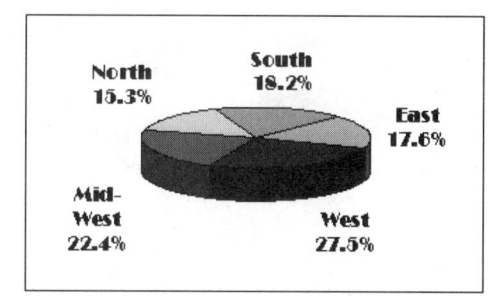

Figure 17. These labels have been formatted to 20-point Broadway; the percentages have been formatted to display one decimal place.

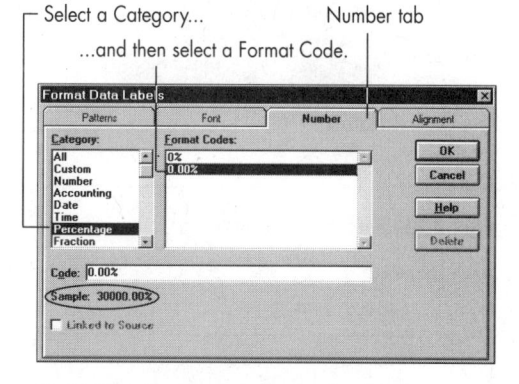

Figure 18. Formatting numbers in data labels

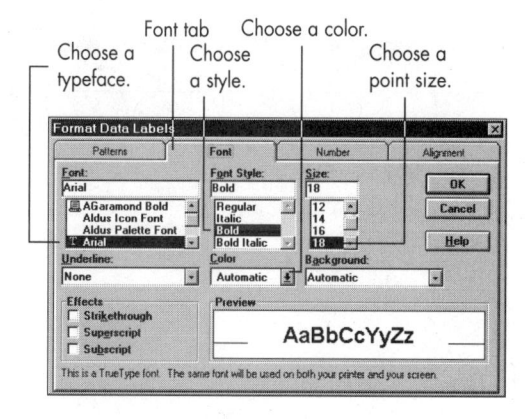

Figure 19. Formatting text in data labels

Formatting Slice Labels

You can format the numbers (percents or values) and the text in the slice labels (Figure 17).

1. Select the slice labels.
2. Select Format/Selected Data Labels.

   or

   Press the right mouse button to display the shortcut menu. Then choose Format Data Labels.

3. To format numbers:
   - Choose the Number tab (Figure 18).
   - From the Category list, choose the appropriate formatting category (such as Number, Percentage, or Currency).
   - In the list of Format Codes, choose the code with the appropriate number of decimal places.

4. To format text:
   - Choose the Font tab (Figure 19).
   - In the Font list, choose the desired typeface (use the scroll bar if necessary).
   - Select the desired Font Style (Regular, Italic, Bold, Bold Italic).
   - In the Size list, choose the desired point size (use the scroll bar if necessary).
   - Choose a color.

5. Click OK.

See also Formatting the Axis Numbers on page 68 and Formatting Graph Text on page 69.

■ Tips

✓ After clicking a format code, look at the Sample (circled in Figure 18) to preview what the number will look like.

✓ If you want to display one decimal place in your percentages, you can create a custom format code: First, choose 0.00% from the Format Codes list and then edit the Code field to read 0.0%.

79

CHAPTER 6

Exploding a Slice

To emphasize one of the pie slices, you can *explode* it as shown in Figure 20.

1. Click the pie to select it.
2. Click the slice you want to explode. You'll see selection handles around it (Figure 21).
3. Place the mouse pointer inside the slice, and drag away from the pie center until the slice is the desired distance from the rest of the pie.

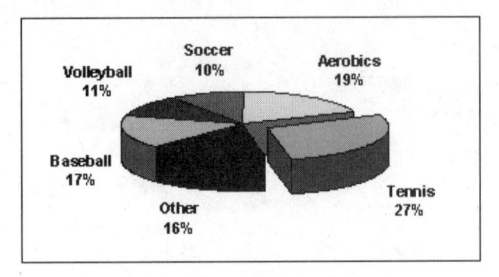

Figure 20. The Tennis slice is exploded from the pie to emphasize that it has the greatest portion of sales.

■ Tips

- ✓ You can explode 2-D and 3-D pie charts.
- ✓ To unexplode a slice, select it and drag it back toward the pie center.
- ✓ To explode all the slices (Figure 22), select the entire pie and drag any slice—all slices will explode.
- ✓ If you want the exploded slice to be in a particular position (for instance, at the 5:00 position on the pie), rotate the pie until the slice is in the desired place.

See Rotating a Pie on page 82.

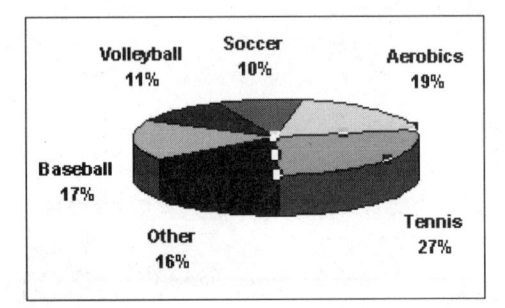

Figure 21. The Tennis slice is selected.

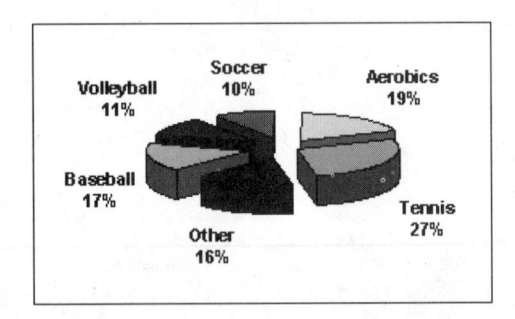

Figure 22. All slices are exploded in this pie chart.

Creating Pie Charts

80

CREATING PIE CHARTS

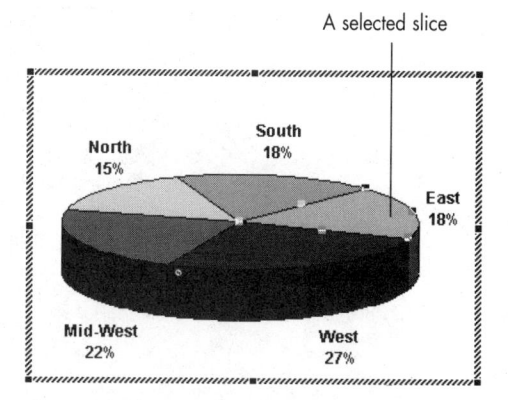

Figure 23. The East slice is selected.

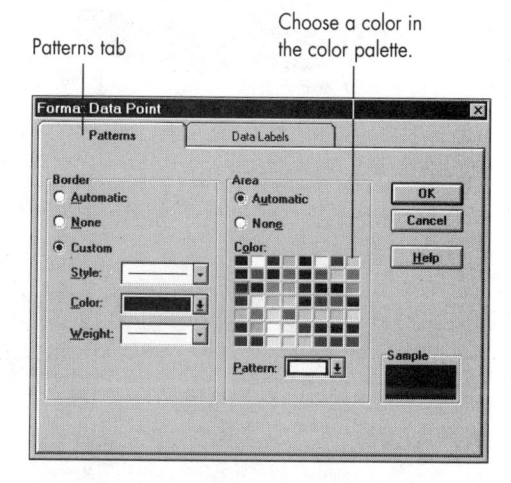

Figure 24. Changing the color of a slice

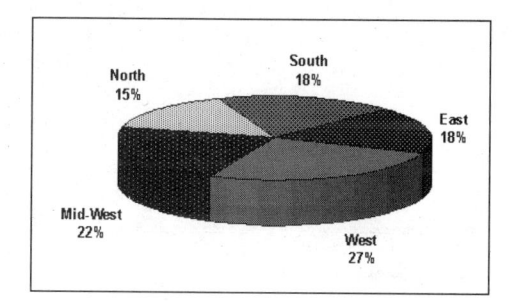

Figure 25. Each slice has a different pattern.

Coloring the Slices

1. Click the pie to select it.
2. Click the slice you want to color. You'll see selection handles around it (Figure 23).
3. Select Format/Selected Data Series.

   or

   Right-click the slice and choose Format Data Point from the shortcut menu.
4. Choose the Patterns tab (Figure 24).
5. Choose a color in the Area Color palette.
6. Click OK.
7. Repeat steps 2 through 6 for each slice.

■ Tip

✓ Slices can also have distinguishing patterns (Figure 25). Click the arrow in the Pattern field to display the pattern palette (Figure 26) and then choose a pattern. The colors in the pattern palette affect the pattern's *foreground* (lines, dots, etc.). The colors in the Area color palette affect the pattern's *background*.

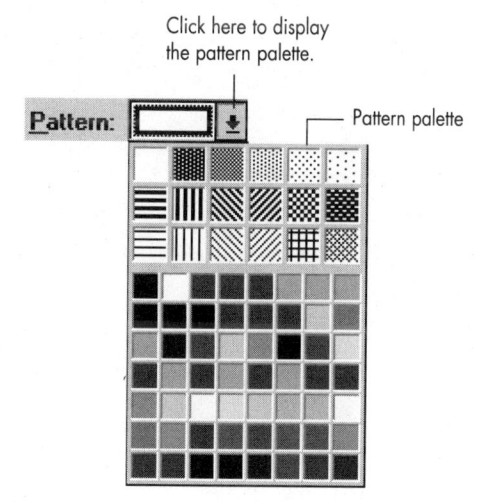

Figure 26. The pattern palette

81

CHAPTER 6

Rotating a Pie

To control the positioning of the slices, you can rotate the pie (Figures 27 and 28).

1. Select Format/1 3-D Pie Group.

   or

   Select Format/1 Pie Group.

2. Choose the Options tab (Figure 29).
3. In the Angle of First Slice field, click the up arrow to rotate the pie clockwise in 10-degree increments, or click the down arrow to rotate the pie counterclockwise.
4. Click OK.

■ Tips

✓ The angle is measured from the 12:00 position on the pie.

✓ Watch the preview box (Figure 29) as you click the arrows in the Angle of First Slice field—the pie rotates with each click.

✓ After rotating the pie, you may want to reposition some of the data labels.

See Repositioning Data Labels on page 55.

✓ After rotating the pie, you may end up with too much space on one side of the chart. To solve this problem, you may want to increase the size of the plot area.

For information on resizing the plot area, see Resizing and Repositioning a Pie on page 84.

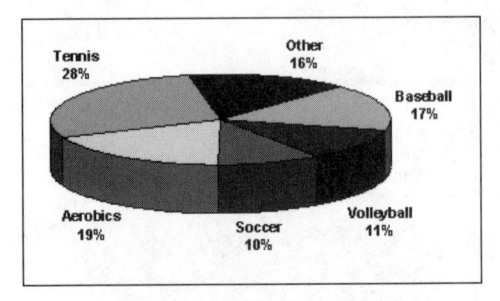

Figure 27. Before rotating the pie (angle=45)

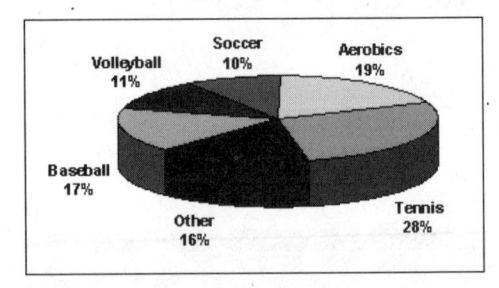

Figure 28. After rotating the pie (angle=225)

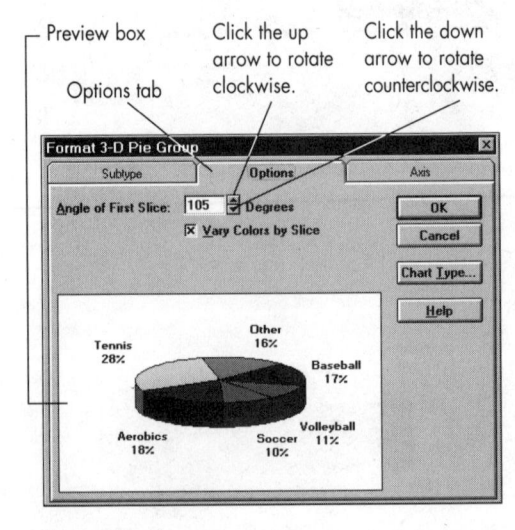

Figure 29. Rotating a pie

Creating Pie Charts

82

CREATING PIE CHARTS

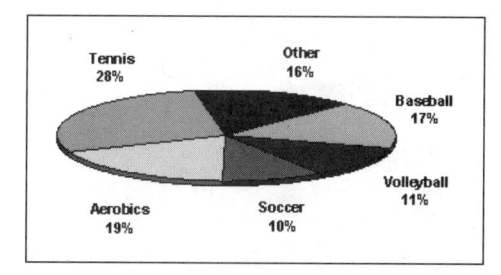

Figure 30. This pie chart has a height of 10%.

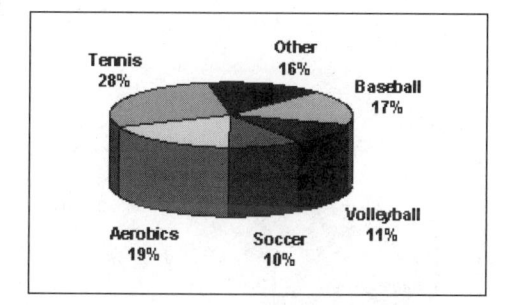

Figure 31. This pie chart has a height of 200%.

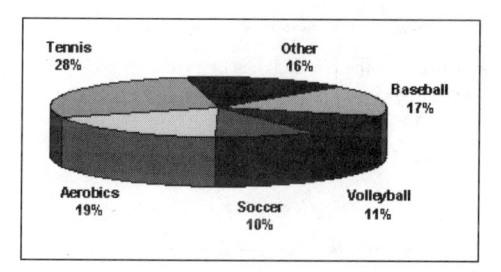

Figure 32. This pie chart has an elevation of 10 (the minimum).

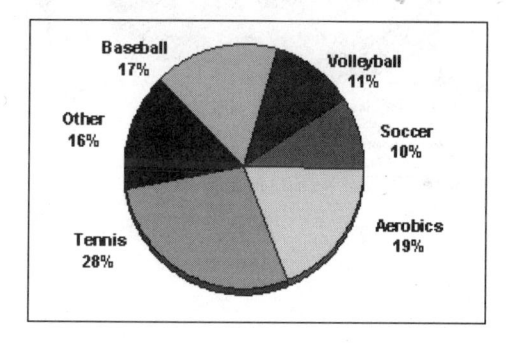

Figure 33. This pie chart has an elevation of 80 (the maximum).

Formatting 3-D Effects

For 3-D pies, you can control the height of the pie (Figures 30 and 31) and the elevation angle at which you are viewing the pie (Figures 32 and 33).

1. Select F_ormat/_3-D View. The Format 3-D View dialog box appears (Figure 34).
2. Click the large up or down arrows to increase or decrease the _Elevation angle.
3. Enter a percentage in the He_ight field. The Height value is a percentage of the default height (100%). For instance, 50% is half the default height and 200% is twice the default height.
4. Click _Apply to see the result of your changes without closing the dialog box.
5. Repeat steps 2 through 4 until you are satisfied with the results.
6. Click OK.

■ Tips

✓ With a low _Elevation value, it is as if you are standing next to the pie and looking at it from the side. With a high value, it is as if you are in an airplane and viewing the pie from up above.

✓ To return to the default settings, click _Default in the Format 3-D View dialog box.

✓ Because you may need to rotate your pie after adjusting the _Elevation and He_ight, the Format 3-D View dialog box has a _Rotation field.

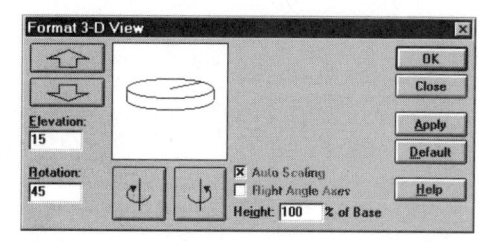

Figure 34. Changing the elevation and height of a 3-D pie chart

CHAPTER 6

Resizing and Repositioning a Pie

After you format and modify a pie chart, you may notice that it seems too small or that it is no longer centered in the chart area (Figure 35). You can solve these types of problems by manipulating the plot area. Figure 36 shows the results.

1. Select the plot area (Figure 37).
2. To enlarge the pie, drag a corner selection handle. You may also want to drag the handle on the opposite corner to finish enlarging the pie.
3. To reposition the pie, drag the border of the selected plot area.

■ Tips

✓ The plot area can be tricky to select because there are so many other items inside or near this area. Click just outside the edge of the pie, but not on a data label (Figure 37). Keep clicking in different places until you successfully select the plot area.

✓ When resizing or moving a pie, the data labels move with their respective slices. However, you may want to manually reposition some of them.

See Repositioning Data Labels on page 55.

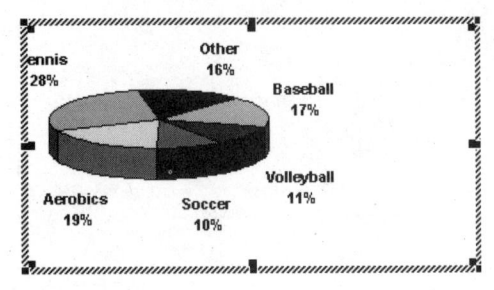

Figure 35. This pie chart is off center and smaller than it could be.

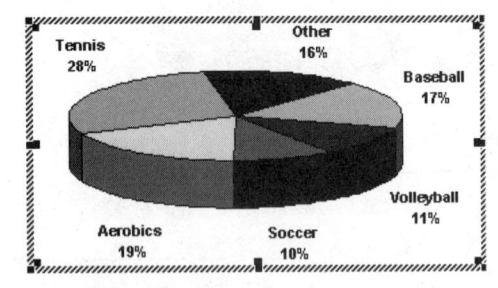

Figure 36. The pie chart has been resized and repositioned.

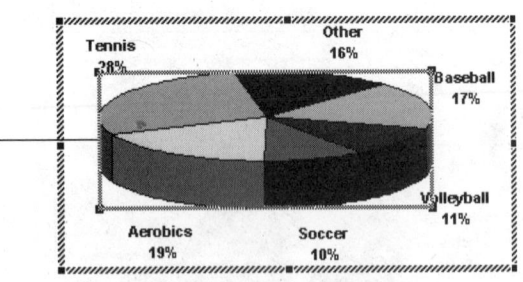

Click near, but not on, the pie to select the plot area.

Figure 37. The selected plot area

CREATING PIE CHARTS

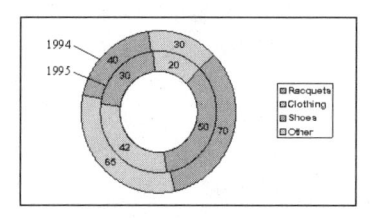

Figure 38. A doughnut chart with two data series

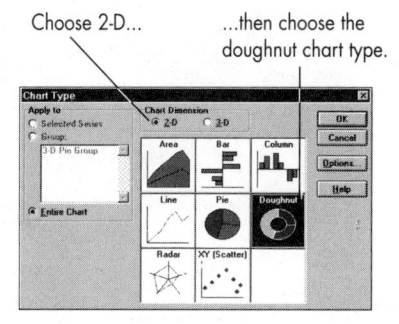

Figure 39. Choosing the doughnut chart type

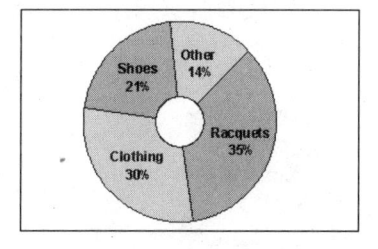

Figure 40. To fit the labels inside the doughnut pieces, the doughnut hole was reduced in size.

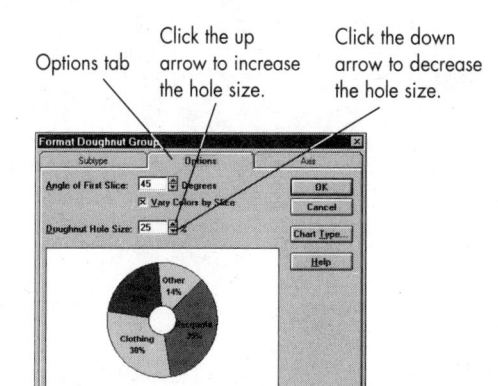

Figure 41. Changing the size of the doughnut hole

Creating a Doughnut

A doughnut chart is more than just a two-dimensional pie chart with a hole in the center: It can also display more than one data series (Figure 38).

1. Insert a graph slide and fill in the data sheet with each data series in a different row.

   See Inserting a Pie Slide on page 76 and Entering Pie Data on page 77.

2. Select F*o*rmat/*C*hart Type. The Chart Type dialog box appears (Figure 39).
3. For the Chart Dimension, choose *2*-D.
4. Click the doughnut chart type.
5. Click OK.

■ Tips

✓ Use *I*nsert/*D*ata Labels to label the doughnut pieces (Figure 40). Notice that the labels are inside the pieces.

   To move the labels outside the pieces, see Repositioning Data Labels on page 55.

✓ Because the legend identifies the doughnut pieces, not the data series, you need to identify the data series yourself. In Figure 38, this was accomplished by typing the labels 1994 and 1995 with PowerPoint's Text tool and drawing the pointers with the Line tool.

Sizing the Doughnut Hole

If there isn't enough room inside the doughnut pieces for the data labels, you can reduce the doughnut hole size.

1. Select F*o*rmat/*1* Doughnut Group.
2. Choose the Options tab (Figure 41).
3. Click the up or down arrows in the *D*oughnut Hole Size field to increase or decrease the size of the hole.
4. Click OK.

85

CHAPTER 6

Creating Two Pies on a Slide

For comparison purposes, it is sometimes useful to display two pie charts on a slide (Figure 42).

See Creating Two Graphs on a Slide on page 57.

■ Tip

✓ Because the pies are smaller when you have two to a slide, you will probably have to reduce the size of the data labels. (This was done in Figure 42.)

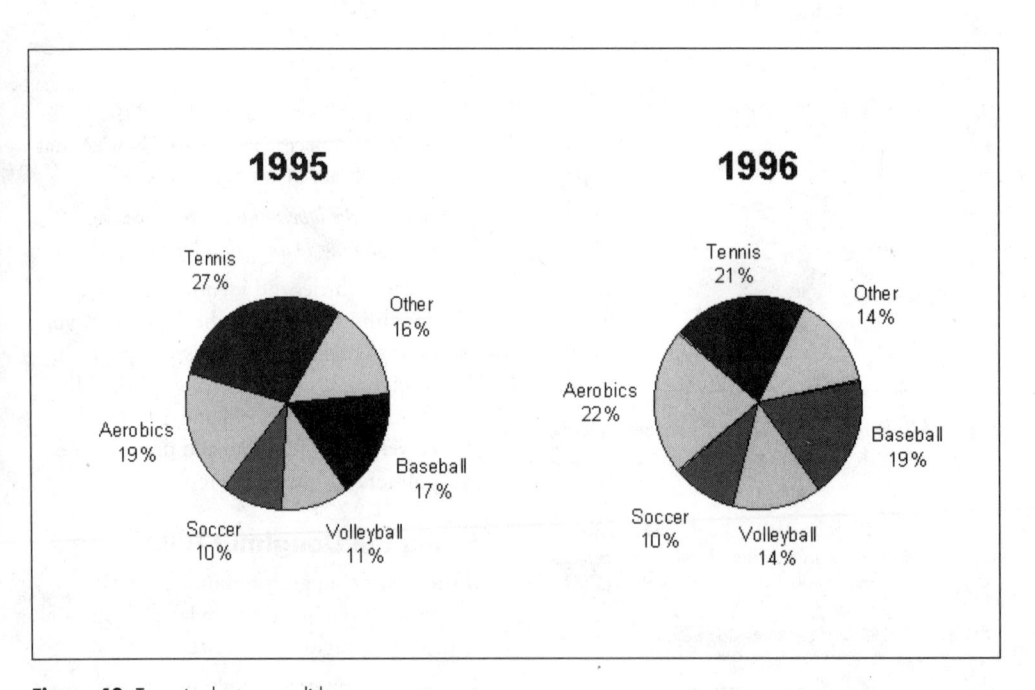

1995

- Tennis 27%
- Other 16%
- Baseball 17%
- Volleyball 11%
- Soccer 10%
- Aerobics 19%

1996

- Tennis 21%
- Other 14%
- Baseball 19%
- Volleyball 14%
- Soccer 10%
- Aerobics 22%

Figure 42. Two pie charts on a slide

BUILDING ORGANIZATION CHARTS

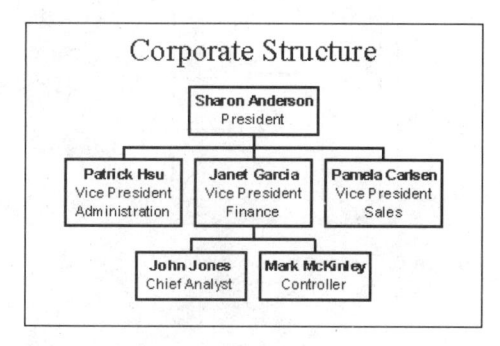

7

Figure 1. An organization chart

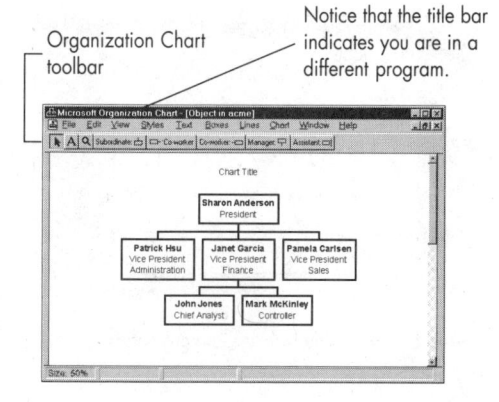

Figure 2. Use Microsoft Organization Chart to create your org charts.

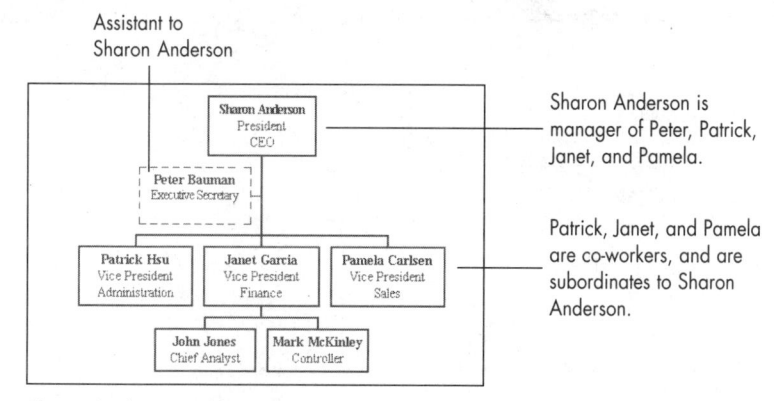

Figure 3. The types of boxes in an org chart

About Organization Charts

The most common use for an organization chart (or *org chart*) is to illustrate a corporation's structure (Figure 1). It identifies the names and titles of the key people in a company or division. You can also use org charts to create a simplified flowchart, an outline of tasks in a project, a family tree, or even a diagram of a hard disk's directory structure.

Org charts are actually created in a separate program called *Microsoft Organization Chart* (Figure 2). You launch Organization Chart by double-clicking the org chart placeholder or an embedded org chart. To return to PowerPoint, choose File/Exit and Return.

Organization charts are made up of managers, subordinates, co-workers, and assistants (Figure 3). A *manager* is someone who has other people—*subordinates*—reporting to him/her. *Co-workers* are subordinates who have the same manager. An *assistant* provides administrative assistance to a manager.

Building Organization Charts

87

CHAPTER 7

Inserting an Org Chart Slide

1. Click the New Slide button at the bottom of the PowerPoint window.
2. In the New Slide dialog box, choose the Organization Chart layout (Figure 4).
3. Click OK. The slide appears with title and org chart placeholders (Figure 5).
4. Click the title placeholder and type the title of your org chart.
5. Double-click the org chart placeholder to create your organization chart. This action launches Microsoft Organization Chart (Figure 6).

■ Tip

✓ When you are ready to return to PowerPoint, click the close button for Microsoft Organization Chart (Figure 6). Choose Yes to update the object.

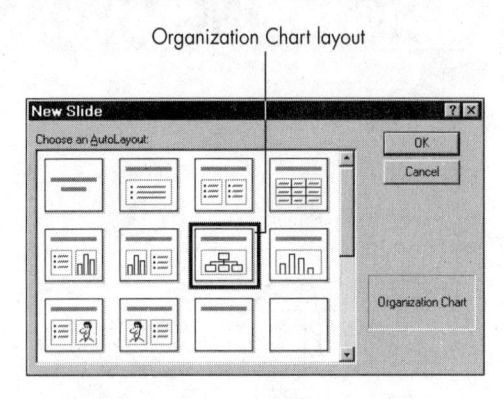

Figure 4. Choosing the Organization Chart layout

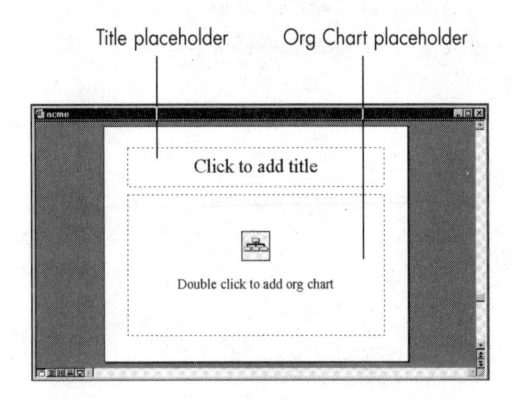

Figure 5. A new slide with title and org chart placeholders

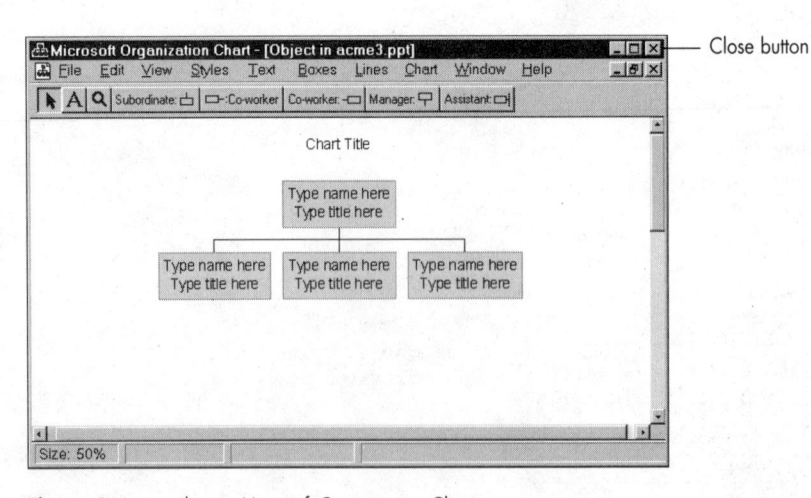

Figure 6. A new chart in Microsoft Organization Chart

Building Organization Charts

88

BUILDING ORGANIZATION CHARTS

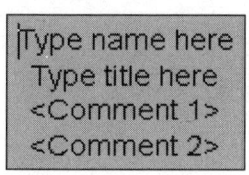

|Type name here
Type title here
<Comment 1>
<Comment 2>

Figure 7. A box before any text is entered

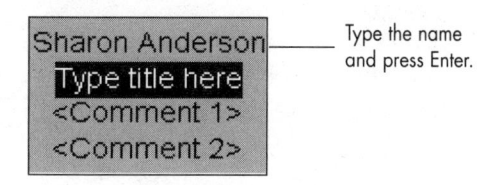

Sharon Anderson — Type the name
Type title here   and press Enter.
<Comment 1>
<Comment 2>

Figure 8. Entering the name

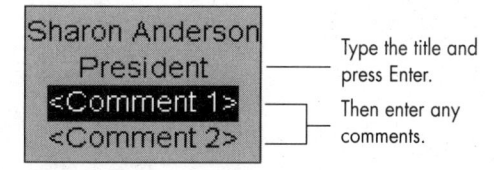

Sharon Anderson — Type the title and
President   press Enter.
<Comment 1>   — Then enter any
<Comment 2>   comments.

Figure 9. Entering the title and comments

Entering Text into Boxes

You can have up to four lines of text in a box: name, title, and two comment lines (Figure 7).

1. Click to select the box into which you want to enter text. If no text is selected, drag across the words "Type name here."
2. Type the name and press Enter (Figure 8). The next line is highlighted.
3. Type the title and press Enter (Figure 9). The next line is highlighted.
4. If needed, type a comment and press Enter.
5. Type an additional comment line, if desired.
6. To close the box, click on another box or click elsewhere in the window.

See next page for information on inserting additional boxes on the org chart.

■ Tips

✓ You can press either Enter or Tab to go to the next line in the box.

✓ To edit the text in a box, click the box to select it; click again in the text to see the text cursor.

✓ Boxes automatically resize to fit the text you type inside. To make a box smaller, choose a smaller point size for the text.

See Formatting Box Text on page 96.

✓ When you are ready to return to PowerPoint, click the close button for Microsoft Organization Chart. Choose Yes to update the object.

89

CHAPTER 7

Inserting a Box

Since the default org chart has only four boxes, it is likely that you will want to insert additional boxes.

1. Click the appropriate box tool (Figure 10) for the type of box you are inserting.
2. Click the existing box to which the new box should be attached (Figure 11).

Figure 12 shows the results.

■ Tips

✓ Note that there are two Add Co-worker tools. The first tool inserts a box to the left, and the second tool inserts one to the right.

✓ To delete a box, select it and press Delete.

✓ If you accidentally insert a box in the wrong location, choose Edit/Undo.

✓ When you are ready to return to PowerPoint, click the close button for Microsoft Organization Chart. Choose Yes to update the object.

Keyboard Shortcuts for Inserting Boxes

F2	Creates of subordinate for the selected box
F3	Creates a co-worker to the left of the selected box
F4	Creates a co-worker to the right of the selected box
F5	Creates a manager for the selected box
F6	Creates an assistant for the selected box

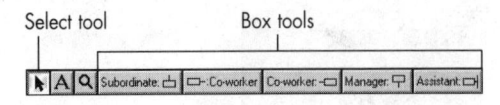

Figure 10. The Org Chart toolbar

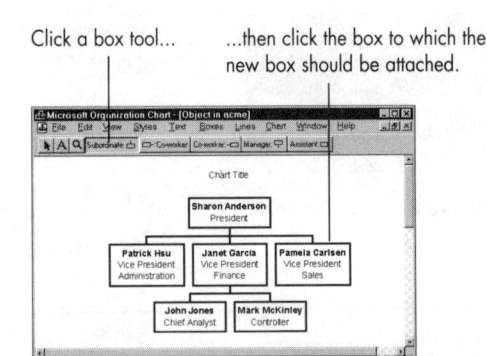

Figure 11. Inserting a subordinate box

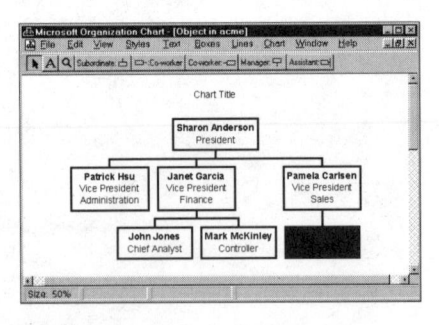

Figure 12. An inserted subordinate box

BUILDING ORGANIZATION CHARTS

Hold down Shift as you click a box tool.

Then click here twice to insert two boxes.

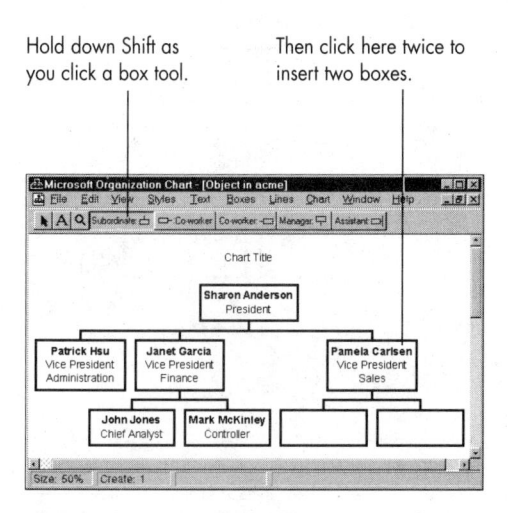

Figure 13. Inserting multiple boxes with the Shift+click technique

Inserting Multiple Boxes

Using the following technique, you can easily insert multiple boxes of the same type.

1. Hold down Shift as you click the appropriate box tool.
2. Click the existing box to which you want to attach the new box (Figure 13).
3. Repeat step 2 for each new box you want to insert.
4. Press Esc to deactivate the box tool.

■ Tips

✓ Another way to insert multiple boxes is to click the box tool multiple times. For example, if you click the Subordinate tool three times and then click a box on your chart, three subordinate boxes will be inserted below the box you clicked (Figure 14).

✓ When you are ready to return to PowerPoint, click the close button for Microsoft Organization Chart. Choose Yes to update the object.

Click the box tool three times...

...then click here once to insert three subordinate boxes.

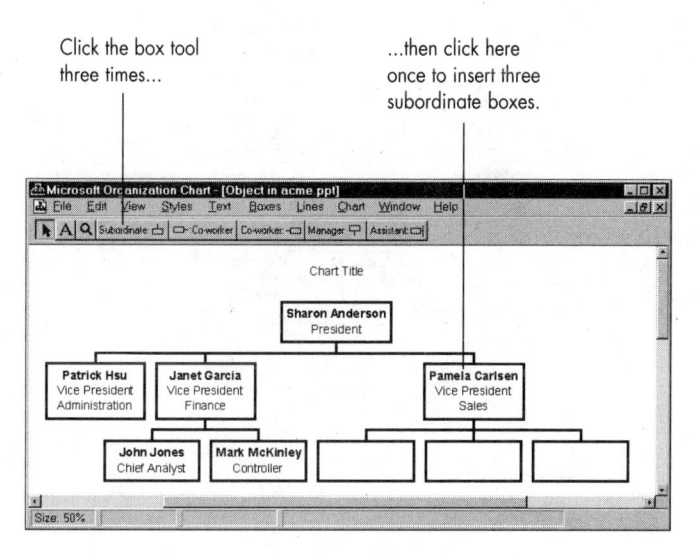

Figure 14. Inserting multiple boxes with the multiple-click technique

91

Rearranging Boxes

You can easily restructure an organization chart by dragging the boxes (Figures 15 and 16).

1. Press Esc or click the background to make sure nothing is selected.
2. Select the box to be repositioned.
3. Point to the box to be moved and drag it over its new manager or co-worker.
4. Release the mouse button.

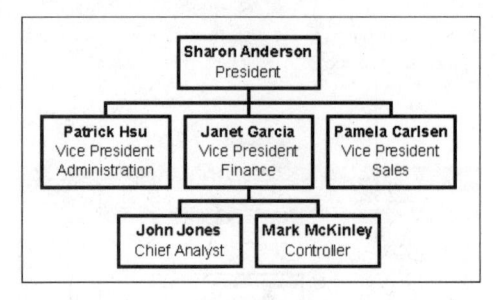

Figure 15. Before moving Mark McKinley

■ Tips

- ✓ As you drag one box over another, the pointer displays an icon to indicate the new positioning of the box:
  - ⇨ Box will be inserted as a co-worker to the right.
  - ⇦ Box will be inserted as a co-worker to the left.
  - ⎵ Box will be inserted as a subordinate.
- ✓ To move an entire branch, drag the manager's box; subordinates automatically move when you move a manager (Figure 17).
- ✓ Another way to move a box is by cutting and pasting. Select the box and choose Edit/Cut. Then, select the box of the new manager and choose Edit/Paste Boxes.
- ✓ When you are ready to return to PowerPoint, click the close button for Microsoft Organization Chart. Choose Yes to update the object.

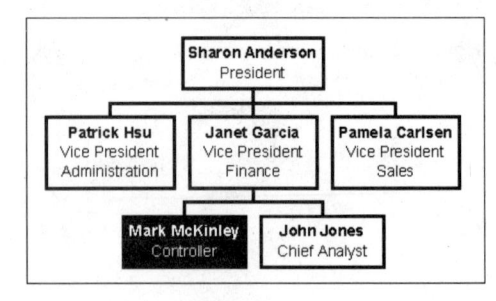

Figure 16. After moving the box to a new location

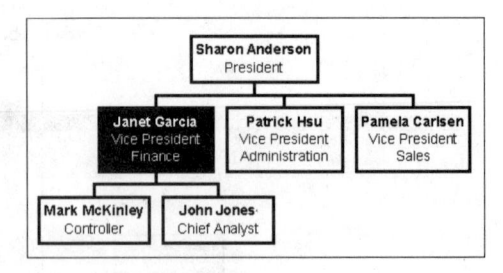

Figure 17. Moving Janet Garcia automatically moves her subordinates.

BUILDING ORGANIZATION CHARTS

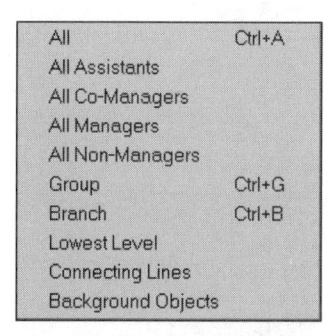

Figure 18. Choose Edit/Select to display this menu.

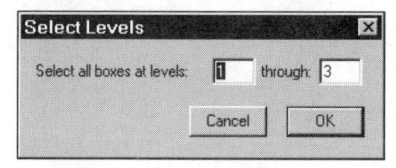

Figure 19. Choose Edit/Select Levels to display this dialog box.

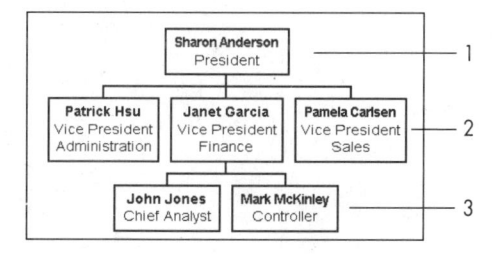

Figure 20. This organization chart has three levels.

Selecting Boxes

To format the boxes in an org chart, you must first select them. To select boxes:

    Shift+click each box.

or

    Draw a marquee around the boxes.

or

    Select Edit/Select and choose the item you wish to select (Figure 18).

or

    Select Edit/Select Levels and enter a range of levels to select (Figures 19 and 20).

Here are a few terms you need to know when selecting boxes (Figure 21):

Group   All boxes with the same manager.

Branch   A box and all the boxes that report to it, all the way to the bottom of the chart.

Co-managers   Those who share responsibility for the same group of subordinates.

■ Tip

✓ Here are some handy keyboard shortcuts: Ctrl+A for selecting all boxes, Ctrl+G for selecting a group, and Ctrl+B for selecting a branch.

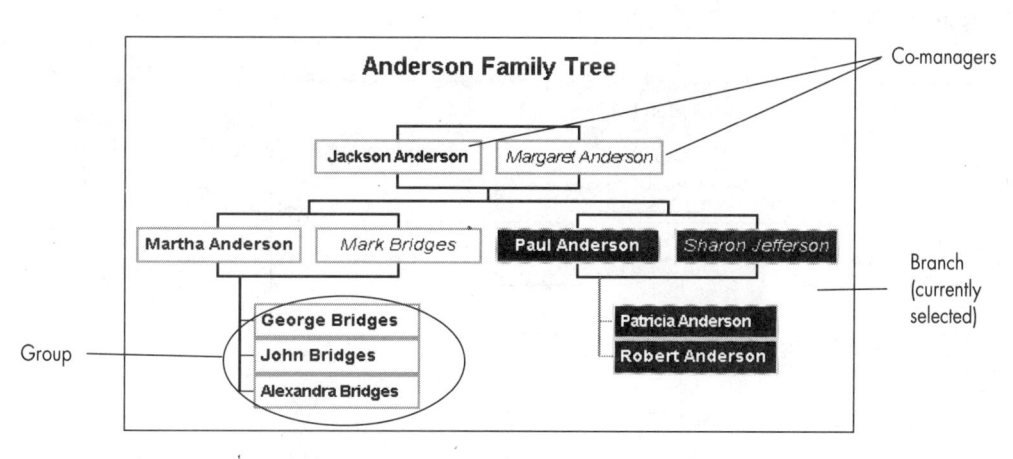

Figure 21. Elements of an organization chart

CHAPTER 7

Choosing a Style

You can choose from a variety of styles for your organization charts. Figures 22 through 24 show several of these styles.

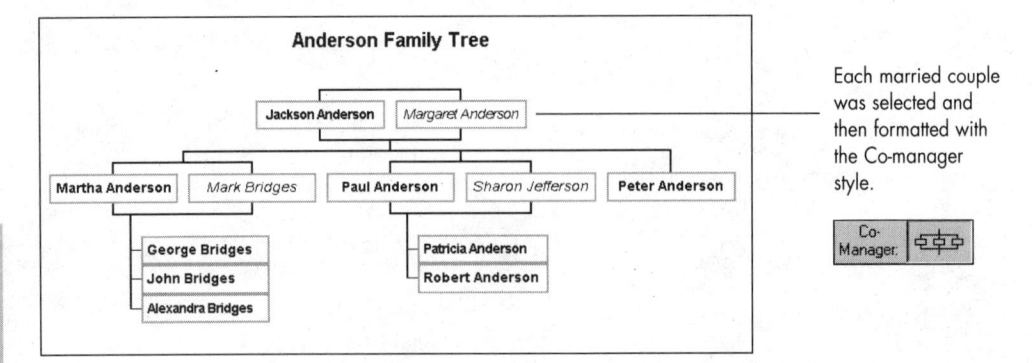

Each married couple was selected and then formatted with the Co-manager style.

Figure 22. The lowest level is vertically oriented; each name is in a box.

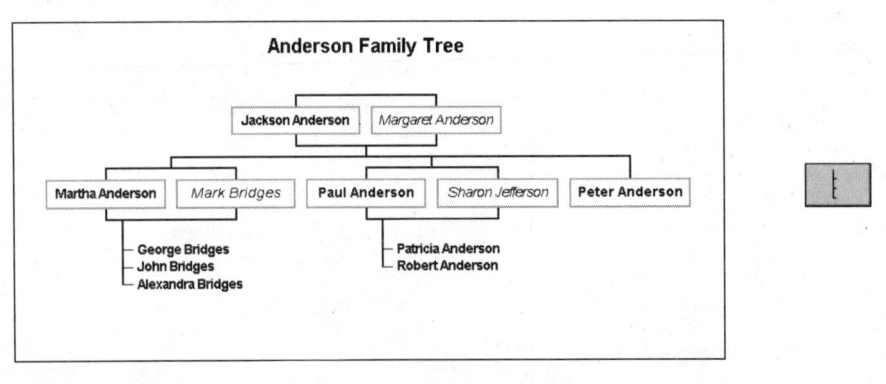

Figure 23. The lowest level is vertically oriented; the names are not boxed.

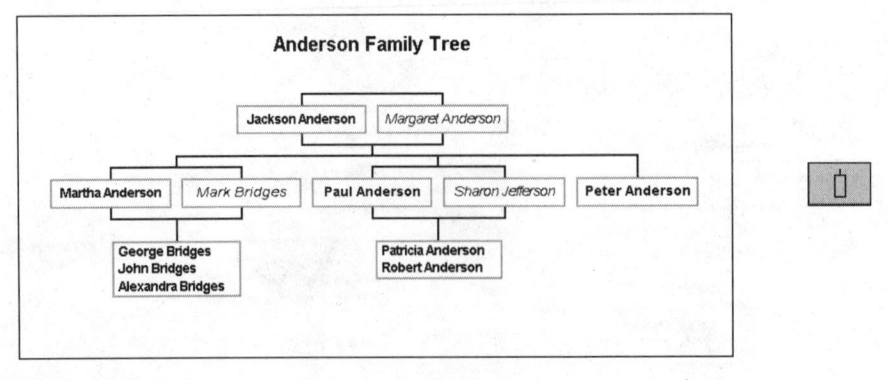

Figure 24. The lowest level is vertically oriented; all names in a group are in one box.

BUILDING ORGANIZATION CHARTS

Choosing a Style (cont'd)

1. Select the boxes (such as a level or a group) for which you want to choose a new style (Figure 25).

   See Selecting Boxes on page 93.

2. Select the Styles menu and choose the desired style (Figure 26).

■ Tips

✓ The styles with vertical orientation are typically used on the lowest level of an organization chart.

✓ Before choosing Group or Branch from the Select menu, click in one of the boxes of the group or branch.

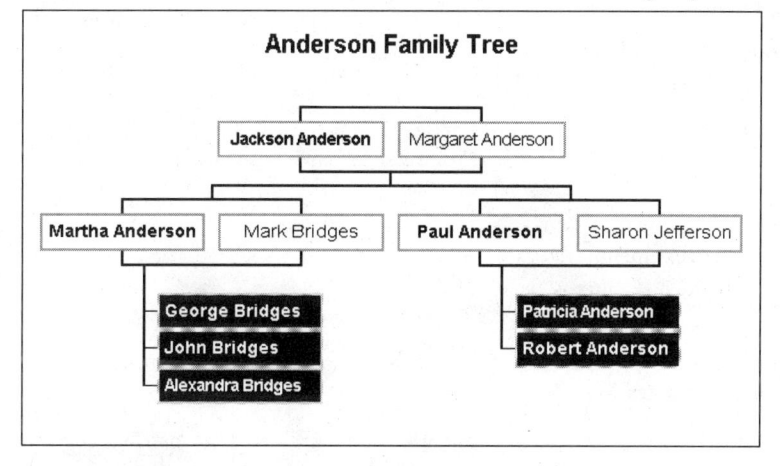

Figure 25. The lowest level of this organization chart is selected.

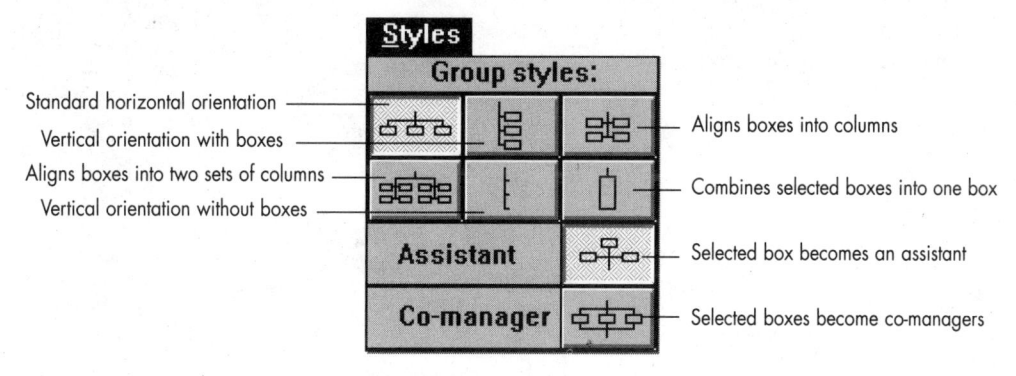

Figure 26. Choosing a style

95

CHAPTER 7

Formatting Box Text

You can format all or any part of the text inside the boxes (Figures 27 and 28).

1. To format a selection of text, click in the box and then drag the text cursor over the characters you want to select.

   or

   To format all the text in one or more boxes, select the boxes.

   See Selecting Boxes on page 93.

2. Select Text/Font. The Font dialog box appears (Figure 29).

3. In the Font list, choose the desired typeface (use the scroll bar if necessary).

4. Select the desired Font Style (Regular, Italic, Bold, or Bold Italic).

5. In the Size list, choose the desired point size (use the scroll bar if necessary).

6. Click OK.

■ **Tips**

✓ You can also change the alignment of text within the boxes. On the Text menu, choose Left, Right, or Center. (Center is the default.)

✓ To avoid the "ransom note" look, use only one typeface on an organization chart.

✓ When you are ready to return to PowerPoint, click the close button for Microsoft Organization Chart. Choose Yes to update the object.

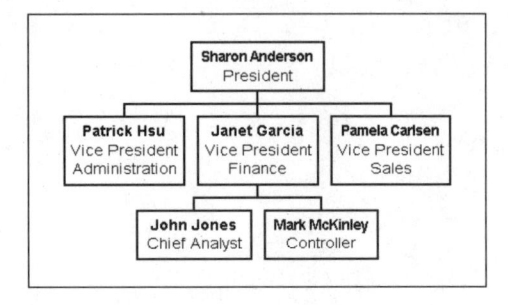

Figure 27. All the names are in bold.

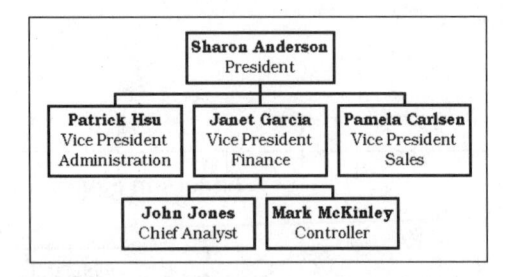

Figure 28. All the box text is formatted to 18-point Bookman.

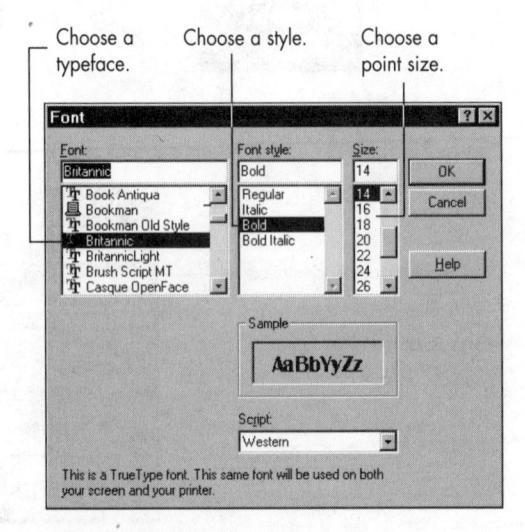

Figure 29. Formatting box text

96

BUILDING ORGANIZATION CHARTS

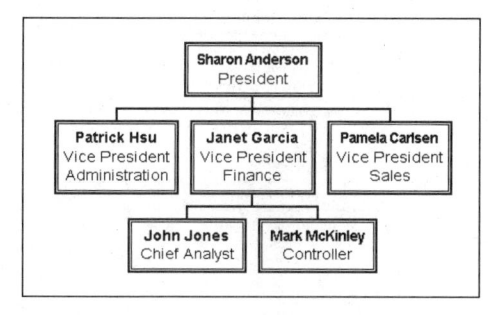

Figure 30. The boxes have a double-line border.

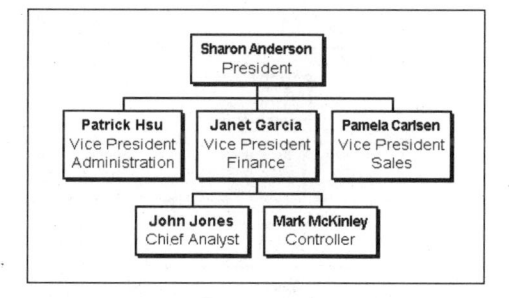

Figure 31. The boxes have drop shadows.

Figure 32. Box borders

Formatting the Boxes

You can choose a different border style (Figure 30), add a drop shadow (Figure 31), or change the color inside your boxes.

1. Select the boxes you want to format.

   See Selecting Boxes on page 93.

2. Use any of the following formatting commands found on the Boxes menu:

   - Select Border Style to change the line style of the borders (Figure 32).
   - Select Shadow to add a shadow effect (Figure 33).
   - Select Color to change the background color of the boxes.

■ Tips

✓ To format all the boxes, select them first with Ctrl+A.

✓ When you are ready to return to PowerPoint, click the close button for Microsoft Organization Chart. Choose Yes to update the object.

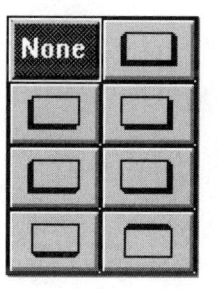

Figure 33. Box shadows

CHAPTER 7

Formatting the Lines

You can adjust the thickness (Figure 34), style (Figure 35), and color of the connecting lines.

1. To format all connecting lines, select Edit/Select/Connecting Lines.

   or

   To format a single line, click the line.

2. Use any of the following formatting commands on the Lines menu:
   - Select Thickness to change the weight of the lines (Figure 36).
   - Select Style to select a different line style (Figure 37).
   - Select Color to change the color of the lines.

■ Tip

✓ When you are ready to return to PowerPoint, click the close button for Microsoft Organization Chart. Choose Yes to update the object.

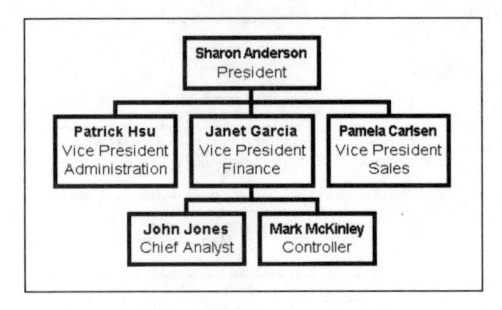

Figure 34. The connecting lines were formatted with one of the wider thicknesses. (The box borders were thickened with the Boxes/Border Style command.)

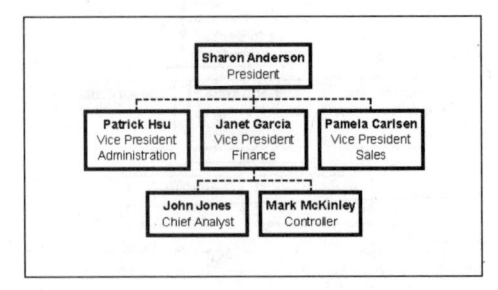

Figure 35. The connecting lines were formatted with a dotted line style.

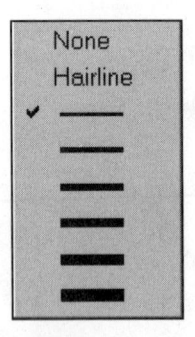

Figure 36. Line thicknesses

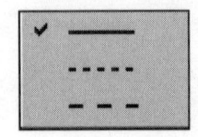

Figure 37. Line styles

BUILDING ORGANIZATION CHARTS

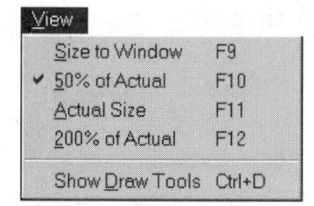

```
View
  Size to Window      F9
✓ 50% of Actual       F10
  Actual Size         F11
  200% of Actual      F12
  Show Draw Tools     Ctrl+D
```

Figure 38. Use the View menu to change your view of the organization chart.

Zooming In and Out

The View menu (Figure 38) offers ways to zoom in (enlarge) or zoom out (reduce) your view of the screen. (It does not affect the printed size of the chart.) The Zoom button is another way to zoom in and out (Figure 39).

Figures 40 through 42 show examples of some of the zoom levels.

Using the Zoom Button

1. Click the Zoom button (Figure 39).
2. Click on the area of the chart you want to magnify or reduce

■ Tip

✓ The Zoom button zooms in to Actual Size and zooms out to Size to Window.

Zoom button (zooms in)   Zoom button (zooms out)

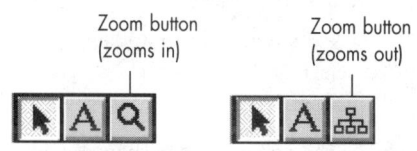

Figure 39. The button for the Zoom tool looks different depending on which view you are currently in.

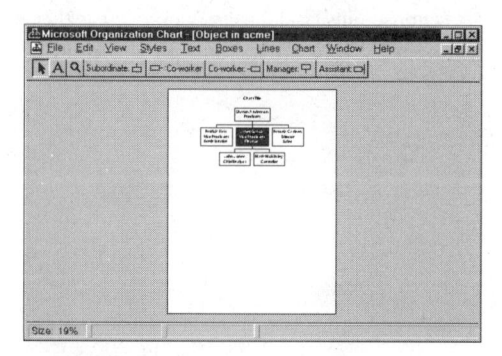

Figure 40. The Size to Window command gives you an overall feel for the chart (though you may not be able to actually read the text).

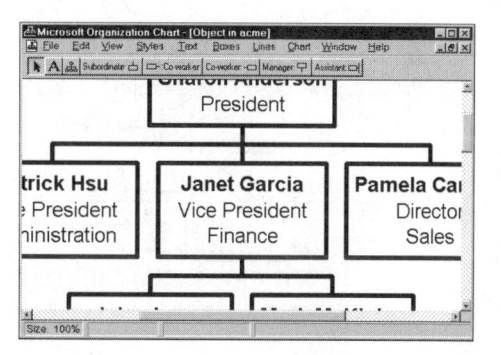

Figure 41. At Actual Size you can see more detail.

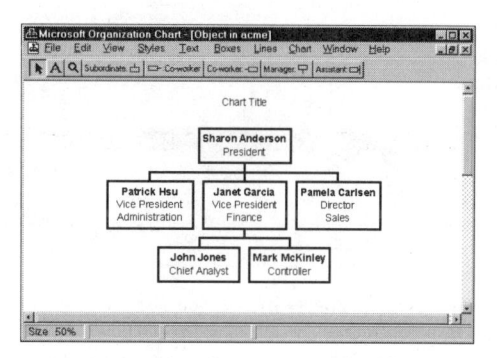

Figure 42. At 50% of Actual you can usually fit the whole chart on the screen and still read the box text.

CHAPTER 7

Double-click the embedded org chart.

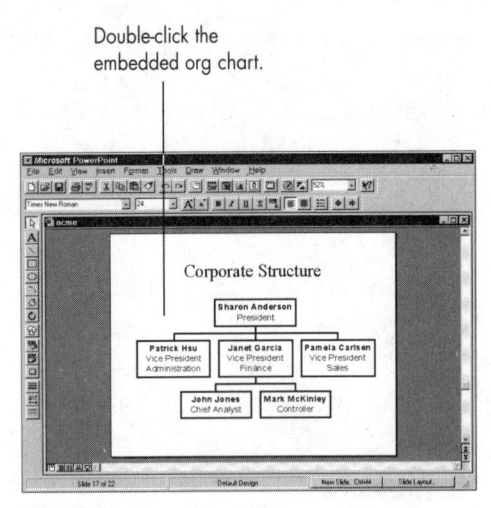

Figure 43. Opening the embedded org chart

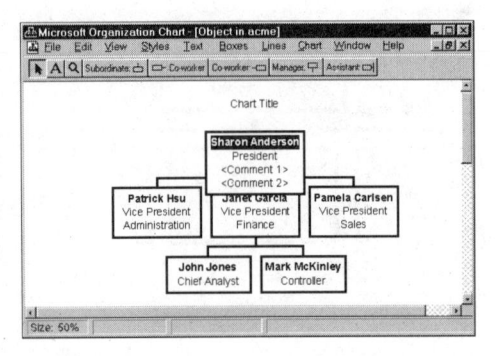

Figure 44. The chart after it is opened in Microsoft Organization Chart

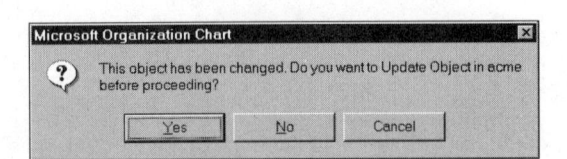

Figure 45. To save the changes you made in Microsoft Organization Chart, be sure to update the object.

Editing an Existing Org Chart

To edit a previously-created org chart, you need to reopen it in Microsoft Organization Chart.

1. In Slide view, double-click the embedded org chart (Figures 43 and 44).
2. Make any desired changes to the chart (insert and/or rearrange the boxes, format the lines and boxes, and so forth).
3. When you are ready to return to PowerPoint, click the close button for Microsoft Organization Chart. Choose Yes to update the object.
4. When asked if you want to update the object, select Yes (Figure 45).

   or

   If you want to abandon the changes you made to the chart, select No.

■ Tip

✓ To update the org chart object without exiting Microsoft Organization Chart, choose File/Update *xxx*, where *xxx* is the name of your PowerPoint presentation.

CREATING TABLES 8

Annual Sales by Salesperson

	1995	1996	Change
Jones	35,600	60,980	25,380
Smith	12,950	23,700	10,750
Black	24,500	27,100	2,600
Johnson	90,000	125,000	35,000
Goldman	54,200	25,400	-28,800
Totals	217,250	262,180	44,930

Figure 1. A four-column table

Medical Plans

	Indemnity Plan	HMO
Services Available	Any doctor	HMO facility
Premium	$50 / month	none
Deductible	$100 / year	none
Co-insurance	80% / 20%	$5 visit

Figure 2. A three-column table

What is the Smart Health Program?	A health care plan designed to maximize your benefits by utilizing a network of participating physicians and hospitals.
Is my physician a provider in the network?	Check with your physician or get a copy of the Smart Health Program Directory of Physicians. To order a copy, call 800-555-2323.
What about claim forms?	The participating provider is responsible for submitting forms for you.

Figure 3. A table with side-by-side paragraphs

About Tables

The best way to present columns of data is in a Table slide. Figures 1 through 3 show examples of the kinds of tables you can create in PowerPoint.

Think of a table as a mini-spreadsheet, similar to the ones you may have created in Microsoft Excel or Lotus 1-2-3. You can even build formulas in PowerPoint tables.

When you create tables in PowerPoint, you actually use the *Microsoft Word* program (Figure 4). When you're in Word, you'll notice that the menu bar contains a Table item instead of a Draw item. The toolbars are different, too—that's how you know that another program is running.

Word is not included with PowerPoint—it must be purchased separately. However, if you have Microsoft Office, Word and PowerPoint are included (along with several other programs).

To create or modify your table, double-click a table placeholder or an embedded table. This action launches Word. To return to PowerPoint, click anywhere on the slide outside of the table.

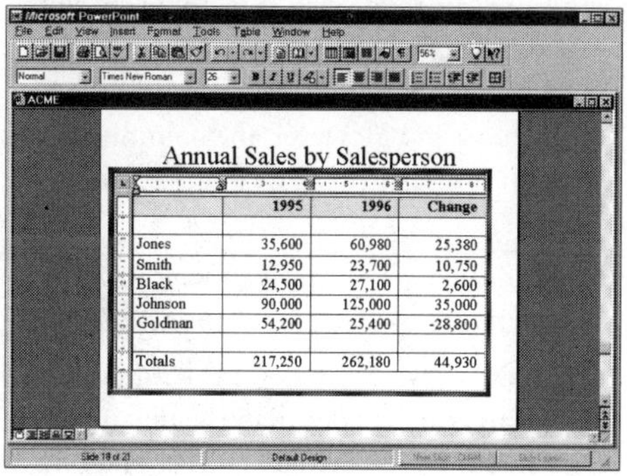

Figure 4. A table being edited in Word for Windows 95

CHAPTER 8

Inserting a Table Slide

PowerPoint offers one AutoLayout for tables (Figure 5).

1. Click the New Slide button at the bottom of the PowerPoint window.
2. In the New Slide dialog box, choose the Table layout (Figure 5).
3. Click OK. The slide appears with title and table placeholders.
4. Click the title placeholder and type the title of your table.
5. Double-click the table placeholder to create your table. You are asked to specify the number of columns and rows (Figure 6).
6. Specify the Number of Columns (maximum of 30) and press Tab.
7. Specify the Number of Rows (maximum of 7) and click OK. A table appears in Word (Figure 7).

■ Tips

✓ Though the maximum number of rows you can specify in the Insert Word Table dialog box is 7, you can insert more rows, if needed, once you are in Word.

See Inserting Rows and Columns on page 109.

✓ The default size of a table is about 8 inches wide by 4.5 inches high. The columns and rows will be evenly spaced in this area. For instance, if you specify 2 columns by 3 rows, each column will be 4 inches wide and each row will be 1.5 inches high. However, the column widths and row heights can be adjusted at any time.

See Adjusting Column Widths on page 106 and Adjusting Row Heights on page 108.

✓ If you know that you want your table to be larger or smaller than the default size, you can adjust the table placeholder by dragging its selection handles.

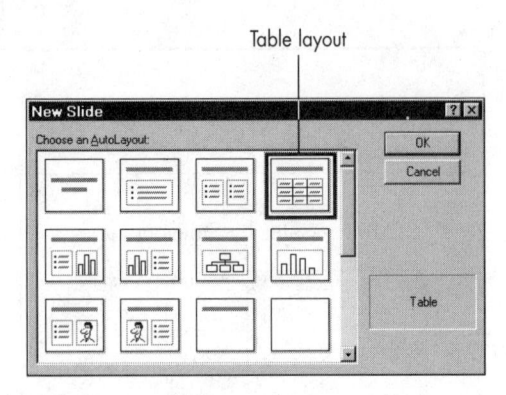

Figure 5. Choosing the Table layout

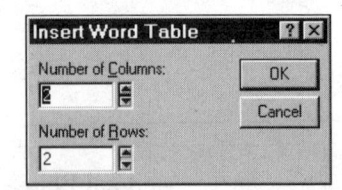

Figure 6. Specify the number of columns and rows in your table.

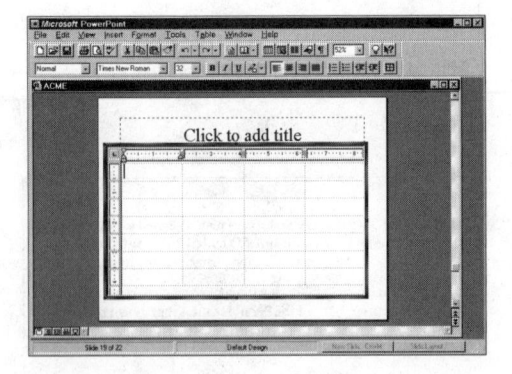

Figure 7. A table in Word for Windows 95

CREATING TABLES

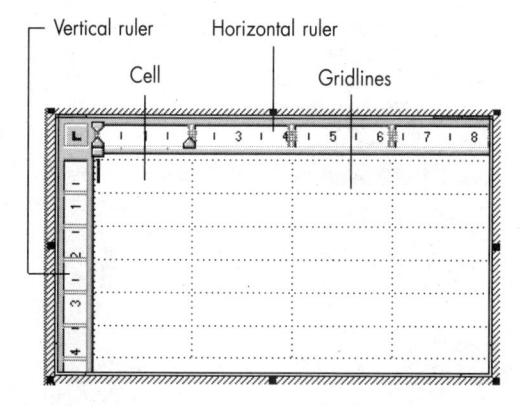

Figure 8. A table is a grid of cells.

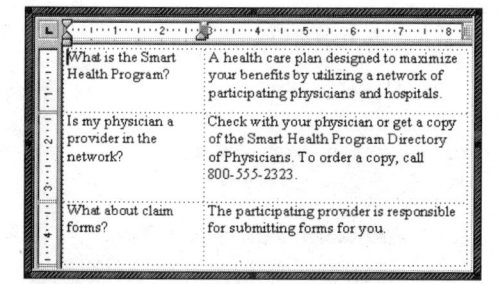

Figure 9. Text automatically wraps within each cell, and the row heights automatically adjust.

Entering Text into a Table

A table is made up of rows and columns; the intersection of a row and column is called a *cell* (Figure 8).

Follow these steps to type text into a table:

1. Click a cell and start typing. Text that is wider than the column width will wrap automatically in the cell (Figure 9).
2. Press Tab to move the cursor to the next cell to the right. Press Shift+Tab to move to the previous cell.
3. After entering text in the last cell in the row, press Tab; this moves the cursor to the first cell in the next row.

■ Tips

- ✓ If you don't see gridlines between cells in your table, select Table/Gridlines.
- ✓ If you don't see the rulers, select View/Ruler.
- ✓ Pressing Enter in a cell drops the cursor down to the next line in the same cell. It does *not* move the cursor to a different cell.
- ✓ You can also position the cursor in a cell by clicking it or by using the arrow keys on the keyboard.
- ✓ Pressing Tab from the last cell in a table inserts a new row and places the cursor in the first cell.
- ✓ If text wraps in a cell but you want it to fit on a single line, there are two solutions: You can either decrease the type size or adjust the column width.

  See Formatting Text on page 111, and Adjusting Column Widths on page 106.
- ✓ The table itself does not have a scroll bar. To move to a cell that has scrolled off the screen, use the arrow keys or press Tab.
- ✓ To return to PowerPoint, click the slide outside of the table, or press Esc.

103

CHAPTER 8

Editing an Existing Table

To edit a previously-created table, you need to reopen it in Microsoft Word.

1. In Slide view, double-click the embedded table (Figures 10 and 11).
2. Make any desired changes to the table (add borders, change the font, adjust column widths, and so forth).
3. To return to PowerPoint, click the slide, outside of the table.

   or

   Press Esc.

■ Tip

✓ The rulers can be displayed or hidden (Figure 12) with the View/Ruler command.

Double-click the embedded table.

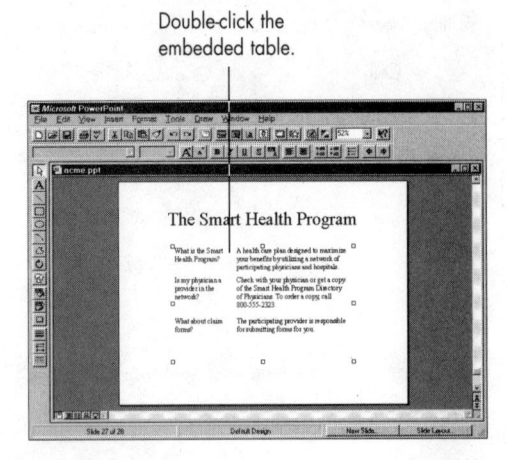

Figure 10. Opening the embedded table in Microsoft Word

Even though the title bar says PowerPoint, you are actually using Word to edit the table.

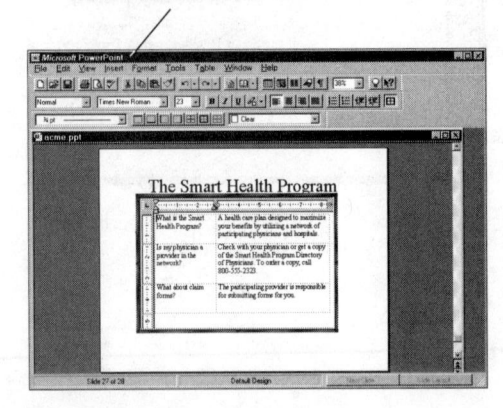

Figure 11. The table after it is opened in Word

Figure 12. A table without the rulers displayed

104

CREATING TABLES

Selecting Cells

You will need to select cells in your table before formatting them. The Table menu (Figure 13) offers ways to select the current row or column, or the entire table.

With the mouse, you can select a range of cells by dragging across them (Figure 14).

You can select an entire column by clicking directly above the column (Figure 15). The mouse pointer becomes a down arrow when it is positioned properly for selecting the column.

To select an entire row (Figure 16), double-click the beginning of the row—to the left of the cell contents. The mouse pointer points up and to the right when it is positioned properly for selecting the row.

■ Tips

- ✓ The keyboard shortcut for selecting the entire table is Alt+5 (on the numeric keypad). For this shortcut to work, Num Lock *cannot* be turned on.
- ✓ A shortcut for selecting a column is to hold down Alt as you click a cell.

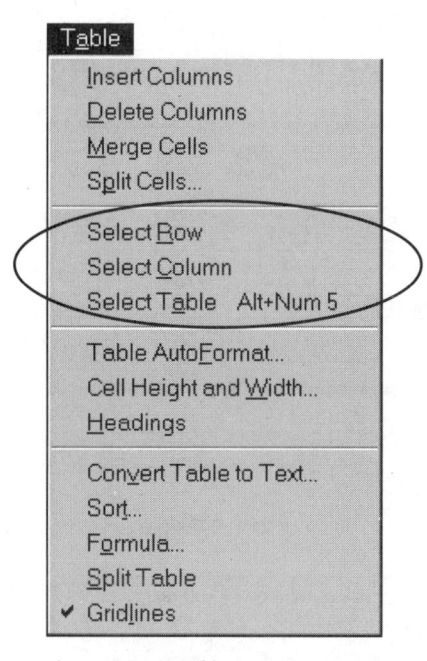

Figure 13. The Table menu contains three commands for selecting all or part of the table.

Figure 14. A selected range.

Figure 15. Selecting an entire column

Figure 16. Selecting an entire row

105

CHAPTER 8

Adjusting Column Widths

By default, all the columns in the table have equal widths. There are three ways to adjust column widths: dragging markers in the ruler (Figure 17), dragging column boundaries (Figure 18), or using the Cell Height and Width dialog box (Figure 19).

When you adjust the width of a column, all columns to the right are resized proportionately. For some alternatives, see Figure 20 on the next page.

■ Tips

- ✓ If the rulers are hidden, select View/Ruler.
- ✓ Click on the table to make sure no cells are selected when you drag the column markers or boundaries. (Otherwise, the width will change for only the selected cells.)
- ✓ Double-click a column marker in the ruler to quickly bring up the Cell Height and Width dialog box.
- ✓ The AutoFit button in the Cell Height and Width dialog box (Figure 19) automatically sets an appropriate width for the column, based on the longest entry in the column.
- ✓ To autofit with the mouse, double-click the right column boundary.
- ✓ If text in one column is right-aligned and the text in the next column is left-aligned, the text will be too close together. One way to fix this problem is to add extra space between columns (Figure 19).

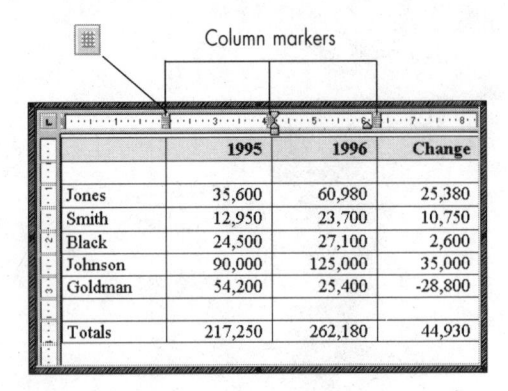

Figure 17. Place the pointer on a column marker. When the pointer changes to double arrows, drag to the right or left.

Figure 18. Dragging the column boundary is another way to adjust the column width.

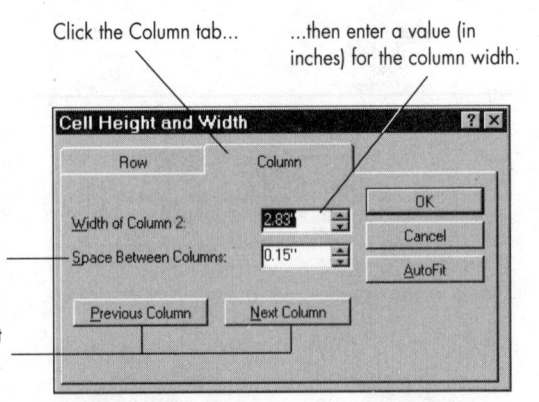

Figure 19. With the Table/Cell Height and Width command, you can enter exact values for your table's column widths.

106

CREATING TABLES

Adjusting Column Widths (cont'd)

Figure 20. Compare each table with the first one.

At first, all columns have the same width.

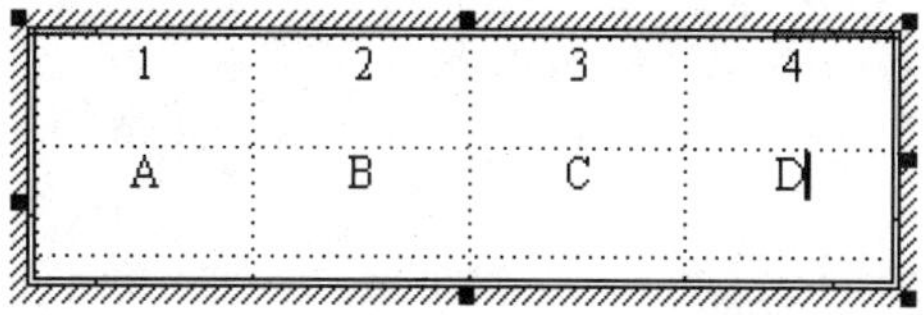

When you drag a column boundary, the columns to the right are resized proportionately. The overall table width is unchanged.

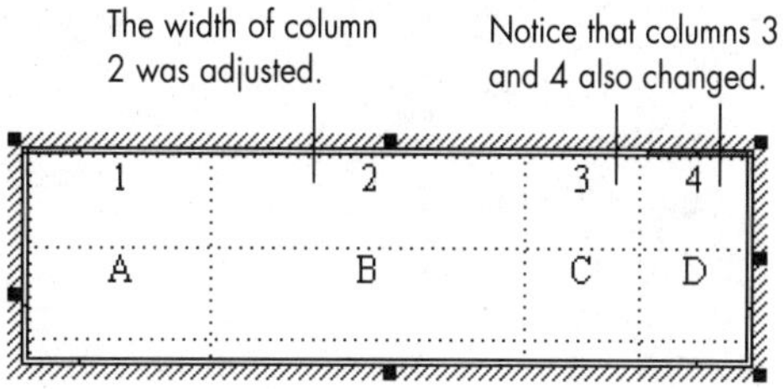

The width of column 2 was adjusted.

Notice that columns 3 and 4 also changed.

When you hold down Shift when dragging a column boundary, only the single column to the right of the boundary is resized. Other columns and the overall table width are unchanged.

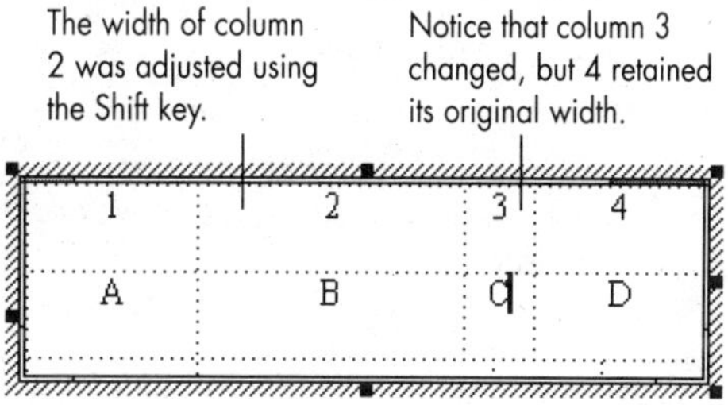

The width of column 2 was adjusted using the Shift key.

Notice that column 3 changed, but 4 retained its original width.

When you hold down Shift and Ctrl when dragging a column boundary, columns to the right do not change size but the overall width of the table changes.

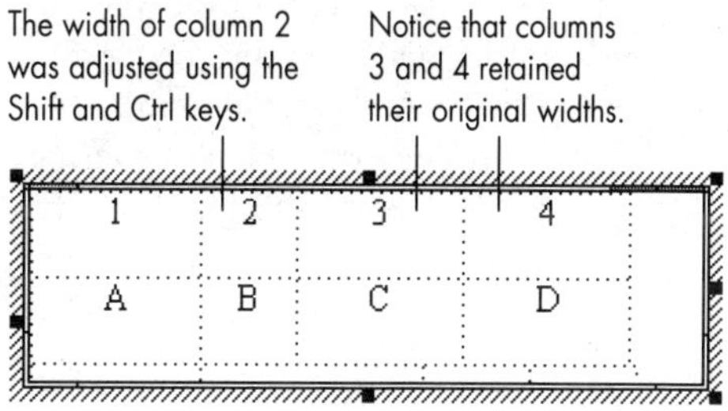

The width of column 2 was adjusted using the Shift and Ctrl keys.

Notice that columns 3 and 4 retained their original widths.

CHAPTER 8

Adjusting Row Heights

By default, all rows are spaced evenly in the table. There are two ways to adjust the row height: You can drag the row's bottom divider line in the vertical ruler (Figure 21) to visually adjust the height, or use the Cell Height and Width dialog box (Figure 22) to enter a precise value. The following steps describe the latter technique.

1. Select at least one cell in the row whose height you want to adjust.
2. Select Table/Cell Height and Width.
3. Click the Row tab (Figure 22).
4. For the Height, choose Exactly.
5. In the At box, specify the number of points for the row height.
6. Click OK.

■ Tips

✓ The row height should be at least the point size of the text; otherwise, the characters will be cut off.

✓ Another way to add extra space between rows is with the Format/Paragraph command. You can add space above or below cells.

See Aligning Text Within a Cell on page 114.

✓ To set all rows to the same height, just click anywhere in the table (no cell should be selected) before displaying the Cell Height and Width dialog box.

✓ If Word won't let you adjust the row height by dragging, it means the Height setting is set to At Least. Go to the Cell Height and Width dialog box and change this setting to Exactly, and specify a value for the At setting. Then you will be able to adjust the row height with the mouse.

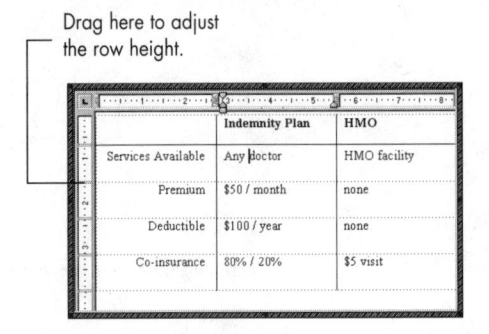

Figure 21. Adjusting the row height visually

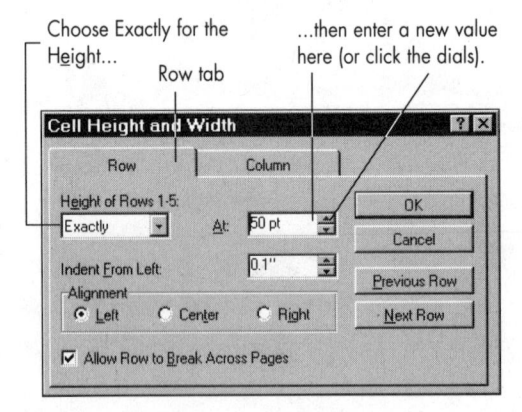

Figure 22. Adjusting the row height precisely

CREATING TABLES

The new row will be inserted above the selected row.

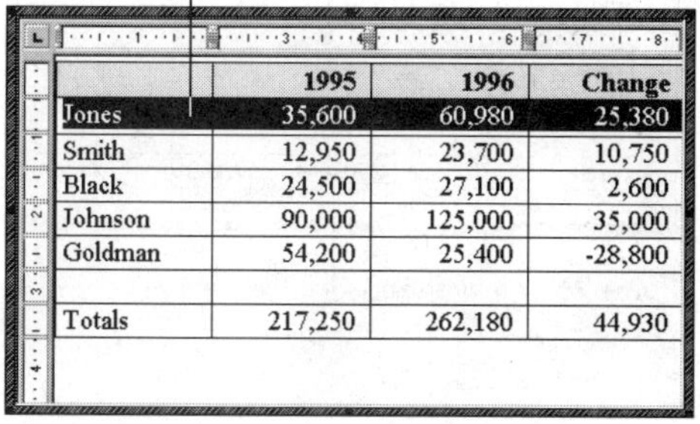

	1995	1996	Change
Jones	35,600	60,980	25,380
Smith	12,950	23,700	10,750
Black	24,500	27,100	2,600
Johnson	90,000	125,000	35,000
Goldman	54,200	25,400	-28,800
Totals	217,250	262,180	44,930

Figure 23. Before inserting a row

Inserted row

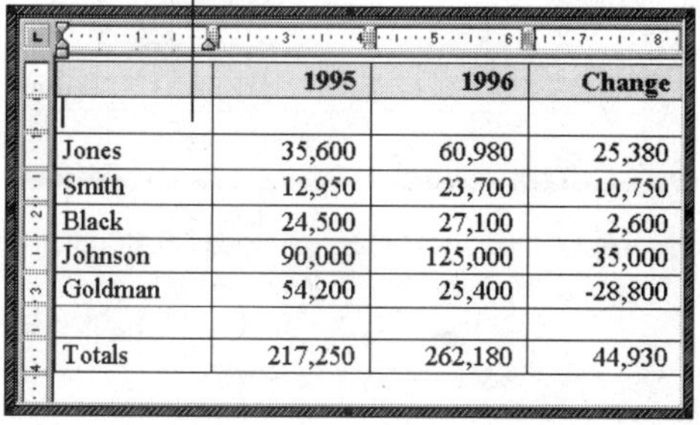

	1995	1996	Change
Jones	35,600	60,980	25,380
Smith	12,950	23,700	10,750
Black	24,500	27,100	2,600
Johnson	90,000	125,000	35,000
Goldman	54,200	25,400	-28,800
Totals	217,250	262,180	44,930

Figure 24. After inserting a row

Insert Rows (or Insert Columns if a column is selected)

Figure 25. The Standard toolbar in Word for Windows 95

Inserting Rows and Columns

If you underestimated the number of rows or columns in your table when initially creating it, you can insert them later. Figures 23 and 24 show a table before and after inserting a row.

Inserting a Row

1. Position the cursor, keeping in mind that rows are inserted *above* the cursor. Click the text cursor anywhere in the row, or select the entire row.

   See Selecting Cells on page 105.

2. Select T*a*ble/*I*nsert Rows.

   or

   Right-click the row and choose Insert Rows from the shortcut menu.

Inserting a Column

1. Select an entire column. (The new column will insert to the *left* of the selected column).

   See Selecting Cells on page 105.

2. Select T*a*ble/*I*nsert Columns.

   or

   Right-click the selected column and choose Insert Columns from the shortcut menu.

■ Tips

✓ You can also insert rows and columns using the Insert button on Word's Standard toolbar (Figure 25).

✓ To insert multiple rows (or columns) in the same location, first select the number of rows (columns) you wish to insert. For instance, to insert two rows, select two rows.

✓ To insert a new row after the last row, position the cursor in the last cell in the table, and press Tab. A new row will appear.

✓ Inserted cells automatically adopt the formatting of neighboring cells.

CHAPTER 8

Deleting Rows and Columns

When you delete rows and columns, you not only remove the contents of the cells, you remove the cells as well (Figures 26 and 27).

1. Select the rows or columns to be deleted (Figure 26).

   See Selecting Cells on page 105.

2. Select Table/Delete Rows or Table/Delete Columns.

   or

   Right-click the selection and choose Delete Rows or Delete Columns from the shortcut menu.

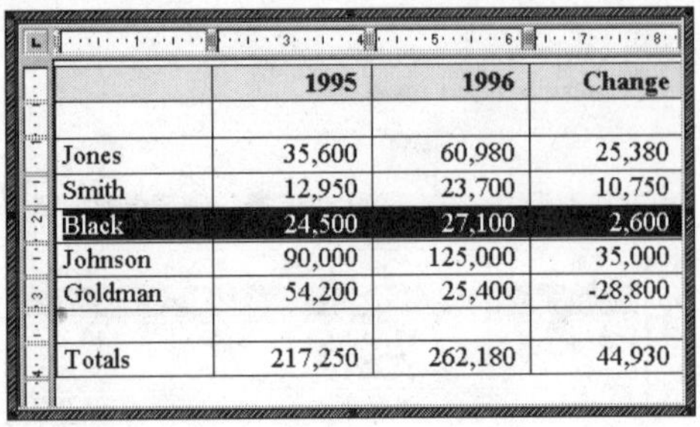

■ Tips

✓ If you accidentally delete rows or columns, immediately choose the Edit/Undo command.

✓ To erase the contents of selected cells, just press Delete. (The empty cells will remain, as shown in Figure 28.)

✓ If you select a cell or part of a row or column, the Table menu includes the command Delete Cells. Choosing this command displays the dialog box shown in Figure 29. Using this bo, you can still delete whole rows or columns.

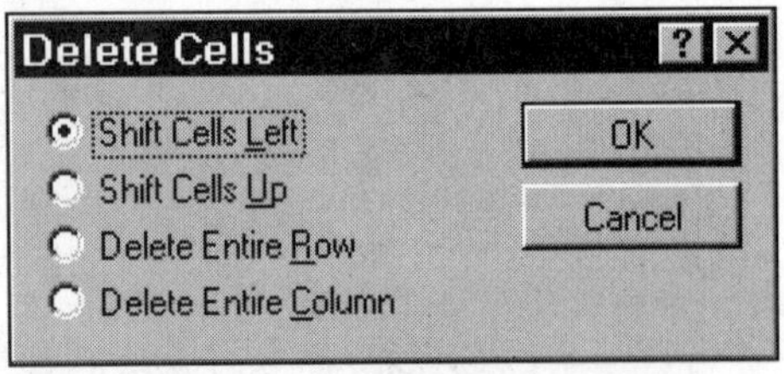

Figure 26. A row is selected for deleting.

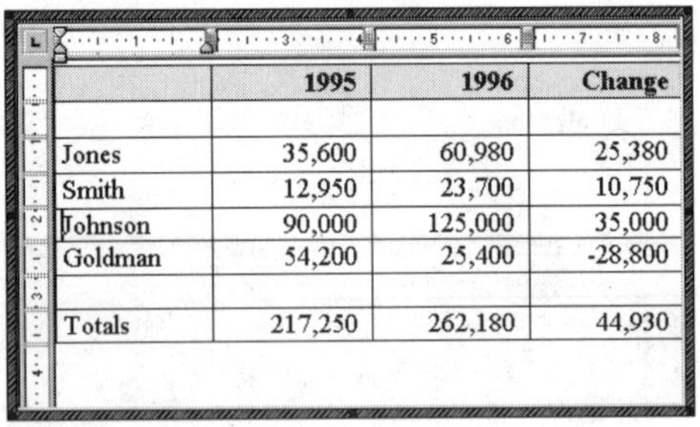

Figure 27. The row that had contained Black's data has been deleted; that row no longer exists.

Figure 29. Select either Delete Entire Row or Delete Entire Column.

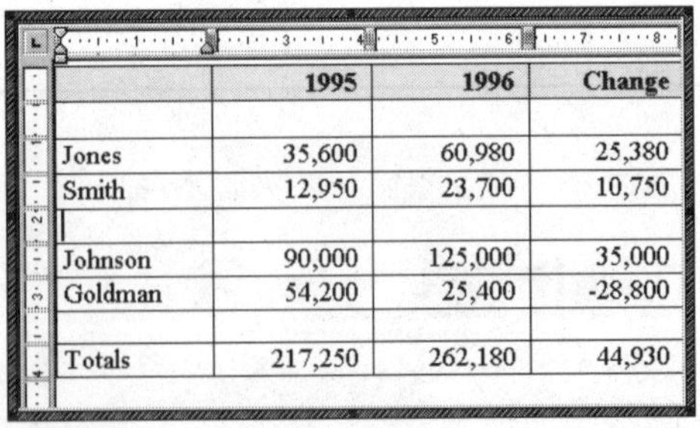

Figure 28. The row that had contained Black's data has been erased by pressing Delete; the row is now empty.

110

CREATING TABLES

	Indemnity Plan	HMO
Services Available	Any doctor	HMO facility
Premium	$50 / month	none
Deductible	$100 / year	none
Co-insurance	80% / 20%	$5 visit

Figure 30. The text is 22-point Times New Roman.

	Indemnity Plan	HMO
Services Available	Any doctor	HMO facility
Premium	$50 / month	none
Deductible	$100 / year	none
Co-insurance	80% / 20%	$5 visit

Figure 31. The text is 20-point Arial.

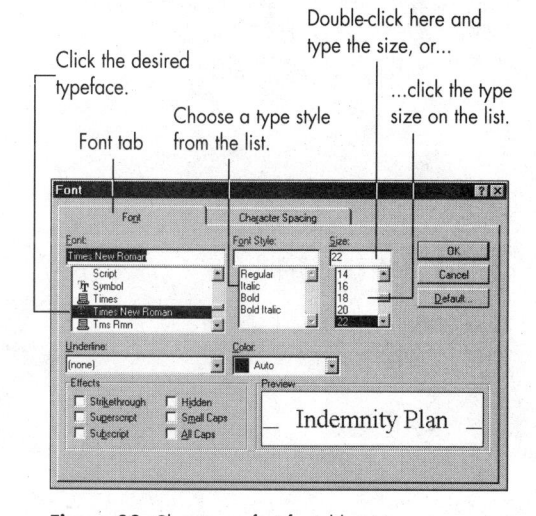

Figure 32. Choosing a font for table text

Formatting Text

You can format the text in the table with a particular typeface, size, and style, among other things (Figures 30 and 31).

1. Select the cells whose text you want to format; or within a cell, drag across the individual characters you want to format.

   See Selecting Cells on page 105.

2. Select Format/Font.

   or

   Right-click the selection, and choose Font from the shortcut menu.

3. Click the Font tab (Figure 32).
4. In the Font list, choose the desired typeface (use the scroll bar if necessary).
5. Select the desired Font Style (Regular, Italic, Bold, or Bold Italic).
6. In the Size list, choose the desired point size (use the scroll bar if necessary).
7. If you like, you can add an underline, or other effect, to the selection.
8. Click OK.

■ Tips

✓ Instead of displaying the Font dialog box, you can use the Font, Font Size, Bold, Italic, and Underline buttons (Figure 33).

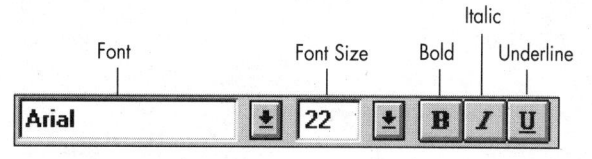

Figure 33. The Formatting toolbar in Word for Windows 95

111

CHAPTER 8

Adding Borders and Shading

The gridlines between cells (Figure 34) in a table do not print—they are there to help you distinguish cells on the screen. To print boundaries between cells, you can add borders (Figure 35). You can also add shading to a range of cells (also Figure 35).

1. Select the cells to which you want to add borders or shading.

    See Selecting Cells on page 105.

2. Click the Borders button (Figure 36). The Borders toolbar appears (Figure 37).

3. Click the arrow in the Line Style field to choose a line thickness and style (Figure 38).

4. Choose one or more border types (Figure 37):

    Top Border Horizontal line on the top of the selected range

    Bottom Border Horizontal line on the bottom edge of the selected range

    Left Border Vertical line on the left side of the selected range

    Right Border Vertical line on the right side of the selected range

    Inside Border Horizontal and vertical lines inside the selected range

    Outside Border Outline around the selected range

    No Border Removes lines from the selected range

5. Choose a shade in the Shading field, if desired (Figure 39).

6. To hide the Borders toolbar again, click the Borders button.

	1995	1996	Change
Jones	35,600	60,980	25,380
Smith	12,950	23,700	10,750
Black	24,500	27,100	2,600
Johnson	90,000	125,000	35,000
Goldman	54,200	25,400	-28,800
Totals	217,250	262,180	44,930

Figure 34. Non-printing gridlines

	1995	1996	Change
Jones	35,600	60,980	25,380
Smith	12,950	23,700	10,750
Black	24,500	27,100	2,600
Johnson	90,000	125,000	35,000
Goldman	54,200	25,400	-28,800
Totals	217,250	262,180	44,930

Figure 35. This table has inside and outside borders; the top row has a 20% shade.

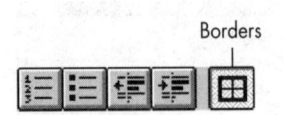

Figure 36. The Formatting toolbar in Word for Windows 95

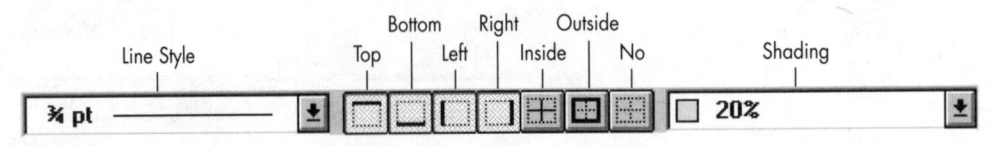

Figure 37. The Borders toolbar

CREATING TABLES

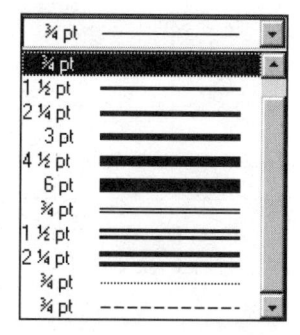

Figure 38. The list of line styles

Adding Borders and Shading (cont'd)

■ Tip

✓ Another way to specify borders is with the Format/Borders and Shading command (Figure 40). However, the Borders toolbar is more intuitive than this dialog box.

See AutoFormatting a Table on page 115 for information on automatically applying borders to a table.

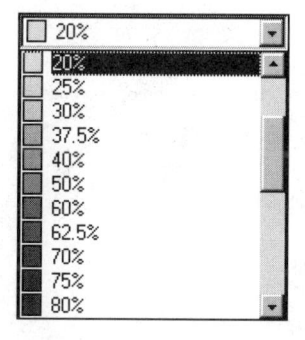

Figure 39. The list of shading percentages and patterns

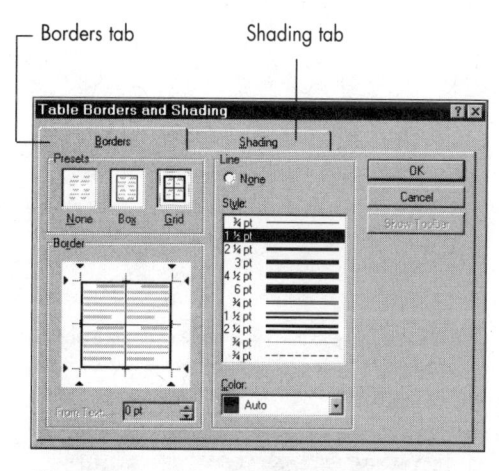

Figure 40. Use the Format/Borders and Shading command to display this dialog box.

CHAPTER 8

Aligning Text Within a Cell

By default, table text is aligned at the top-left edge of each cell (Figure 41). Using Word's paragraph formatting commands, you can adjust the horizontal and vertical alignment of text within a cell (Figure 42).

To control the horizontal alignment, use the alignment buttons (Figure 43). To add padding to the left or right of the text, drag the indent markers in the ruler (Figure 44). Finally, to control the vertical alignment, use the F*o*rmat/*P*aragraph command to add space before or after the paragraph (Figure 45).

You must select cells before formatting them.

See Selecting Cells on page 105.

■ Tip

✓ The rulers can be turned on and off with the *V*iew/*R*uler command.

	Indemnity Plan	HMO
Services Available	Any doctor	HMO facility
Premium	$50 / month	none
Deductible	$100 / year	none
Co-insurance	80% / 20%	$5 / visit

Figure 41. Notice how close the text is to the cell borders.

	Indemnity Plan	HMO
Services Available	Any doctor	HMO facility
Premium	$50 / month	none
Deductible	$100 / year	none
Co-insurance	80% / 20%	$5 visit

Figure 42. By changing indents, alignment, and paragraph spacing, you can improve the appearance of this table.

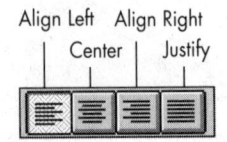

Figure 43. The Formatting toolbar in Word for Windows 95

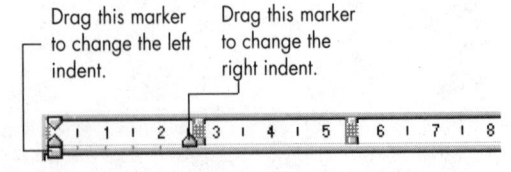

Figure 44. Drag the indent markers to position text horizontally in a cell.

Figure 45. Use F*o*rmat/*P*aragraph to position text horizontally and vertically in a cell. These are the settings used to format the table in Figure 42.

CREATING TABLES

	1995	1996	Change
Jones	35,600	60,980	25,380
Smith	12,950	23,700	10,750
Black	24,500	27,100	2,600
Johnson	90,000	125,000	35,000
Goldman	54,200	25,400	-28,800
Totals	217,250	262,180	44,930

Figure 46. An unformatted table

	1995	1996	Change
Jones	35,600	60,980	25,380
Smith	12,950	23,700	10,750
Black	24,500	27,100	2,600
Johnson	90,000	125,000	35,000
Goldman	54,200	25,400	-28,800
Totals	217,250	262,180	44,930

Figure 47. The List 4 AutoFormat

Click a format... ...and see an example of it in the Preview box.

Select which aspects of the format to apply.

Apply special formatting to select areas.

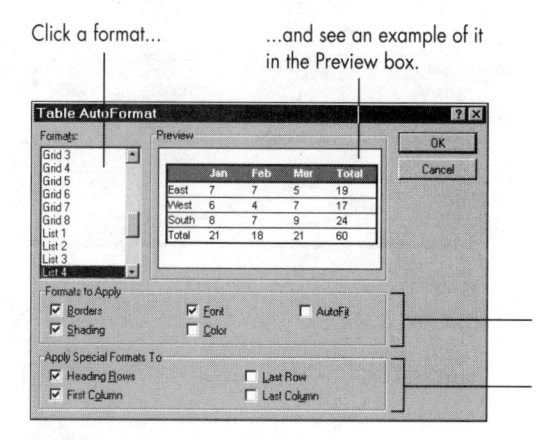

Figure 48. Selecting an AutoFormat

AutoFormatting a Table

With Word's AutoFormat feature, you can add borders, shading, and other formatting attributes by choosing one of several dozen predesigned formats. Figures 46 and 47 show a table before and after choosing an AutoFormat. This feature not only is a big time-saver, but you can also be assured of a well-designed format.

1. Select Table/Table AutoFormat.
2. Click different formats in the Formats list, and look at the Preview box to see what each one looks like (Figure 48).
3. Choose the aspects of the format you want to apply: Borders, Shading, Font, Color, and/or AutoFit.
4. Select whether you want to apply special formatting to the Heading Rows, First Column, Last Row, and/or Last Column.
5. Click OK.

■ Tips

✓ You may want to turn off the AutoFit checkbox in the Table AutoFormat dialog box, if you have already adjusted the column widths manually. The AutoFit option will sometimes make the columns too narrow and will reduce the table width.

✓ Many formats offer unique formatting for the first and last rows and columns. As you preview a format, enable and disable the various options under Apply Special Formats To while looking at the Preview box. This box lets you see how the table will look with these options.

Creating Tables

115

CHAPTER 8

Summing Columns

Just as with spreadsheet applications, Word tables can perform calculations. The main difference is that formulas are not typed directly into a cell—they are entered in the Formula dialog box (Figure 49).

1. Click the cell at the bottom of the column where you want the total to appear (Figure 50).
2. Select Table/Formula.
3. Enter =SUM(ABOVE) in the Formula box.
4. Click OK.

The result is shown in Figure 51.

■ Tips

✓ To sum a row, the formula is =SUM(LEFT).

✓ In addition to the SUM function, there are 21 other functions available, such as AVERAGE, MAX, and MIN. The Paste Function field lists these functions. Choosing a function from the list displays it in the Formula box.

✓ You can also enter formulas that perform calculations on individual cells, such as =B3-C3.

To sum a column, enter this function in the Formula box.

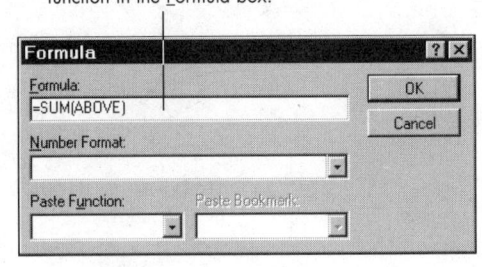

Figure 49. Entering a formula to sum a column

Figure 50. Click where you want the formula to appear.

Figure 51. The result of the calculation

ADDING GRAPHIC OBJECTS   9

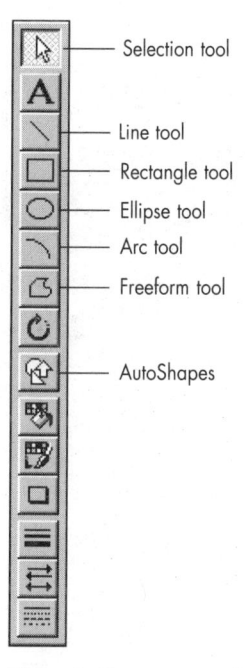

- Selection tool
- Line tool
- Rectangle tool
- Ellipse tool
- Arc tool
- Freeform tool
- AutoShapes

Figure 1. The Drawing toolbar

Types of Graphic Objects

Graphic elements will contribute variety and interest to your slides. There are several ways to add graphic objects. First, you can use the Drawing toolbar (Figure 1) which offers tools for drawing lines, boxes, circles, arcs, and so forth. With the AutoShapes toolbar (Figure 2), you can easily create predefined objects such as arrows, stars, diamonds, and triangles.

The second way to add graphic objects is by inserting *clip art* images that come with PowerPoint (Figure 3). You have hundreds to choose from.

See Inserting Clip Art on page 128.

Finally, you can import other graphic files—for example, an image created in CorelDRAW or Microsoft Paint.

See Inserting Graphic Files on page 131 and Pasting Graphics on page 132.

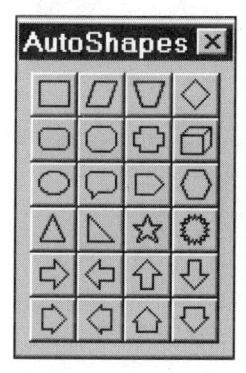

Figure 2. You can add any of these autoshapes to your slides.

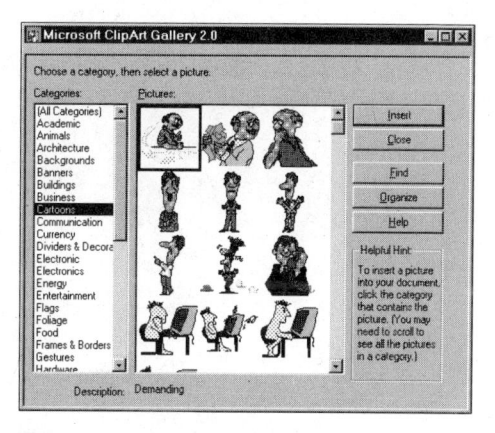

Figure 3. Use ClipArt Gallery to insert images on your slides.

117

CHAPTER 9

Drawing Lines

Figure 4 illustrates how lines can become a graphic element on a slide.

1. In the Drawing toolbar, click the Line tool (Figure 5).
2. Place the mouse pointer (a crosshair) where you want to begin the line.
3. Hold down the mouse button as you drag in the direction you want the line to follow.
4. Release the mouse button when the line is the desired length.

■ Tips

- ✓ To make sure the line is perfectly straight (horizontally or vertically), hold down the Shift key as you draw the line.
- ✓ To draw several lines, double-click the Line tool. When you are finished drawing lines, press Esc.
- ✓ To change the length or angle of the line, click on the line to select it (Figure 6), and drag a selection handle. To change the length without changing the angle, hold down Shift as you drag a handle.
- ✓ To reposition the line, select it and drag it into position. (Make sure you don't drag a selection handle or you will change the length of the line.)

To change the line thickness, see Formatting Lines on the opposite page.

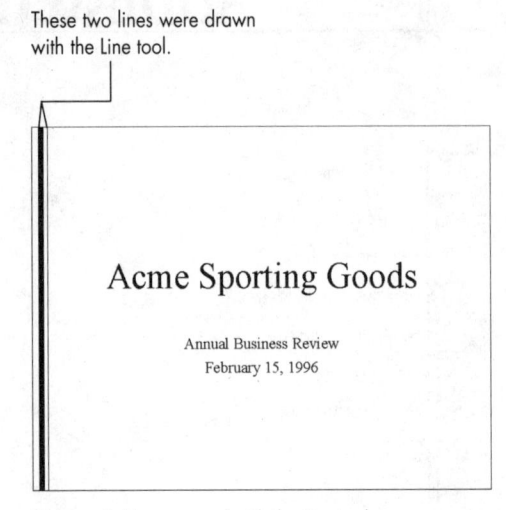

These two lines were drawn with the Line tool.

Figure 4. Lines created with the Line tool

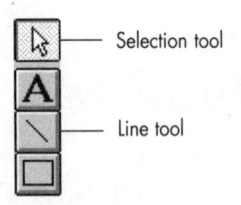

Figure 5. The Drawing toolbar

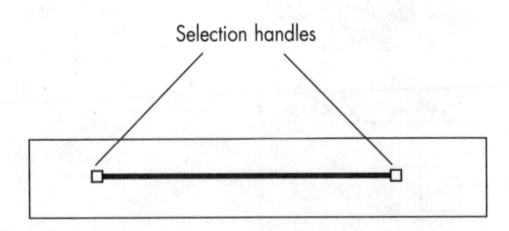

Figure 6. When a line is selected, selection handles appear at each end.

ADDING GRAPHIC OBJECTS

Formatting Lines

There are a variety of ways to format lines and borders. For instance, you can change the line thickness (Figure 7), choose a double-line style, create a dashed line, or add an arrowhead (Figure 8).

1. Select the line or shape to be formatted.
2. Select F*o*rmat/Colors and L*i*nes.

    or

    Right-click the line or shape to be formatted and choose Colors and Lines from the shortcut menu.

    The Colors and Lines dialog box appears (Figure 9).

3. In the *C*olor field, choose a color.
4. In the *S*tyle list, click the sample line with the thickness or style you prefer.
5. If desired, click one of the sample lines in the *D*ashed list.
6. To create an arrow, choose one of the styles in the *A*rrows list.
7. Click OK.

■ Tips

✓ To select more than one line, hold down Shift as you click each one.

✓ You can also format lines with the Line Color, Line Style, Arrowheads, and Dashed Lines tools in the Drawing toolbar (Figure 10).

Figure 7. The lines on this slide have different thicknesses.

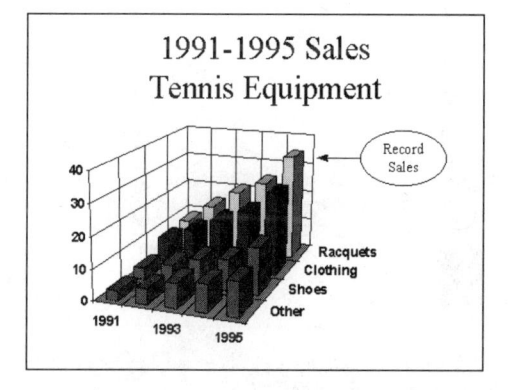

Figure 8. A line was turned into an arrow by giving it an arrowhead style.

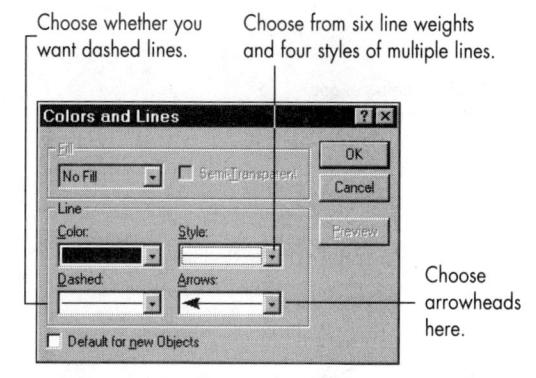

Choose whether you want dashed lines.

Choose from six line weights and four styles of multiple lines.

Choose arrowheads here.

Figure 9. In the Colors and Lines dialog box, you can choose line styles and colors, create dashed lines, and add arrowheads.

— Line Color
— Line Style
— Arrowheads
— Dashed Lines

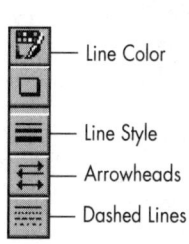

Figure 10. The Drawing toolbar

CHAPTER 9

Drawing Rectangles and Squares

Using the Rectangle tool (Figure 11), you can create rectangles and squares. Figure 12 shows an example of how a rectangle can be used on a slide.

1. In the Drawing toolbar, click the Rectangle tool (Figure 11).
2. Place the mouse pointer (a crosshair) where you want to begin the rectangle.
3. Hold down the mouse button as you drag towards the opposite corner of the box (Figure 13).
4. Release the mouse button when the box is the desired size.

■ Tips

✓ To create a perfect square, hold down Shift as you draw the rectangle.

✓ To create several rectangles, double-click the Rectangle tool. When you are finished drawing rectangles, press Esc.

✓ To change the size of an object, click on it and drag a selection handle (Figure 14).

✓ To reposition the object, select it and then drag it into position. (Make sure you don't drag a selection handle or you will change the size of the object.)

✓ To type centered text inside a selected rectangle, just start typing. The text is actually part of the rectangle.

✓ To change the border, use the F<u>o</u>rmat/ Color and <u>L</u>ines command.

See Formatting Lines on page 119.

See also Filling an Object on page 122.

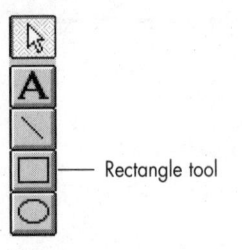

Figure 11. The Drawing toolbar

The gray rectangle was drawn on top of the black rectangle.

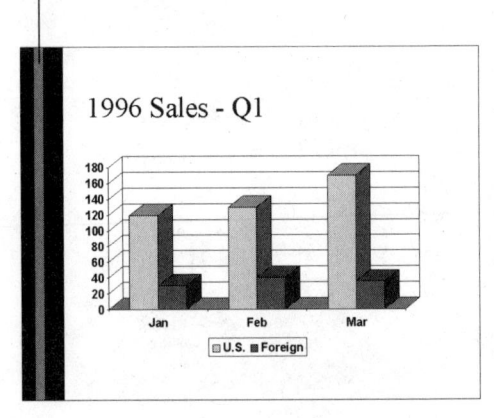

Figure 12. The Rectangle tool created the black and gray boxes on this slide.

Begin dragging at one corner of the box...

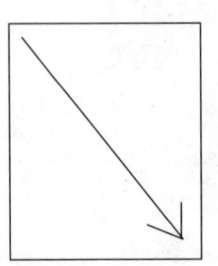

...then drag to the opposite corner until the box is the desired size.

Figure 13. Drawing a box

Selection handles

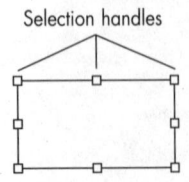

Figure 14. A selected rectangle

ADDING GRAPHIC OBJECTS

— Ellipse tool

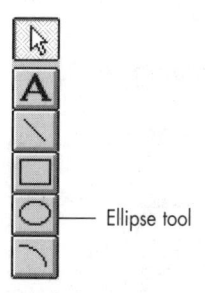

Figure 15. The Drawing toolbar

Drawing Ellipses and Circles

Using the Ellipse tool (Figure 15), you can create ellipses and circles. Figure 16 shows an example of how an ellipse can be used to annotate a slide.

1. In the Drawing toolbar, click the Ellipse tool (Figure 15).
2. Place the mouse pointer (a crosshair) where you want to begin the ellipse.
3. Hold down the mouse button as you drag in a diagonal direction (Figure 17).
4. Release the mouse button when the ellipse is the desired size.

■ Tips

✓ To create a perfect circle, hold down Shift as you drag to draw the ellipse.

✓ To create several ellipses, double-click the Ellipse tool. When you are finished drawing ellipses, press Esc.

✓ To change the size and position of an ellipse, see the tips for Drawing Rectangles and Squares on the previous page.

✓ To change the ellipse's border, use the Format/Color and Lines command.

✓ To type centered text inside a selected ellipse, just start typing. The text is actually part of the ellipse. This technique was used in Figure 16. (The text does not wrap, however—you must press Enter after each line.)

See Formatting Lines on page 119.

See also Filling an Object on the next page.

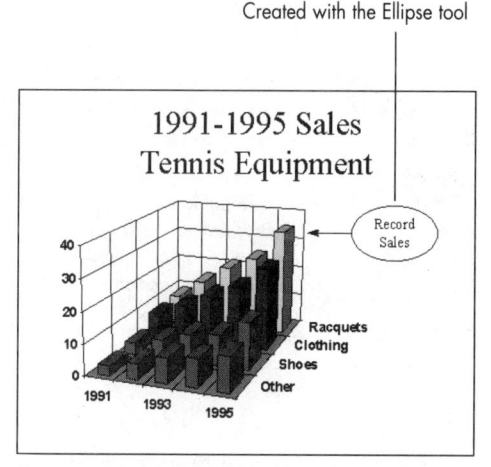

Created with the Ellipse tool

Figure 16. An ellipse encloses a graph annotation (*Record Sales*).

Begin dragging at one edge of the ellipse...

...then drag diagonally until the ellipse is the desired size.

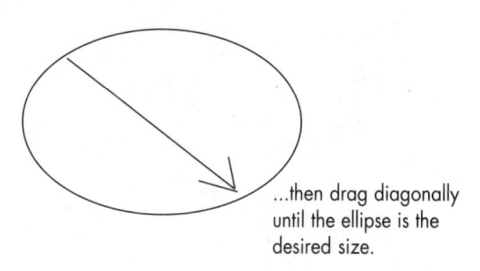

Figure 17. Drawing an ellipse

CHAPTER 9

Filling an Object

You can choose a fill color or pattern for the rectangles, circles, arcs, freeform objects, and autoshapes you create in PowerPoint.

1. Select the object you want to fill.
2. Select Format/Colors and Lines. The Colors and Lines dialog box appears (Figure 18).

   or

   Right-click the object and choose Colors and Lines from the shortcut menu.

3. Display the Fill list (Figure 19) by clicking this field.
4. Choose a color, or click Other Color to display the large color palette (Figure 20).

   or

   Click Patterned on the Fill list, and then choose a pattern in the Pattern Fill dialog box (Figure 21).

   or

   Click Textured on the Fill list, and then choose a texture (such as marble or cork) in the Textured Fill dialog box (Figure 22).

   or

   To remove the fill, choose either No Fill for a transparent object or Background for an opaque object (Figure 23).

5. Click OK.

   For information on creating shades, refer to Creating a Shaded Background on page 150.

■ Tips

✓ Another way to choose a fill color or pattern is with the Fill Color button (Figure 24).

✓ To remove the outline around an object, click the Line Color button (Figure 24) and choose No Line.

Click here to display the Fill list.

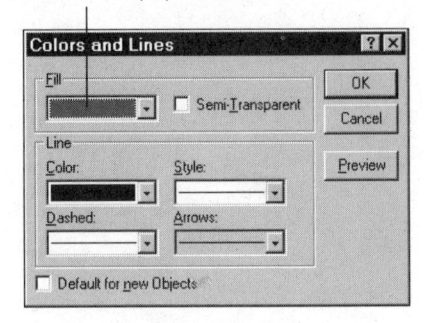

Figure 18. The Colors and Lines dialog box

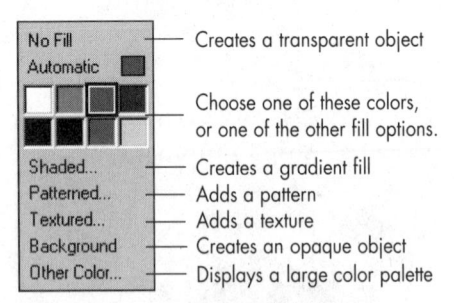

Figure 19. Choosing a color or other type of fill for an object

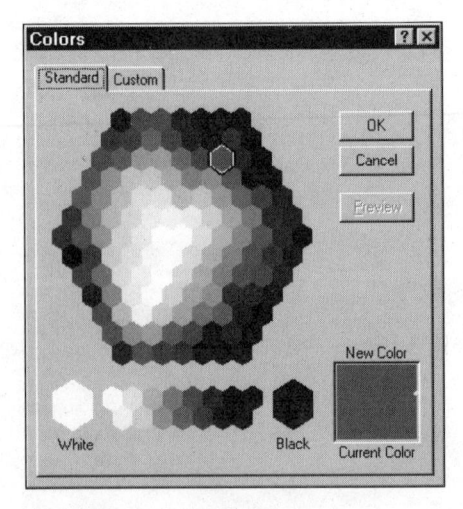

- No Fill — Creates a transparent object
- Choose one of these colors, or one of the other fill options.
- Shaded... — Creates a gradient fill
- Patterned... — Adds a pattern
- Textured... — Adds a texture
- Background — Creates an opaque object
- Other Color... — Displays a large color palette

Figure 20. The large color palette

122

ADDING GRAPHIC OBJECTS

Filling an Object (cont'd)

Choose a pattern style.

Choose a color for the pattern itself.

Choose a color for behind the pattern.

Figure 21. Choosing a pattern

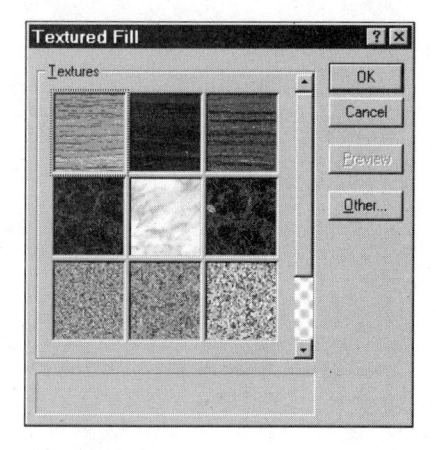

Figure 22. Choosing a texture

This ellipse has no fill.

This ellipse has a Background fill.

Fill Color
Line Color

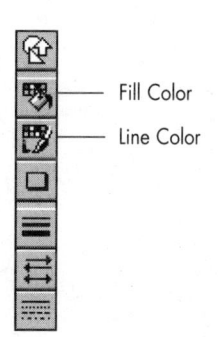

Figure 24. The Drawing toolbar

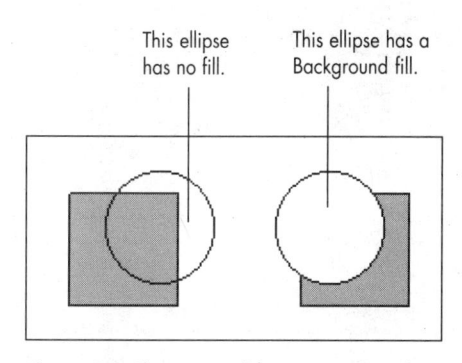

Figure 23. Choose No Fill for a transparent object and choose Background fill for an opaque object.

Adding Graphic Objects

123

CHAPTER 9

Adding a Drop Shadow

A drop shadow can add a feeling of depth to an object. Figure 25 shows a rectangle with a drop shadow.

1. Select the object you want to shadow.
2. Click the Shadow On/Off button (Figure 26).
3. To adjust the color and offset of the shadow, select Format/Shadow (Figure 27).
4. Click OK.

■ **Tip**

✓ You can add drop shadows to any closed object drawn in PowerPoint (ellipses, rectangles, polygons, and AutoShapes).

Figure 25. This rectangle has a drop shadow.

Shadow On/Off

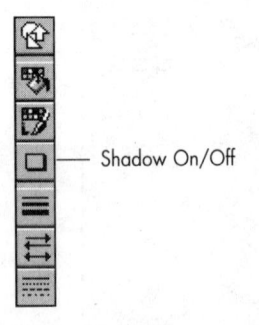

Figure 26. The Drawing toolbar

Click here to choose a color for the shadow.

Click the up arrows to see more shadow; click the down arrows to see less.

Figure 27. Adjusting the color and offset of a drop shadow

124

ADDING GRAPHIC OBJECTS

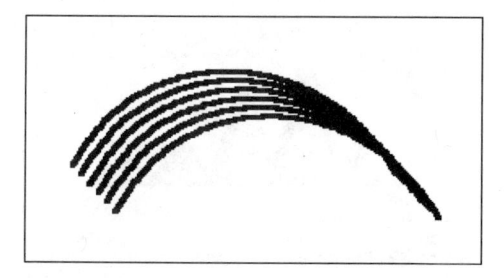

Figure 28. These arcs were created with the Arc tool.

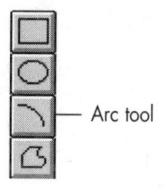

— Arc tool

Figure 29. The Drawing toolbar

Original arc   Reshaped arc
Adjustment handle
Adjustment handle

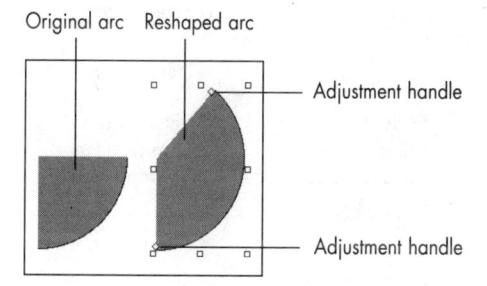

Figure 30. Filled arcs, before and after reshaping

Original arc   Resized arc
Selection handles

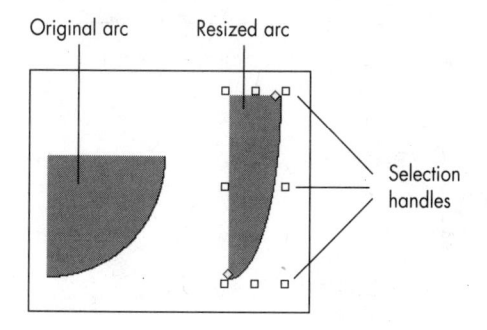

Figure 31. Filled arcs, before and after resizing

Drawing Arcs

Figure 28 shows a series of arcs you can create in PowerPoint. Here's how to create arcs:

1. Click the Arc tool (Figure 29).
2. Click at the beginning of the arc and drag to the end.

or

Hold down one of the following *constraint keys* as you drag:

- Shift (to draw a quarter of a circle)
- Ctrl (to center the arc on the starting point)
- Shift+Ctrl (to draw a quarter of a circle and center the arc on the starting point)

■ Tips

✓ To draw several arcs, double-click the Arc tool. When you are finished drawing arcs, press Esc.

✓ To extend or contract the arc, select it and drag one of the two adjustment handles (Figure 30).

✓ To resize the arc, select it and drag one of the eight selection handles (Figure 31).

To rotate the arc, see Rotating Objects on page 145.

To fill the arc (as in Figures 30 and 31), see Filling an Object on page 122.

To change the line thickness or style of the arc, see Formatting Lines on page 119.

125

CHAPTER 9

Creating Polygons and Freehand Drawings

The Freeform tool lets you create your own shapes, such as the one in Figure 32. In addition to creating a series of connected line segments, this tool also can be used to create freehand drawings, if you are artistically inclined (Figure 33).

Your shapes and drawings can be open or closed (Figure 34).

Creating Connected Line Segments

1. Click the Freeform tool (Figure 35).
2. Click at each point of the shape you want to draw—PowerPoint draws a line segment between each point.
3. To finish the drawing, click on or near the first point (to create a closed shape) or double-click (to create an open shape).

Creating a Freehand Drawing

1. Click the Freeform tool (Figure 35).
2. Place the crosshair pointer at the starting point of the drawing.
3. Hold down the mouse button—you'll see a drawing pencil appear.
4. Drag the mouse to draw with the pencil.
5. To finish the drawing, put the pencil on or near the starting point (to create a closed drawing) or double-click (to create an open drawing).

■ Tips

- ✓ Closed shapes are automatically filled; open shapes are not. Use the Fill Color tool (Figure 35) to remove or change the fill of a selected object.

    See Filling an Object on page 122 for information on changing the fill color.

- ✓ Double-click a freeform shape to see vertexes (control handles). Drag a vertext to adjust the shape. (It often helps to zoom in.)

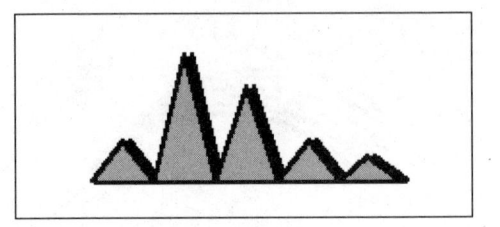

Figure 32. This geometric mountain range was created with the Freeform tool.

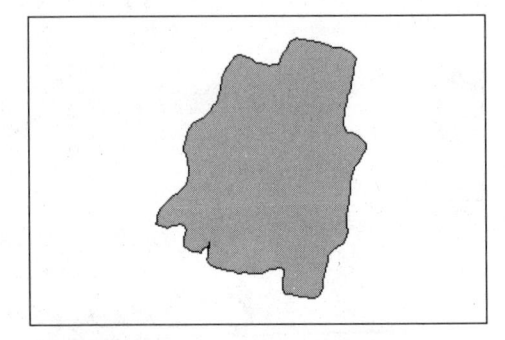

Figure 33. Hmmm...your author is obviously not artistically inclined and should stay clear of freehand drawing!

Click near starting point to create a closed shape.

Double-click at ending point to create an open shape.

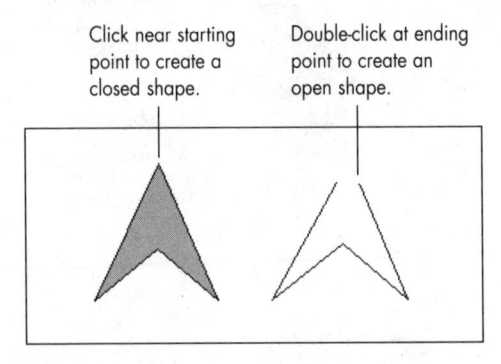

Figure 34. You can create closed or open shapes.

— Freeform tool

— Fill Color tool

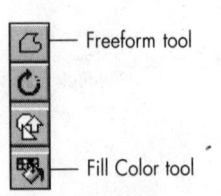

Figure 35. The Drawing toolbar

Adding Graphic Objects

126

ADDING GRAPHIC OBJECTS

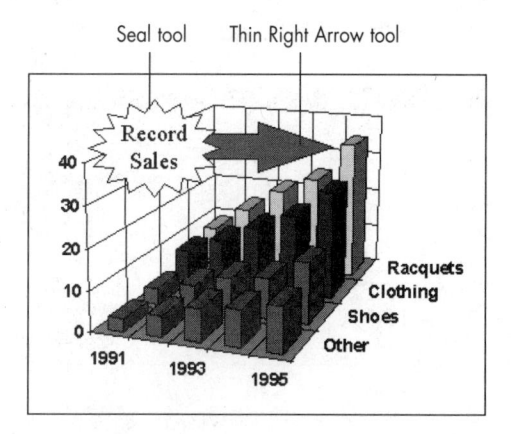

Figure 36. This graph was annotated with two autoshapes.

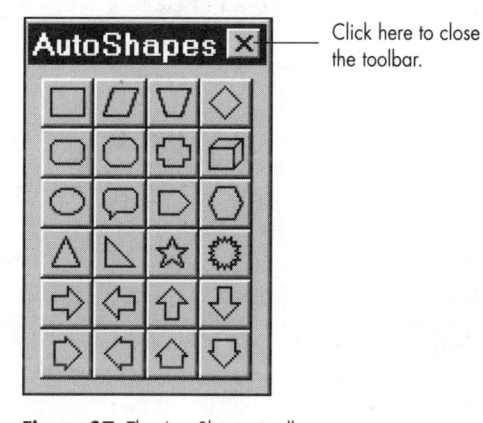

Figure 37. The AutoShapes toolbar

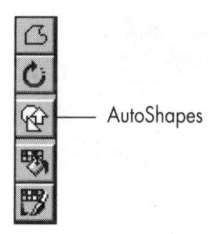

Figure 38. The Drawing toolbar

Using AutoShapes

PowerPoint comes with a set of built-in shapes, called *AutoShapes*, that you can add to any slide. The graph in Figure 36 has been enhanced with a couple of these shapes. Figure 37 shows the complete set of AutoShapes.

1. Click the AutoShapes button (Figure 38) to display the toolbar.
2. In the AutoShapes toolbar (Figure 37), click the desired tool.
3. Place the mouse pointer where you want to begin the object. (The pointer changes to a crosshair.)
4. Hold down the mouse button as you drag diagonally to create the object.
5. Release the mouse button when the object is the desired size.

■ Tips

✓ To type centered text inside a selected AutoShape, just start typing. The text is actually part of the AutoShape object. This technique was used to type "Record Sales" in Figure 36. (The text does not wrap, however—you must press Enter after each line.)

✓ To replace an existing AutoShape with another, select it and choose the Draw/Change AutoShape command; then choose the desired shape. The new shape will have the same size, text (if any), and line and fill attributes as the AutoShape it replaces.

✓ To create a shape whose height is equal to its width, hold down Shift as you draw the object.

✓ You can customize many of the AutoShapes by dragging the diamond adjustment handle.

See Filling an Object on page 122 for information on changing the fill color.

127

CHAPTER 9

Adding Graphic Objects

Inserting Clip Art

PowerPoint comes with hundreds of *clip art* images that you can add to your slides. There are two ways to insert clip art.

When adding a new slide, you can choose one of the two clip art AutoLayouts (Figure 39). These layouts will insert a clip art placeholder (Figure 40); double-clicking this placeholder will bring up *Microsoft ClipArt Gallery* (Figure 41) from which you can select a clip art image.

Or, if you want to add clip art to an existing slide, use the Insert Clip Art button (Figure 42). This button inserts a placeholder and immediately launches ClipArt Gallery.

Once you are in ClipArt Gallery, follow these steps to choose an image:

1. Click a category (such as Animals or Backgrounds). Use the scroll bar to see additional categories.
2. Select a picture and click Insert.

   or

   Double-click a picture.

■ Tips

✓ To resize a clip art image, select it and drag a *corner* selection handle. If you drag a *middle* handle the image will not maintain its original proportions.

✓ To move the image, select it and drag it into position. Make sure that you don't drag a selection handle, or you will resize the image.

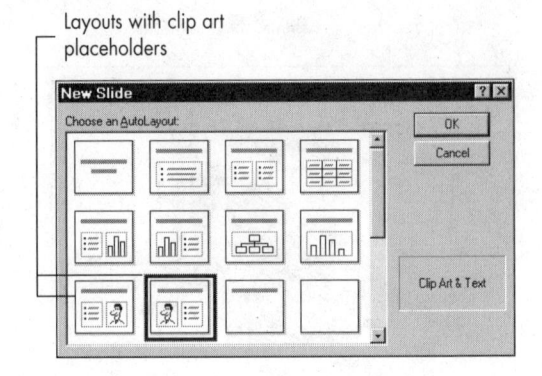

Figure 39. Choosing a layout with a clip art placeholder

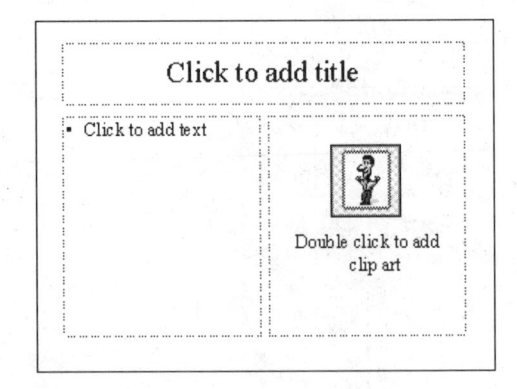

Figure 40. A slide with a clip art placeholder

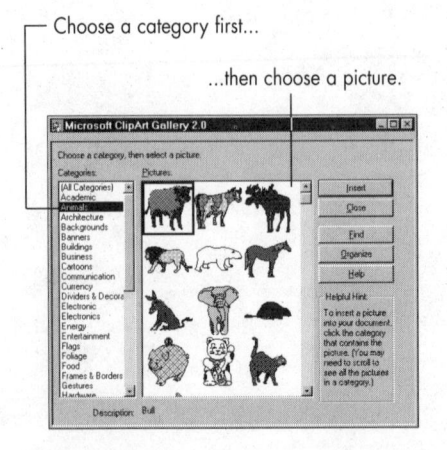

Figure 41. Choosing a picture in ClipArt Gallery

Figure 42. The Standard toolbar

128

ADDING GRAPHIC OBJECTS

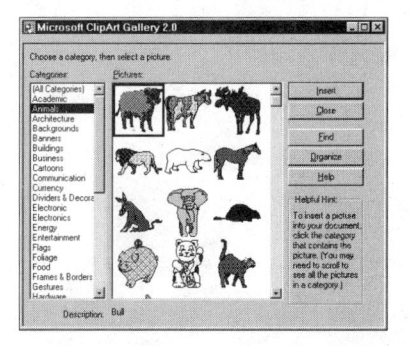

Figure 43. To search for clip art, click the Find button.

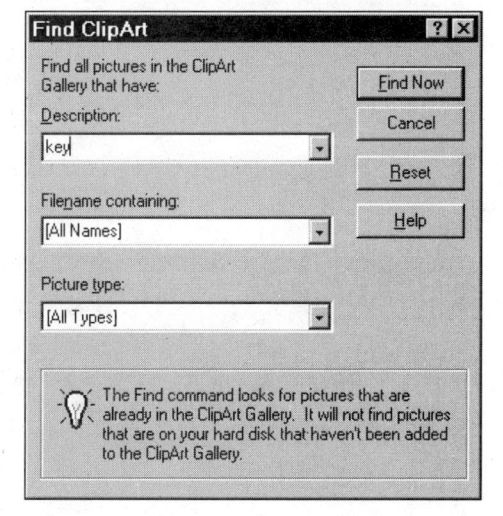

Figure 44. In this example, we are searching for pictures with the letters *key* in their description.

Searching for Clip Art

An easy way to locate a particular clip art image is to have ClipArt Gallery search for it. Because each image has a short description associated with it, you can search for images based on a word in the description.

See the previous page for information on inserting a clip art placeholder.

1. In ClipArt Gallery, click Find (Figure 43).
2. In the Find ClipArt dialog box (Figure 44), enter a word in the Description box.

   or

   Enter a file name or part of a file name in the box under Filename Containing.
3. Click Find Now. ClipArt Gallery now displays all pictures that match your specifications (Figure 45).
4. Click the picture you want and choose Insert.

■ Tip

✓ ClipArt Gallery displays only the pictures that match the conditions you entered in the Find ClipArt dialog box. To go back to viewing all the clip art again, click All Categories in the Categories list.

ClipArt Gallery found every image that had *key* in its description, such as...

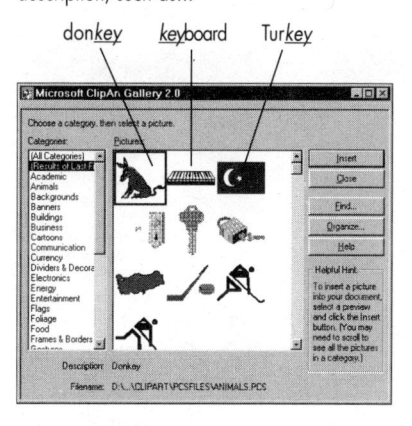

don*key*   *key*board   Tur*key*

Figure 45. The results of the search

Adding Graphic Objects

129

CHAPTER 9

Using the AutoClipArt Feature

Another way to locate clip art is with PowerPoint's new AutoClipArt feature.

1. In Slide view, go to the slide to which you want to add clip art.
2. Select Tools/AutoClipArt. The AutoClipArt dialog box appears (Figure 46).
3. Select a word that corresponds to the type of clip art for which you are searching.
4. Choose the View Clip Art button. Images that match the specified category appear in the Microsoft ClipArt Gallery (Figure 47).
5. Click the desired image and then choose Insert to copy the image to your slide.

   or

   If you don't see an image that works for your slide, choose Close.
6. Choose Cancel to close the AutoClipArt dialog box.

■ Tip

✓ After inserting the clip-art image, you may need to move and resize the image.

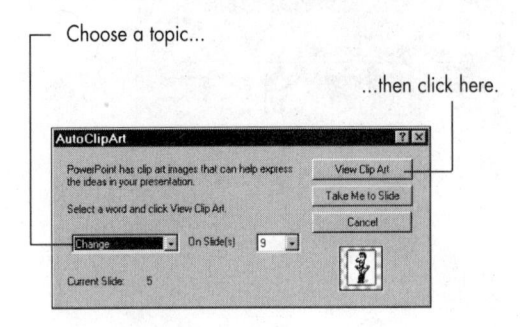

Figure 46. Choosing a topic

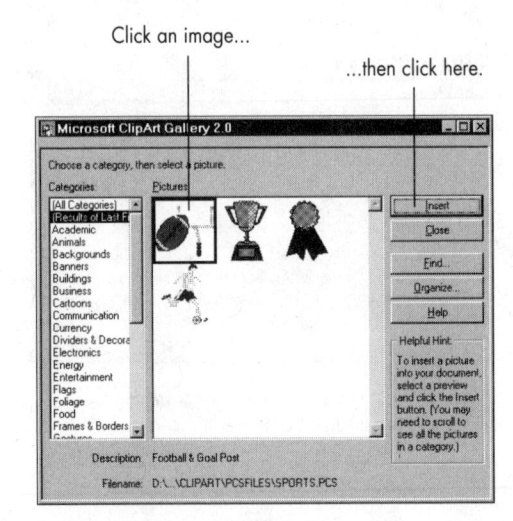

Figure 47. Selecting an image

Adding Graphic Objects

130

ADDING GRAPHIC OBJECTS

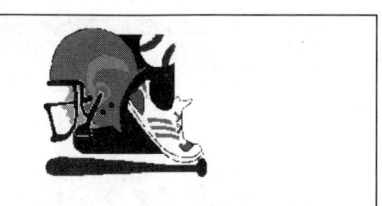

Figure 48. This sport graphic is an imported Windows Metafile.

Choose another drive or folder here...

...or, use the Up One Level tool.

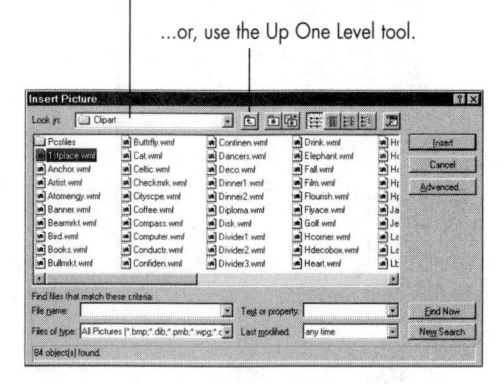

Figure 49. Inserting a graphic file

Inserting Graphic Files

You may want your slides to include graphic files that you have created or purchased. Figure 48 shows a graphic that has been imported to a PowerPoint slide.

1. Display the slide on which you want to insert the graphic file.
2. Select Insert/Picture. The Insert Picture dialog box appears (Figure 49).
3. In the Files of Type field, choose a specific type of graphic format, such as Windows Metafile. (This step is optional because, by default, all pictures are displayed.)
4. To insert a file from another drive or a different folder, use the Look In field or the Up One Level tool.
5. Click the name of the graphic file.
6. Click Insert.

■ Tips

✓ To resize a graphic image, select it and drag a *corner* selection handle. If you drag a *middle* handle the image will not maintain its original proportions.

✓ To move the image, select it and then drag it into position. Make sure that you don't drag a selection handle, or you will resize the image.

See Pasting Graphics on the next page for another way to insert graphics.

131

CHAPTER 9

Adding Graphic Objects

Pasting Graphics

If you have created a graphic image in another program (such as CorelDRAW), you may want to use the copy-and-paste routine to bring it into PowerPoint (Figure 50). One advantage to using this method is that the image becomes an *embedded object* (like org charts, graphs, and tables) that can be easily modified.

1. Select the graphic in the source application, and use Edit/Copy to copy it to the Windows Clipboard.
2. Switch to PowerPoint and display the slide on which you want to insert the graphic.
3. Select Edit/Paste.

■ **Tip**

✓ As with any embedded object, you can modify it by double-clicking the object. PowerPoint will then launch the application that created the image and display the graphic, ready for editing. When you exit the source application, the graphic will be updated automatically in PowerPoint.

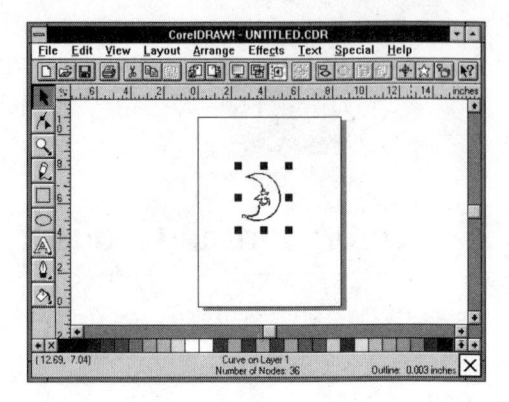

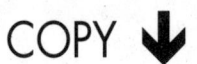

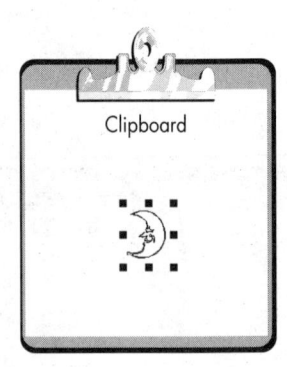

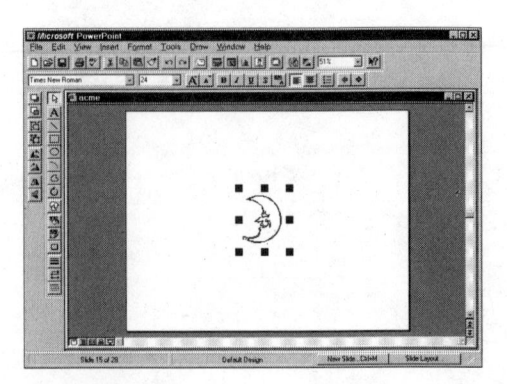

Figure 50. Pasting a graphic from CorelDRAW into PowerPoint

MANIPULATING GRAPHIC OBJECTS 10

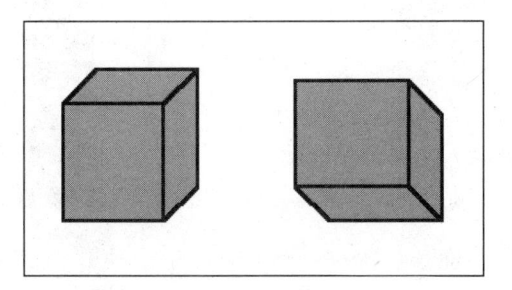

Figure 1. The cube on the right has been rotated.

About Graphic Manipulation

PowerPoint offers a number of ways to manipulate the graphic objects you created with the drawing tools, as well as the images you imported from ClipArt Gallery and other programs.

The figures on this page demonstrate some of the techniques you can use to manipulate graphic objects. Objects can be flipped, rotated (Figure 1), scaled (Figure 2), cropped (Figure 3), aligned (Figure 4), and recolored.

In this chapter, you will also learn how to use PowerPoint's rulers, guides, and grid snap feature to place objects; copy graphic attributes; group a set of objects; and change the stacking order of objects.

Figure 2. The star on the right has been scaled to 50% of its original size.

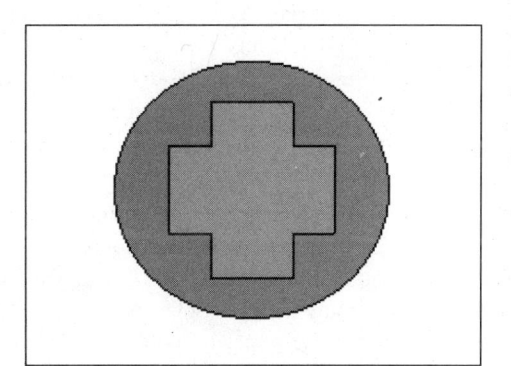

Figure 4. Alignment commands were used to center the cross exactly in the center of the circle.

Figure 3. The clip-art image of a woman has been cropped to show just her head and shoulders.

133

CHAPTER 10

Using Rulers and Guides

To help you precisely position graphic objects, you can use *rulers* and *guides* (Figure 5). For example, in Figure 6, the ruler helped position the squares exactly 1 inch apart, and a guide was used to align the boxes along the baseline.

The View menu (Figure 7) allows you to turn rulers and guides on and off.

To display the rulers, select View/Ruler. The horizontal ruler appears above the slide; the vertical ruler appears to the left. Notice that the zero point is at the center of each ruler. This enables you to measure distances from the center of the slide.

To display the guides, select View/Guides. You can drag the individual guides to intersect at any position on the slide.

■ Tips

✓ You can turn the guides on and off with Ctrl+G.

✓ As you drag the guides, a measurement appears in the guide (Figure 5); this measurement represents the distance from the zero point. Thus, if you want to place objects exactly 1.25 inches down from the center of the slide, you can easily drag the horizontal guide to this position (with or without the ruler displayed).

✓ A broken line appears in the rulers to represent the position of the mouse pointer on the slide. Use this line to help you measure the size of objects as you draw them, or to position objects as you drag them.

✓ When positioning an object horizontally, be sure to drag the *left* border, so that the broken line in the ruler reflects the left edge of the object. (By the same token, drag from the *top* when measuring vertically.)

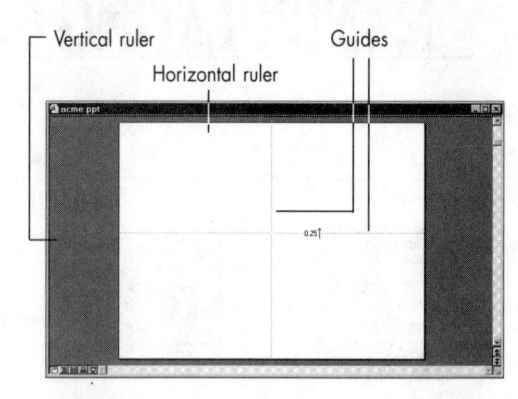

Figure 5. The rulers and guides

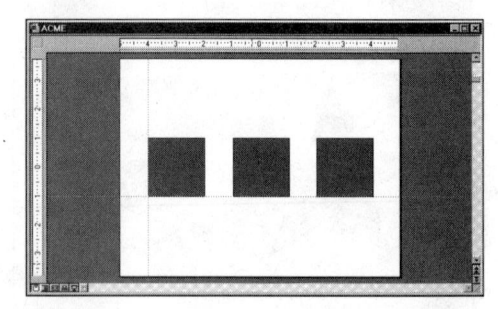

Figure 6. The horizontal ruler made it easy to space the boxes 1 inch apart; the horizontal guide helped align the boxes along the bottom.

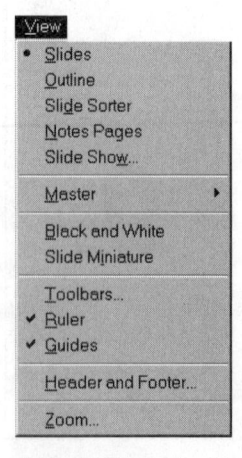

Figure 7. The check marks next to Ruler and Guides indicate these screen elements are currently displayed.

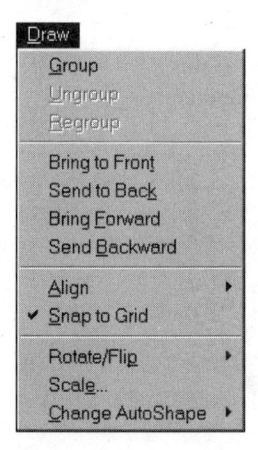

Figure 8. The check mark indicates that Snap to Grid is enabled.

Using Grid Snap

Another tool that helps position objects is the *grid*, a series of invisible, horizontal and vertical lines, about 1/12 inch apart. Whenever you draw, size, or move an object, the object borders jump to the grid, as though they were magnetized.

The grid is always there, although you can never actually see it. To activate the magnetic effect of the grid, use the Draw/Snap to Grid command. To see if grid snap is enabled, pull down the Draw menu; if there is a check mark next to Snap to Grid, the feature is already enabled (Figure 8).

■ Tips

✓ If PowerPoint is not letting you position an object exactly where you want it, grid snap may be interfering and you may want to disable it.

✓ The effect of jumping from one gridline to the next is more apparent in zoomed-in views.

See Zooming In and Out on the next page.

✓ Because you don't actually see the gridlines, grid snap is not as useful as it could be.

✓ To temporarily disable grid snap when positioning an object, hold down Alt as you drag.

CHAPTER 10

Zooming In and Out

As you are drawing, sizing, and moving objects, you may want to zoom in to make sure they are positioned properly. Though objects may look fine when zoomed out (Figure 9), zooming in may help you discover small inaccuracies (Figure 10).

There are three ways to zoom in and out:

- Click the arrow in the Zoom Control field (Figure 11) to display a list of zoom percentages. Then click the desired number. Use "Fit" to fit the whole slide in the window.

    or

- Click the percentage in the Zoom Control field, type a number between 10 and 400, and press Enter.

    or

- Select View/Zoom and choose the desired zoom percentage in the Zoom dialog box (Figure 12).

■ Tip

✓ To zoom in on a particular area of the slide, click an object in this area before choosing a zoom percentage; the selected object will then be in view and you won't have to scroll to see it.

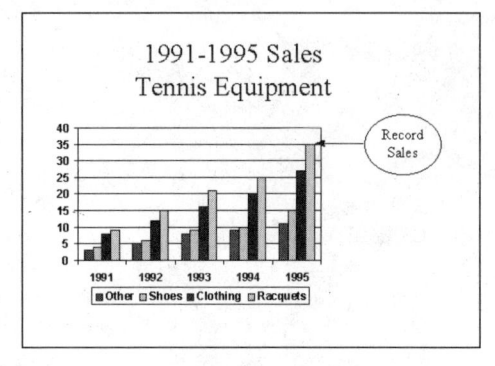

Figure 9. At a 50% zoom, the arrow looks perfectly straight.

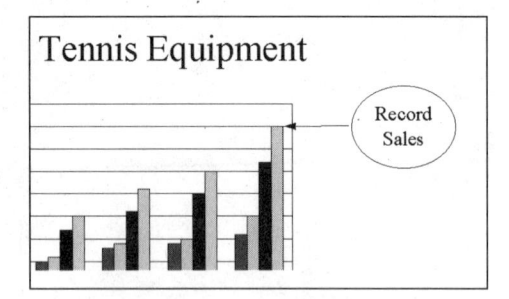

Figure 10. When you zoom in to 100%, you can see that the arrow is crooked.

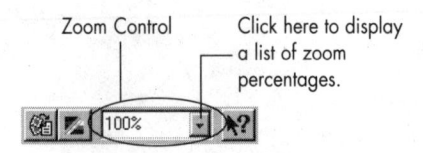

Figure 11. The Standard toolbar

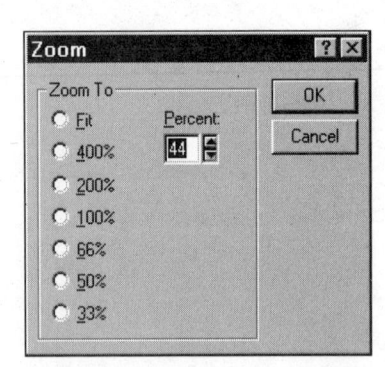

Figure 12. Choose a zoom percentage, or enter any value between 10 and 400 in the Percent field.

MANIPULATING GRAPHIC OBJECTS

Slide miniature

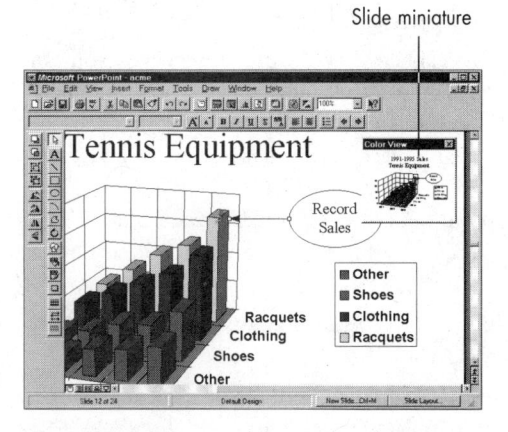

Figure 13. Displaying a slide miniature when you are zoomed in helps you see how your changes affect the entire slide.

Close button

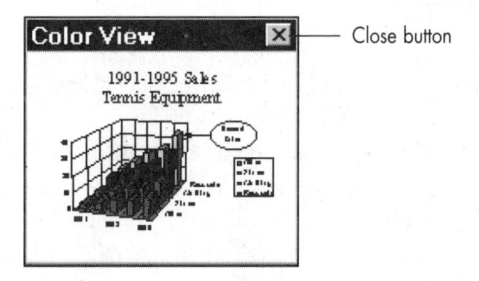

Figure 14. A slide miniature

Displaying a Slide Miniature

When you are zoomed in while in Slide view, it's helpful to display a *slide miniature* so you can see the complete slide as you are working on the detail (Figure 13). Slide miniatures are a new feature to PowerPoint for Windows 95.

1. Select View/Slide Miniature. A slide miniature of the current slide appears (Figure 14).

2. Click the slide miniature to toggle between color view and black and white view.

3. To remove the slide miniature, click the close button on the slide miniature window.

■ Tip

✓ If the slide miniature is blocking your work area, you can position it elsewhere in the PowerPoint window by dragging its title bar.

137

CHAPTER 10

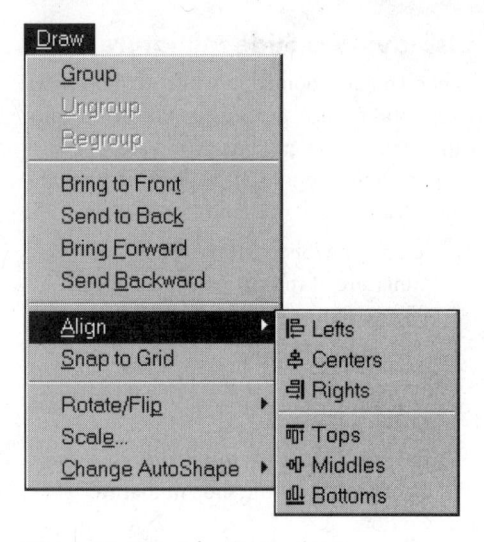

Figure 15. Options for aligning objects

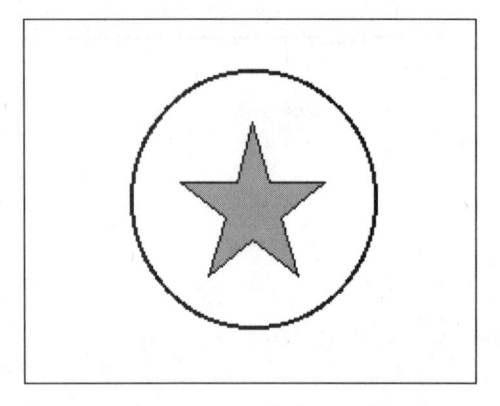

Figure 16. The star is centered—horizontally and vertically—inside the circle.

Figure 17. The seven lines are aligned on the left.

Aligning Objects

As explained on the preceding pages, you can use guides and rulers to help line up several objects. However, perhaps the easiest way to align objects is automatically with the Draw/Align command (Figure 15). For example, you can center one object inside another (Figure 16) or align a group of objects on the left (Figure 17).

1. Click to select the first object you want to align.
2. Hold down Shift as you click additional objects to be aligned.

   or

   Drag around the objects to be selected.
3. Select Draw/Align.
4. Choose one of the alignment options.

■ Tips

✓ The first set of Align options (Lefts, Centers, and Rights) aligns the objects horizontally; the second set (Tops, Middles, and Bottoms) aligns vertically.

✓ To center one object inside another, you need to issue two alignment commands: one to align the objects horizontally (Centers) and the other to align vertically (Middles).

MANIPULATING GRAPHIC OBJECTS

Grouping Objects

When you have several objects that you want to manipulate as a single unit, you can *group* them. Once the objects are grouped, you can move, resize, scale, flip, and rotate the group as if it were a single object.

1. Click to select the first object you want in the group. Then hold down Shift as you click additional objects to be grouped (Figure 18).

   or

   Drag around the objects.

2. Select Draw/Group.

The group is now treated as a single object (Figure 19).

■ Tips

✓ You can also group objects with the Group Objects button on the Drawing+ toolbar (Figure 20), or by pressing Ctrl+Shift+G.

✓ To disassemble the group and modify the objects separately, use Draw/Ungroup, the Ungroup Objects button, or Ctrl+Shift+H.

✓ To recreate a disassembled group, you do not need to reselect the objects. Press Esc to deselect, and choose Draw/Regroup.

✓ To select all the objects on a slide, press Ctrl+A.

✓ For more complex drawings, you can create groups within groups.

Figure 18. All the objects in this design are selected.

Figure 19. After grouping, one set of selection handles surrounds the design.

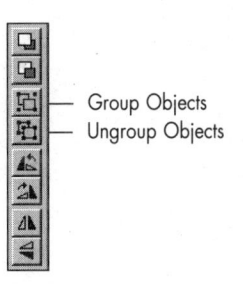

Figure 20. The Drawing+ toolbar

— Group Objects
— Ungroup Objects

139

CHAPTER 10

Copying Graphic Attributes

Use the Format Painter button (Figure 21) to copy attributes from one object to another. All formatting characteristics can be copied, such as color, pattern, shadow, and line thickness.

1. Select the object whose attributes you want to copy (Figure 22).
2. Click the Format Painter button (Figure 21). The pointer changes to an arrow with a paintbrush.
3. Click the object to which you want to apply the attributes (Figure 23).

■ Tips

✓ You can also use the Format Painter tool to copy text attributes (such as font, size, and style) between text boxes.

✓ Format Painter cannot copy attributes of images imported or pasted from other applications.

✓ To copy the object as well as its attributes, use the Copy and Paste buttons (Figure 21).

✓ To copy attributes to more than one object, select the object with the desired format to be copied, and double-click the Format Painter button. Click as many objects as you want to format, and when done, press Esc.

Figure 21. The Standard toolbar

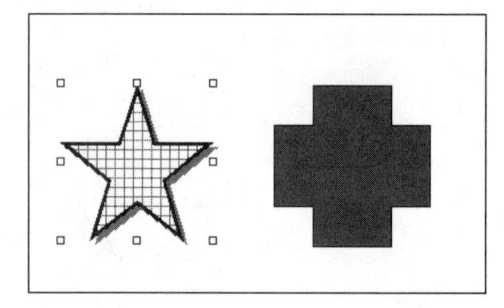

Figure 22. The star has attributes you want to copy to the cross.

The cross now has a thick border, a shadow, and a pattern fill.

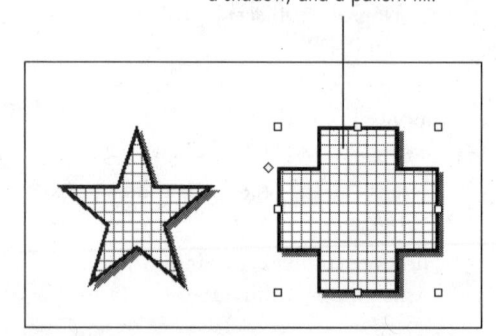

Figure 23. After applying the format with the Format Painter tool, the cross has the same attributes as the star.

MANIPULATING GRAPHIC OBJECTS

Lists all original fill and background colors, but not line colors.

Lists all original colors in the picture.

Click here to choose a new color.

Click here to preview new colors.

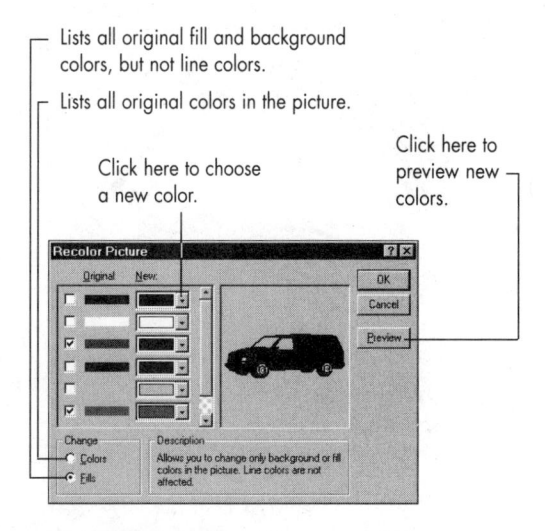

Figure 24. Recoloring a picture

Clicking here displays a small color palette.

For more choices, click here to display a large palette (Figure 26).

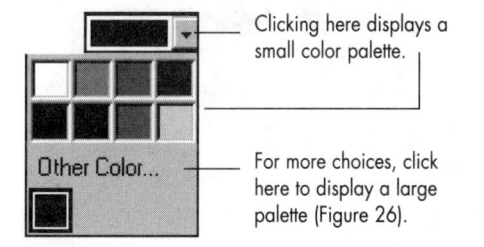

Figure 25. Choosing a new color

Standard tab

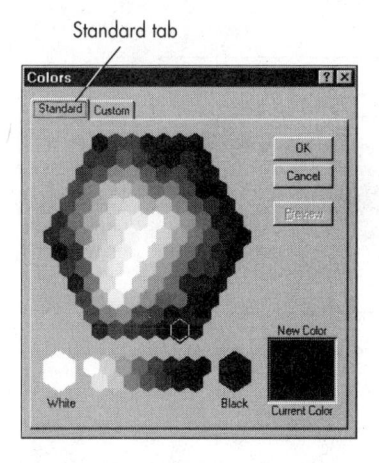

Figure 26. The Other Color dialog box displays a palette with a wide variety of colors.

Recoloring a Picture

You can change the colors of an inserted graphic or clip-art image using the Tools/Recolor command. Recoloring a picture simply involves replacing one color with another.

1. Select the picture to be recolored.
2. Select Tools/Recolor. The Recolor Picture dialog box appears (Figure 24).
3. Choose whether you want to change all Colors (fills and lines) or just the Fills.
4. In the Original column, locate the color you want to replace. This column lists all the original colors used in the picture.
5. Click the arrow in the adjacent New field to display the small palette.
6. Choose a new color (Figure 25).

   or

   Click Other Color to display a large palette of additional colors (Figure 26). Choose the new color from this palette and then click OK.
7. Repeat steps 4 through 6 for any other colors you want to change.
8. Click OK.

■ Tips

✓ To see how the picture looks with the new colors, click the Preview button (Figure 24).

✓ You must ungroup a group before you can recolor it.

See Grouping Objects on page 139.

Manipulating Graphic Objects

141

CHAPTER 10

Scaling an Object

Scaling resizes an object by a designated percentage and ensures that the object maintains its original proportions. This feature is similar to the enlarge and reduce buttons on your copy machine.

Figure 27 shows a group of objects before and after scaling. You can scale objects drawn in PowerPoint, as well as pictures you have inserted.

1. Select the object or group to be scaled.
2. Select Draw/Scale. The Scale dialog box appears (Figure 28).
3. In the Scale To field, specify a percentage. A number greater than 100 enlarges the object; a number less than 100 reduces.
4. To see how the object looks with the new scale factor, click the Preview button in the Scale dialog box.
5. Click OK.

■ Tips

✓ To scale an object or group manually, hold down Shift as you drag a corner selection handle. The Shift key ensures that the object's original proportions are maintained. (This isn't necessary for clip art or inserted pictures.)

✓ Because you can scale your designs at any time, you don't have to worry about the final size of your artwork as you are creating it.

✓ To scale more than one object at a time, group them first. If you select multiple objects without grouping them, they may lose their relative arrangement (Figure 29).

See Grouping Objects on page 139.

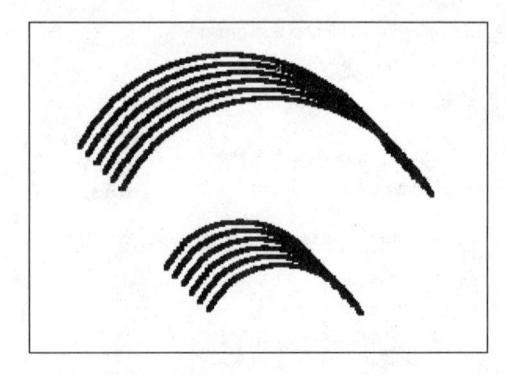

Figure 27. The design at the top is the original size; the copy at the bottom has been scaled to 50%.

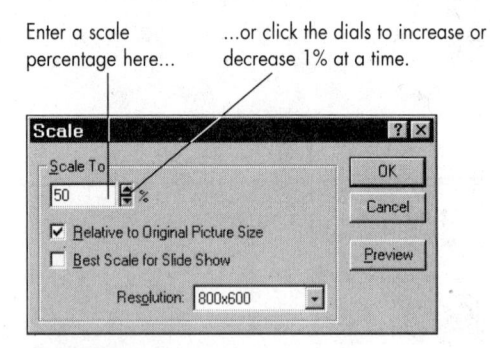

Enter a scale percentage here...   ...or click the dials to increase or decrease 1% at a time.

Figure 28. Scaling an object

The original set of objects

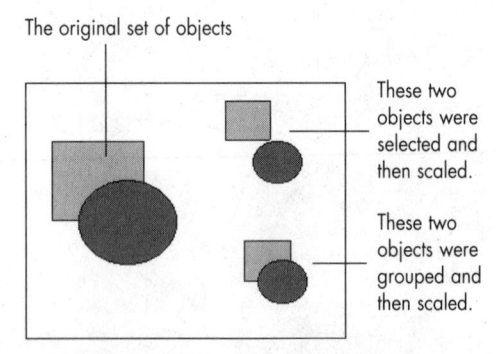

These two objects were selected and then scaled.

These two objects were grouped and then scaled.

Figure 29. For best results, group multiple objects before scaling.

Manipulating Graphic Objects

142

MANIPULATING GRAPHIC OBJECTS

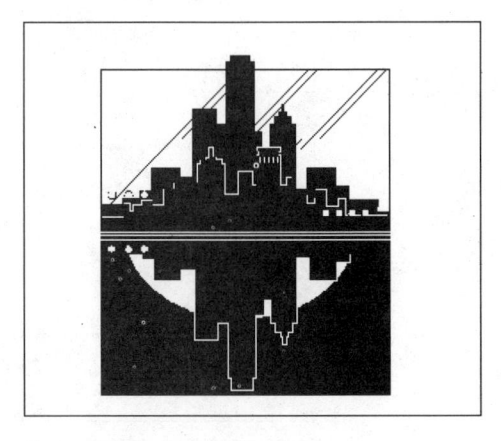

Figure 30. The original picture

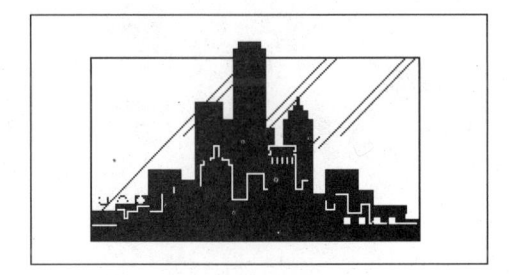

Figure 31. The bottom half of the picture was cropped out.

Figure 32. The cropping pointer

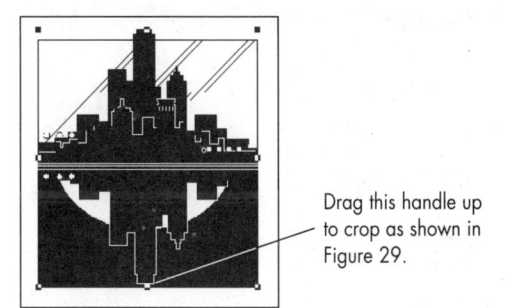

Figure 33. Drag the selection handles to crop the picture.

Drag this handle up to crop as shown in Figure 29.

Cropping a Picture

Cropping is a term that refers to trimming away an unwanted section of a picture. For example, if a graphic displays a person's full body, you can crop it so that only the person's face appears. Figures 30 and 31 show another example of cropping. Note that you can crop only the edges of the picture—you cannot crop out anything in the middle.

1. Select the picture to be cropped.
2. Select Tools/Crop Picture. The pointer changes to the shape shown in Figure 32.
3. Place the cropping pointer on a selection handle (Figure 33), and click and drag toward the middle of the picture until you have trimmed away the unwanted portion.
4. If necessary, drag other selection handles to crop other portions.
5. When you are finished cropping, click an empty area of the slide, or press Esc.

■ Tips

✓ When you crop, you are temporarily hiding part of the picture. At any time, you can crop outwards to redisplay the hidden portion.

✓ You may want to zoom in for more accuracy in cropping.

See Zooming In and Out on page 136.

143

CHAPTER 10

Changing the Stack Order

As you draw objects or place pictures on a slide, PowerPoint layers them one on top of another. In Figure 34, you can see how the clouds and airplane are on different layers.

To control the order in which the objects are stacked, use commands on the Draw menu (Figure 35). The Bring Forward and Send Backward commands are also available as buttons on the Drawing+ toolbar (Figure 36).

■ Tips

✓ Send Backward moves the selected object down one layer in the stack. Send to Back places the object on the bottom of the stack (Figure 37).

✓ Bring Forward moves the selected object up to the next layer in the stack. Bring to Front places the object on the top of the stack.

✓ Choosing the Send Backward command several times will ultimately produce the same results as choosing Send to Back once. Likewise, selecting Bring Forward several times is the equivalent of choosing Bring to Front.

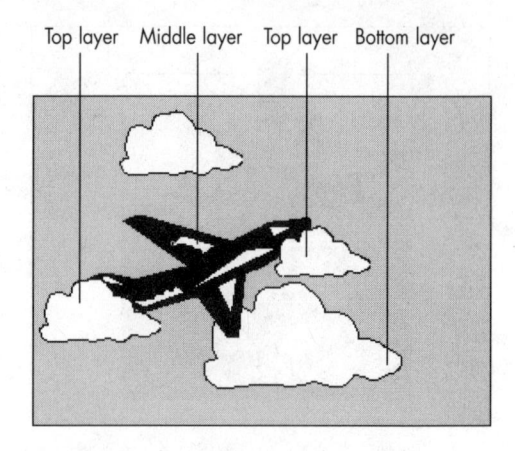

Figure 34. Overlapping objects are layered.

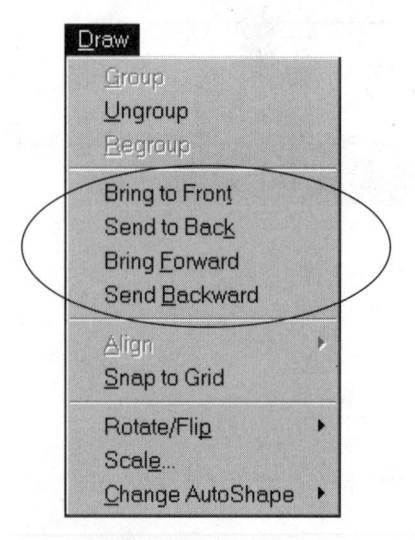

Figure 35. The circled commands let you change the stack order of the selected object.

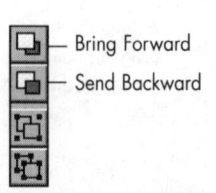

Figure 36. The Drawing+ toolbar

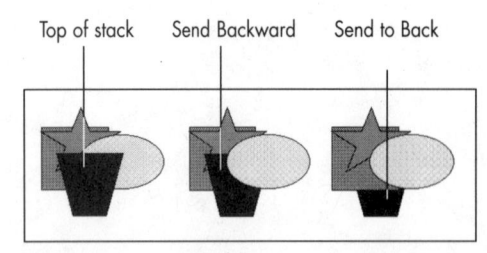

Figure 37. The difference between the effects of Send Backward and Send to Back

144

MANIPULATING GRAPHIC OBJECTS

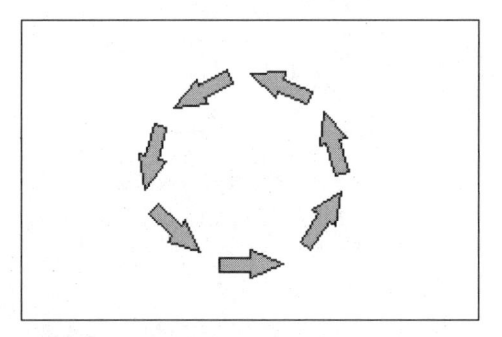

Figure 38. To create this circle of arrows, each arrow was rotated.

— Free Rotate tool

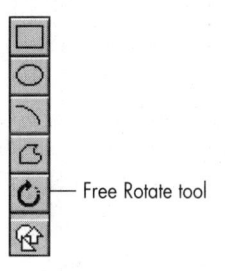

Figure 39. The Drawing toolbar

Place the pointer on a selection handle, and begin dragging.

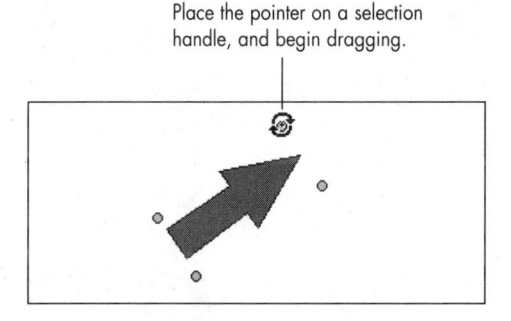

Figure 40. Rotating an object

— Rotate Left
— Rotate Right

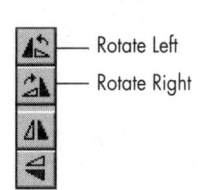

Figure 41. The Drawing+ toolbar

Rotating Objects

Figure 38 shows an example of rotated objects.

1. Select the object to be rotated.
2. Select the Free Rotate tool (Figure 39). You will see the Free Rotate pointer next to the mouse pointer.
3. Place the tip of the mouse pointer (Figure 40) on a green resize handle. Drag in a clockwise or counterclockwise direction.
4. Release the mouse button when you have finished rotating.
5. If you want to rotate the object further, repeat steps 3 and 4.
6. Click off the object or press Esc to deactivate the Free Rotate tool.

■ Tips

✓ The Drawing+ toolbar contains two additional tools for rotating objects (Figure 41). Rotate Left rotates the object 90 degrees counterclockwise, and Rotate Right rotates 90 degrees clockwise.

✓ Anther way to rotate is with the Rotate/Flip command on the Draw menu. The options shown in Figure 42 operate exactly the same as the buttons on the toolbars.

✓ You cannot rotate clip art or other pictures unless you first convert them to PowerPoint objects. To do so, ungroup the graphic and immediately group it again.

See Grouping Objects on page 139.

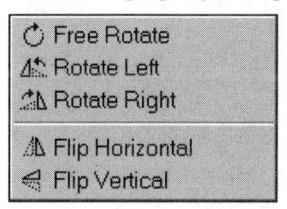

Figure 42. Choose the Rotate/Flip command on the Draw menu to display this submenu.

145

CHAPTER 10

Flipping Objects

You can flip objects horizontally (Figure 43) and vertically (Figure 44).

1. Select the object to be flipped.
2. On the Draw menu, select Rotate/Flip.
3. Choose either Flip Horizontal or Flip Vertical.

■ Tips

- ✓ You can also flip objects with the Flip Horizontal and Flip Vertical buttons on the Drawing+ toolbar (Figure 45).
- ✓ You cannot rotate clip art or other pictures unless you first convert them to PowerPoint objects. To do so, ungroup the graphic and immediately group it again. Figure 46 shows a clip art image that was flipped horizontally.

    See Grouping Objects on page 139.
- ✓ If text is attached to the shape being flipped, it flips also.

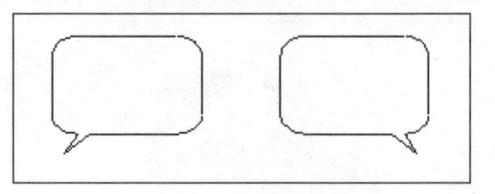

Figure 43. The balloon on the left is the original object; the balloon on the right has been flipped horizontally.

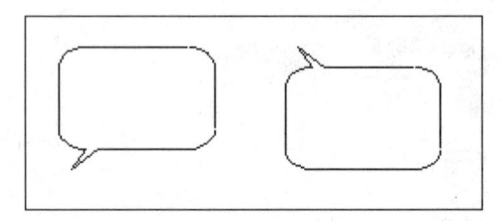

Figure 44. The balloon on the left is the original object; the balloon on the right has been flipped vertically.

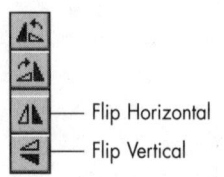

Figure 45. The Drawing+ toolbar

Figure 46. The original clip-art image is on the left; the image on the right was flipped horizontally.

MAKING GLOBAL CHANGES 11

>
> Agenda
> 1995 Annual Business Review
> - Introduction
> - Corporate Goals
> - 1995 Sales Performance
>   - By Region
>   - By Product Line
> - 1996 Budget

Figure 1. The original slide, before global formatting

>
> **Agenda**
> **1995 Annual Business Review**
> - Introduction
> - Corporate Goals
> - 1995 Sales Performance
>   - By Region
>   - By Product Line
> - 1996 Budget

Figure 2. After editing the Slide Master

Formatting a Presentation

This chapter shows you how to quickly format an entire presentation—without having to change each slide.

Some global changes, such as replacing fonts and changing colors or backgrounds, are done with commands on the Format or Tools menu.

Other changes, such as formatting slide titles and adding logos or page numbers, are done by editing the *Slide Master*. The Slide Master contains default formatting, as well as any background items you want repeated on each slide. Figures 1 and 2 show a slide before and after modifying the Slide Master. While these figures show just one slide, bear in mind that *all* slides would be formatted similarly.

Perhaps the most dramatic global change you can make to your presentation is to apply a *template*. A template controls the color scheme, text formatting, and repeating graphic elements—and it's applied with a single command. Figure 3 shows the same slide after applying a template.

>
> Agenda
> 1995 Annual Business Review
> - Introduction
> - Corporate Goals
> - 1995 Sales Performance
>   - By Region
>   - By Product Line
> - 1996 Budget

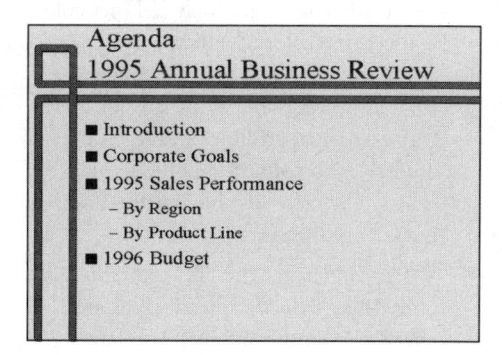

Figure 3. After applying a template

CHAPTER 11

Changing the Default Colors in a Presentation

There are several slide elements whose colors you can change globally: the slide background, slide titles, text and lines, drop shadows, and object fills. Any new slides you create will use the new color scheme.

1. Select Format/Slide Color Scheme.
2. Click the Custom tab. The Custom page of the Color Scheme dialog box appears as shown in Figure 4.
3. In the Scheme Colors area, click the box associated with the element you want to change. For instance, click the Title Text box.
4. Click the Change Color button. A color palette appears, as shown in Figure 5.
5. Click a color cube and then click OK.
6. Repeat steps 3 through 5 for each element you want to change.
7. Click Apply to All to apply the new colors to the entire presentation.

■ Tips

✓ Instead of clicking the Change Color button for an element, you can display the color palette by double-clicking the color box.

✓ When you change the Text & Lines color, it affects the color of bullet, graph, org chart, and table text. It also changes the color of object borders, lines inside graphs (such as gridlines and legend borders), and connecting lines in org charts. The color of table borders does not change, however.

✓ When you change the Fills color, only the objects using the default fill color are affected. Objects for which you have assigned a specific color will retain that color.

First, choose a slide element.

Then, click here to choose a color.

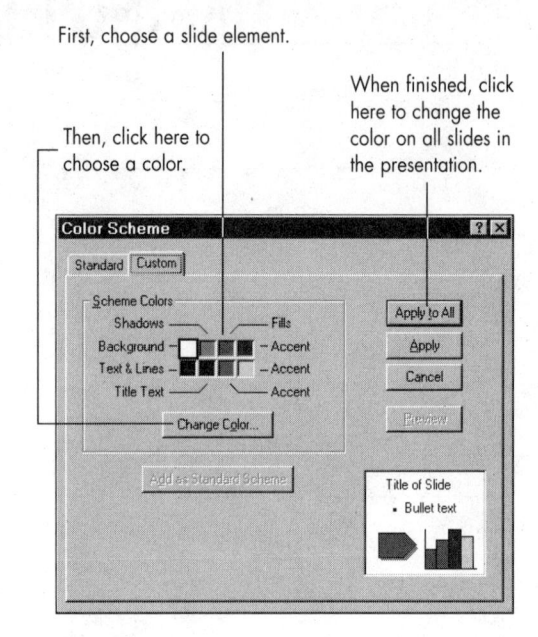

When finished, click here to change the color on all slides in the presentation.

Figure 4. Changing color globally

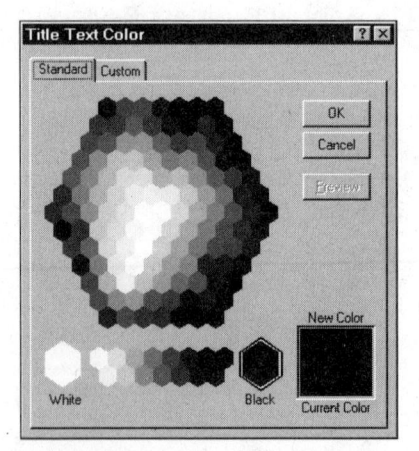

Figure 5. Choosing a color

Making Global Changes

MAKING GLOBAL CHANGES

First, assign new colors to slide elements.

Then, click here to create a scheme.

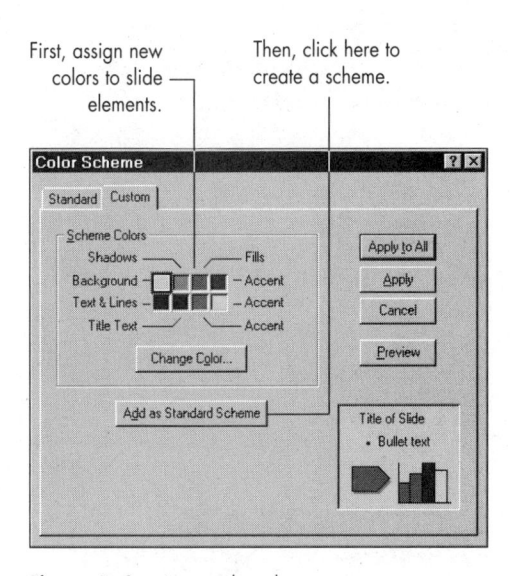

Figure 6. Creating a color scheme

Click the Standard tab.

Your new scheme appears here.

Figure 7. Applying a color scheme

Creating Color Schemes

In PowerPoint for Windows 95, you can create your own color schemes and apply them to either individual slides or the entire presentation.

1. Select Format/Slide Color Scheme.
2. Click the Custom tab. The Custom page of the Color Scheme dialog box appears (Figure 6).
3. Choose colors for the various slide elements.

   See Changing the Default Colors in a Presentation on the previous page.
4. When you're finished assigning colors, click the Add as Standard Scheme button.
5. Click the Standard tab. Your new color scheme is now listed on the Standard page of the Color Scheme dialog box (Figure 7).
6. To apply the new scheme, select it and then click Apply to All (for all slides) or Apply (for one slide).

■ Tip

✓ If you're not happy with the colors after you apply a new color scheme, you can immediately select Edit/Undo to restore your previous color scheme.

149

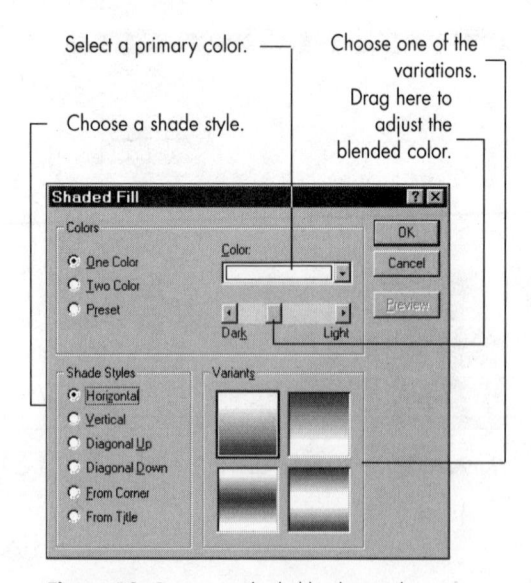

Creating a Shaded Background

A *shade* is a gradual progression from one color to another. Figure 8 shows a slide with a shaded background. Shades have a primary color of your choosing and are blended with different amounts of black or white. Alternatively, you can blend any two colors, as explained on the next page.

1. Select Format/Custom Background.
2. In the Custom Background dialog box, click the drop-down list (Figure 9) and choose Shaded from the list of fills. The Shaded Fill dialog box appears (Figure 10).
3. Click the One Color button.
4. To choose the shade's primary color, click the Color field and choose one of the sample colors or click Other Color to choose from a color palette.
5. Choose one of the Shade Styles (Horizontal, Vertical, etc.).
6. Click one of the Variants (these are variations of the style you selected in step 5).
7. To adjust the blended color, drag the scroll box in the Dark/Light slider.
8. Click OK and then choose Apply to All.

■ Tips

✓ As you darken the blended color, you are adding more black. As you lighten, you are adding more white.

✓ You may need to adjust your color scheme after creating a shaded background. For example, for a dark shade, you might want to choose white for slide titles, text, and lines.

See Changing Default Colors in a Presentation on page 148.

Figure 8. This slide has a shaded background.

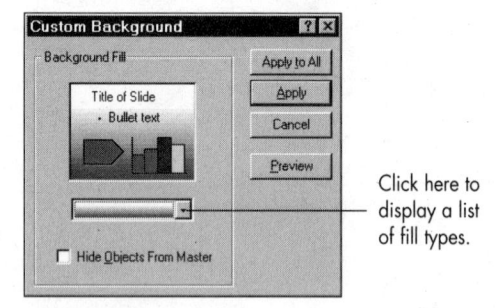

Figure 9. Choosing a shaded fill

Figure 10. Creating a shaded background

MAKING GLOBAL CHANGES

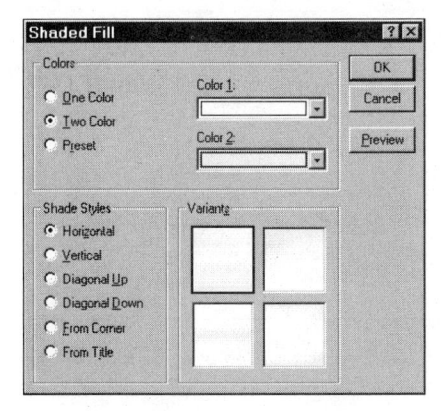

Figure 11. Creating a blend with two colors.

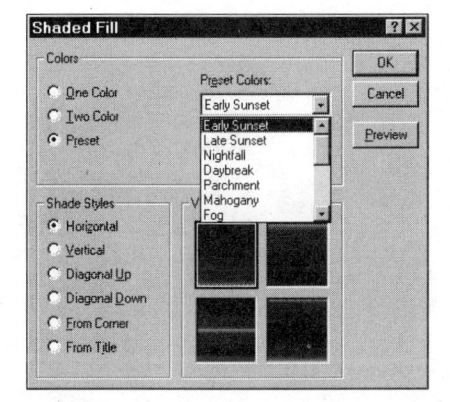

Figure 12. Choosing one of the preset shades.

Creating a Two-Color Shade

In PowerPoint for Windows 95, you can blend two different colors to create vibrant backgrounds for your presentations.

1. Select Format/Custom Background.
2. In the Custom Background dialog box, click the drop-down list (Figure 9) and choose Shaded from the list of fills.
3. In the Shaded Fill dialog box, choose Two Color (Figure 11).
4. To choose the shade's first color, click the Color 1 field and select one of the sample colors or click Other Color to choose from a color palette.
5. To choose the shade's second color, click the Color 2 field and select a color.
6. Choose one of the Shade Styles (Horizontal, Vertical, etc.).
7. Click one of the Variants (these are variations of the style you selected in step 6).
8. Click OK and then choose Apply to All.

■ Tip

✓ Another way to create a multicolor shade is with the Preset option. Choose Preset instead of Two Color, and then choose one of the samples from the Preset Colors list (Figure 12).

Making Global Changes

151

CHAPTER 11

Replacing a Font

Suppose you want all your slide text to be Arial instead of Times New Roman (Figures 13 and 14). You can accomplish this task easily with the Tools/Replace Fonts command.

1. Select Tools/Replace Fonts. The Replace Font dialog box appears (Figure 15).
2. In the Replace field, choose the font you want to replace in the presentation.
3. In the With field, choose the new font.
4. Click the Replace button.
5. Repeat steps 2 through 4 to replace other fonts.
6. Click Close.

■ Tips

✓ The Replace Fonts command does not substitute typefaces in graphs, tables, and org charts.

✓ To replace the font in only the slide titles or only the bullet text, you need to edit the Slide Master.

See Changing the Default Format for Text on page 155.

Retail Store Comparison
Acme Stores vs. XYZ Stores

Acme	XYZ
■ 1200 stores	■ 750 stores
■ Convenient locations in every major city	■ Few locations in East
■ Everyday low prices	■ Suggested retail prices
■ Monthly sales	■ Seasonal sales only

Figure 13. The current font for text on this slide (and all other slides) is Times New Roman.

Retail Store Comparison
Acme Stores vs. XYZ Stores

Acme	XYZ
■ 1200 stores	■ 750 stores
■ Convenient locations in every major city	■ Few locations in East
■ Everyday low prices	■ Suggested retail prices
■ Monthly sales	■ Seasonal sales only

Figure 14. After replacing fonts, the text on this slide (and on all other slides) is in Arial.

Click here to list all fonts used in the presentation.

Click here to list all fonts available on your system.

Replace Font

Replace: Times New Roman

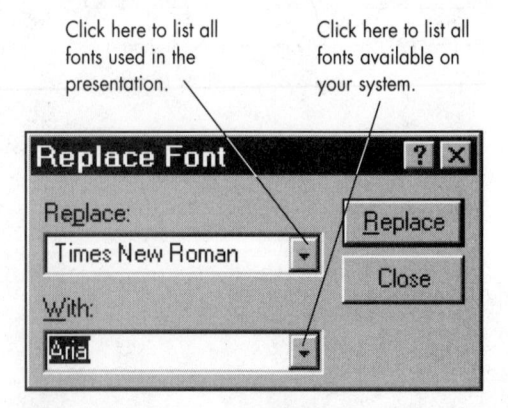

With: Arial

[Replace] [Close]

Figure 15. Replace one font with another using the Tools/Replace Fonts command.

Making Global Changes

MAKING GLOBAL CHANGES

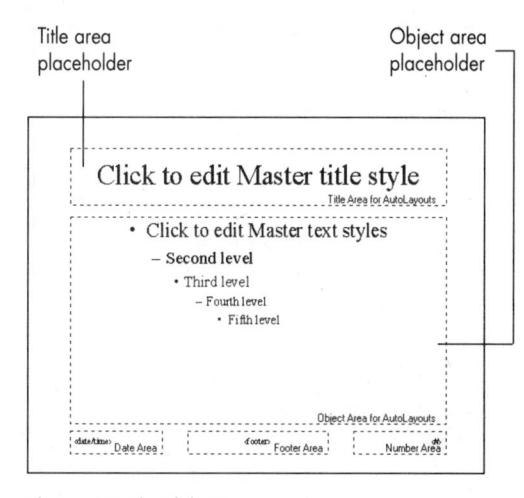

Figure 16. The Slide Master

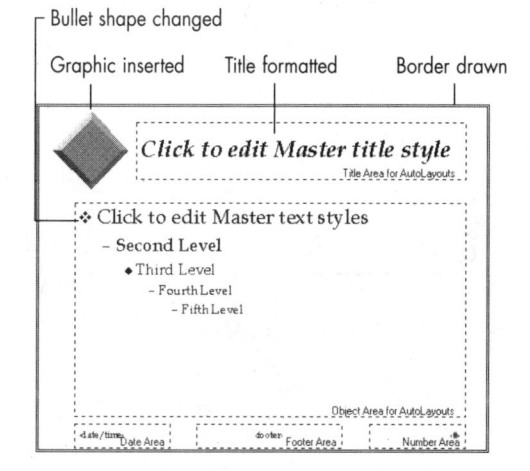

Figure 17. A formatted Slide Master

Figure 18. The View buttons

Editing the Slide Master

The Slide Master (Figure 16) contains the default formatting for your presentation, as well as any background items you want to appear on each slide. Any changes you make to the Slide Master automatically affect all slides in your presentation. When you format the Master title and Master text, you are actually formatting all the titles and text in your presentation (except in tables, graphs, and org charts).

Figure 17 is an example of a formatted Slide Master. To edit the Slide Master, follow these steps.

1. Select <u>V</u>iew/<u>M</u>aster.
2. Choose <u>S</u>lide Master. The Slide Master appears (Figure 16).
3. Make desired changes to the Master.

   See Changing the Default Format for Text, Adding Background Items, and Inserting Footers on pages 155–157.

4. When you're finished, click the Slide View button (Figure 18). All slides now have the formatting and background items you added to the Master.

The following pages show some common ways to edit the Slide Master.

■ Tips

✓ A quick way to display the Slide Master is to hold Shift as you click the Slide View button (Figure 18).

✓ Another change you can make to the Slide Master is to adjust the size and position of the title area and object area placeholders. (These placeholders are pointed out in Figure 16).

   See Manipulating Text Placeholders on page 33.

✓ If you want title slides formatted differently than other slides, insert a Title Master.

   See Inserting a Title Master on page 154.

Making Global Changes

153

CHAPTER 11

Inserting a Title Master

Frequently, you will want your title slides to be formatted differently than other slides in your presentation. For instance, your Slide Master may contain graphic elements that aren't appropriate for title slides (Figure 19). In PowerPoint for Windows 95, you can create a special Master just for your title slides.

1. Select View/Master.
2. Choose Slide Master. The Slide Master appears.
3. Select Insert/New Title Master. A new Master is inserted (Figure 20).

   or

   Click the New Title Master button at the bottom of the window.
4. Make desired changes to the Master.

   See Changing the Default Format for Text and Adding Background Items on pages 155 and 156.
5. When you're finished, click the Slide View or Slide Sorter button. All title slides will now have the formatting and background items you added to (or deleted from) the Title Master.

■ **Tip**

✓ To switch between the Title Master and the Slide Master, press Page Up and Page Down. You can also use the View/Master command.

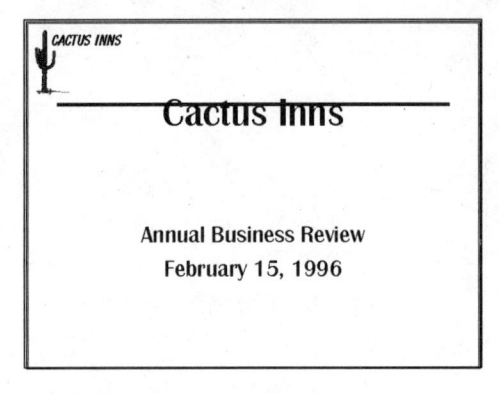

Figure 19. The logo and rule at the top of this title slide are from the Slide Master; they look out of place on a title slide.

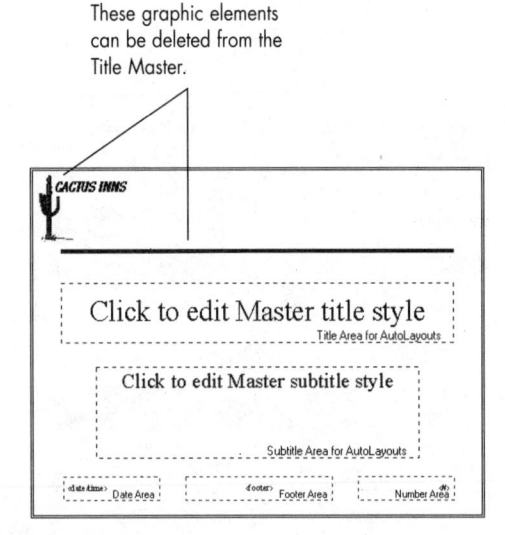

Figure 20. The Title Master

Making Global Changes

154

MAKING GLOBAL CHANGES

Agenda
1995 Annual Business Review
- Introduction
- Corporate Goals
- 1995 Sales Performance
  - By Region
  - By Product Line
- 1996 Budget

Figure 21. This slide uses the default Slide Master.

Agenda
1995 Annual Business Review
- **Introduction**
- **Corporate Goals**
- **1995 Sales Performance**
  - **By Region**
  - **By Product Line**
- **1996 Budget**

Figure 22. The same slide after formatting the Slide Master—all are formatted similarly.

Click this line to format first-level bullets in Bulleted List slides.

Click this line to format slide titles.

Click to edit Master title style
Title Area for AutoLayouts

■ Click to edit Master text styles
  ➢ Second level
    • Third level
      – Fourth level
        • Fifth level

Object Area for AutoLayouts

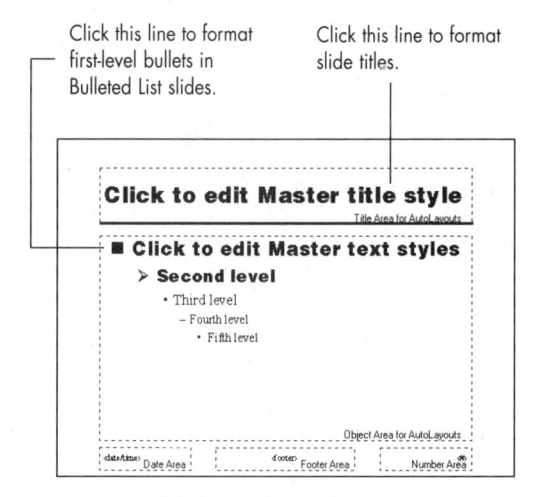

date/time Date Area *footer* Footer Area *#* Number Area

Figure 23. The formatted Slide Master

Changing the Default Format for Text

Suppose you want all your slide titles to be in a larger type size and aligned on the left, all first-level bullets to be squares, and all bullet text to be anchored in the middle. By making these changes on the Slide Master, you only need to format the text once—all new and existing slides will conform to the modified format.

Figures 21 and 22 show a slide before and after editing the Slide Master. Figure 23 shows the modified Slide Master.

1. Select <u>V</u>iew/<u>M</u>aster/<u>S</u>lide Master.
2. To format slide titles, click the Master title and make desired changes. (You do not need to select all the text.)

   See pages 41–45 for information on formatting text.

3. To format first-level bullets in Bulleted List slides, click where it says "Click to edit Master text styles" and make desired changes.

   See Changing Bullets on page 39, Adjusting the Bullet Placement on page 40, and Setting Anchor Points in a Text Placeholder on page 44.

4. To format other bullet levels, click the line (such as "Second level") and make desired changes.
5. Click the Slide View button when you're finished.

■ Tips

✓ When you format text directly on a slide, your formatting overrides the Slide Master. Therefore, for consistent formatting throughout your presentation, try to use direct formatting as little as possible.

✓ If you format a slide before modifying the Slide Master, the slide will retain its direct formatting and not conform to the Master.

155

Adding Background Items

When background items are placed on the Slide Master, they are repeated on every slide in the presentation. Common background items are company names and logos, borders, rules, and graphics.

Figure 24 shows several examples of background items you may want repeated on every slide.

1. Select <u>V</u>iew/<u>M</u>aster/<u>S</u>lide Master. The Slide Master appears.

2. Do any of the following to add background items:

   - Use tools on the Drawing toolbar to create lines and boxes on the Master.
     See Drawing Lines on page 118 and Drawing Rectangles on page 120.

   - Use the Text tool to insert text placeholders on the Master.
     See Creating a Text Placeholder on page 32.

   - Use the <u>I</u>nsert/<u>C</u>lip Art or <u>I</u>nsert/<u>P</u>icture commands to add graphics to the Master.
     See Inserting Clip Art on page 128 and Inserting Graphic Files on page 131.

3. When you're finished, click the Slide View button.

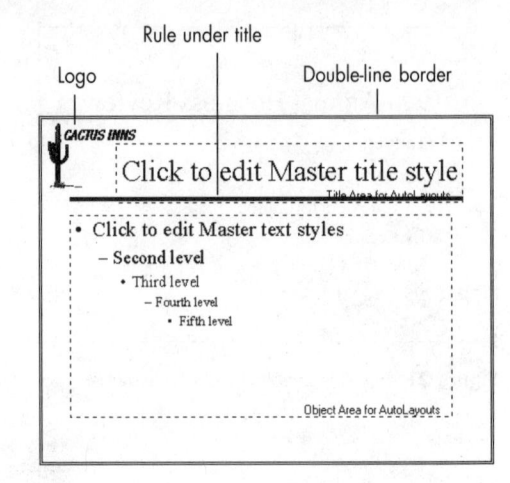

Figure 24. Background items added to a Slide Master

■ Tips

✓ To create the border shown in Figure 24, use the Rectangle tool to draw a box around the slide, and choose No Fill. Use the <u>F</u>ormat/Colors and <u>L</u>ines command to choose a line style.

✓ If you're using a Title Master, you may choose to add background items to it also.

MAKING GLOBAL CHANGES

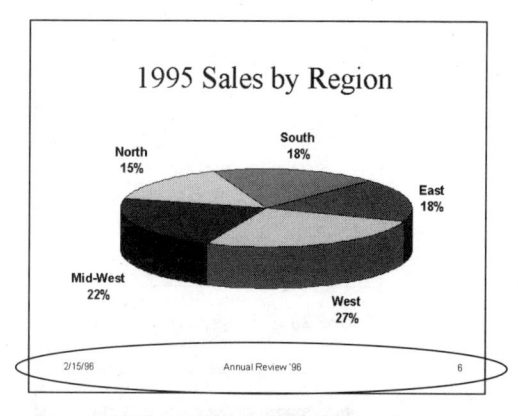

Figure 25. This slide, and all other slides in the presentation, contain footers with the date, presentation title, and slide number.

Figure 26. The Date Area, Footer Area, and Number Area placeholders on the Slide Master

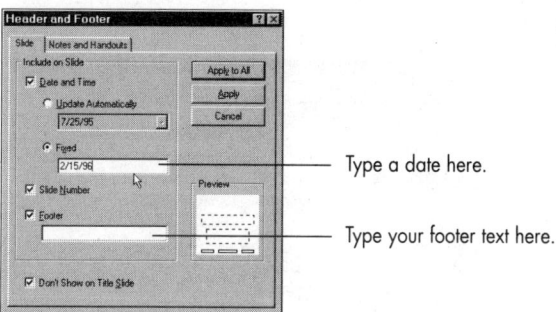

Figure 27. Specifying which elements to include in the footer

Inserting Footers

With a single command, you can place a footer on each slide containing the date, customizable text (such as the presentation title), and/or the slide number (Figure 25). The Slide Master already contains three placeholders for the footer (Figure 26), although the information is not actually placed on the slides until you indicate which elements you want to use.

1. From any view, select View/Header and Footer. The Header and Footer dialog box appears (Figure 27).
2. Turn on the check boxes for Date and Time, Slide Number, and/or Footer.
3. Click Update Automatically to use the current date, or Fixed to use a date that you type in.
4. If you checked Footer, type your footer text in the empty text box (Figure 27).
5. To prevent the footer from appearing on title slides, turn on the check box for Don't Show on Title Slide.
6. Click Apply To All.

■ Tips

✓ To format the footer text, go to the Slide Master and format each footer placeholder.

✓ To change the starting page number, select File/Slide Setup, and specify a new number under Number Slides From.

157

CHAPTER 11

Applying a Template

A *template* is a presentation in which the Slide Master and color scheme have been specifically designed for a particular look so that it can be easily cloned in other presentations. By applying a template, you can instantly change the format of the text, add background items to each slide, and adjust the colors used in the presentation. PowerPoint comes with over 30 templates.

Figure 28 shows a slide before a template has been applied; Figure 29 shows the same slide after applying a template.

1. Click the Apply Design Template tool in the Standard toolbar (Figure 30).

   or

   Select F*o*rmat/Apply Design Te*m*plate.

   or

   Double-click the template name at the bottom of the window ("Default Design" if you haven't applied a template yet).

2. If necessary, navigate to the Presentation Designs folder. This folder is a subfolder of the MSOFFICE\TEMPLATES folder.

3. Click a template file name (Figure 31). A preview of this template is shown in the preview box.

4. Preview other templates, and when you find one you like, click *A*pply.

■ Tips

✓ You can also choose a template as you are creating a new presentation.

   See Choosing a Template on page 18.

✓ A template can be any .pot or .ppt file. Thus, if you want the current presentation to look like another you've previously created, choose this file name for the presentation template.

✓ The name of the template applied to the current presentation is listed at the bottom of the window.

Figure 28. Before applying a template

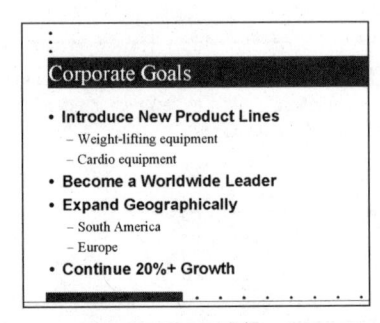

Figure 29. After applying the template named Contemporary.pot

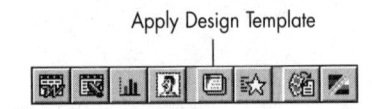

Figure 30. The Standard toolbar

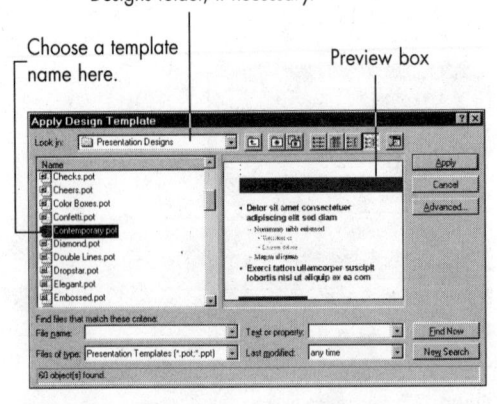

Figure 31. Choosing a template to apply

Making Global Changes

WORKING IN OUTLINE VIEW 12

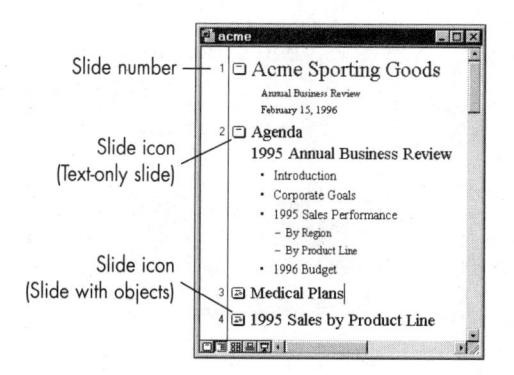

Figure 1. Outline view

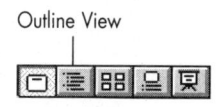

Labels: Slide number; Slide icon (Text-only slide); Slide icon (Slide with objects)

Figure 2. The View buttons

Figure 3. The Outlining toolbar

Introducing Outline View

Outline view displays each slide's title and main text, such as bulleted items, in class outline form (Figure 1). Outline view is ideal for seeing the structure of your presentation and for reordering slides. It also offers a quick way to type a series of Bulleted List slides. In this chapter, you will see how easy it is to type lists, insert new slides, and move slides around.

Switch to Outline view by clicking the Outline View button (Figure 2) or by selecting the View/Outline command. While in Outline view, the Outlining toolbar appears on the screen (Figure 3).

The *slide icon* to the left of each slide's title (Figure 1) indicates whether the slide contains only text or an object such as a graph, table, org chart, or picture. Clicking the slide icon once selects the entire slide (so that you can move, copy, or delete it); clicking it twice displays that slide in Slide view.

See page 204 for information on printing outlines.

159

CHAPTER 12

Hiding Text Formatting

As you can see in Figure 4, Outline view shows text formatting and displays the actual bullet symbols for Bulleted List slides. Since you aren't as concerned with formatting when you are in Outline view, you may wish to hide the formatting (Figure 5).

Use the Show Formatting button (Figure 6) to toggle the formatting on and off.

■ Tips

✓ When formatting is hidden, you can see more slides in the outline.

✓ Another way to hide and display formatting is with the slash key (/) on the numeric keypad.

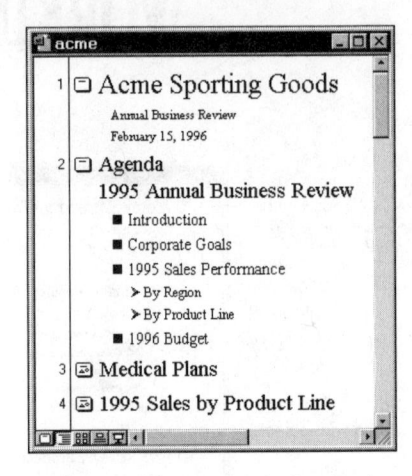

Figure 4. Text formatting is displayed in this outline.

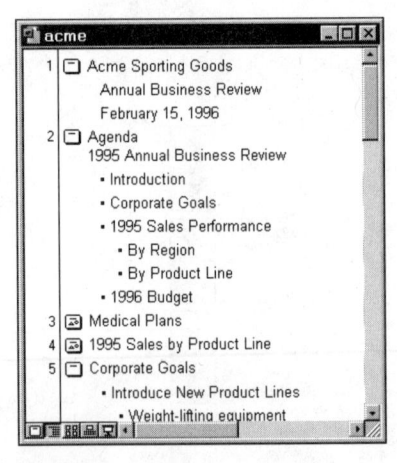

Figure 5. Formatting is hidden in this outline.

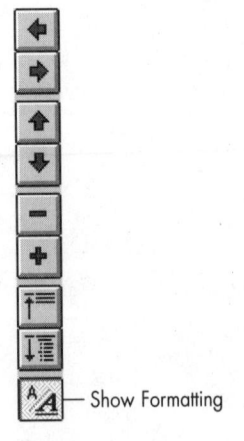

Figure 6. The Outlining toolbar

160

WORKING IN OUTLINE VIEW

A gray line indicates the slide is collapsed.

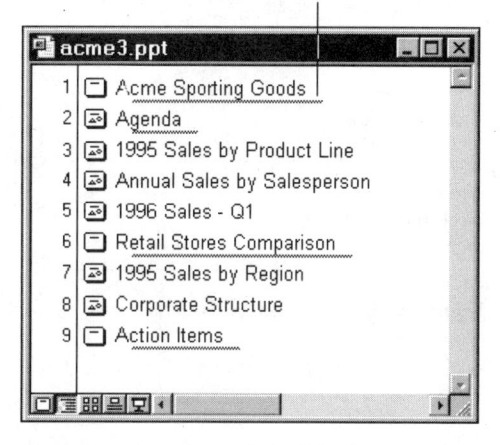

```
acme3.ppt
1  Acme Sporting Goods
2  Agenda
3  1995 Sales by Product Line
4  Annual Sales by Salesperson
5  1996 Sales - Q1
6  Retail Stores Comparison
7  1995 Sales by Region
8  Corporate Structure
9  Action Items
```

Figure 7. In this outline, only the slide titles are displayed.

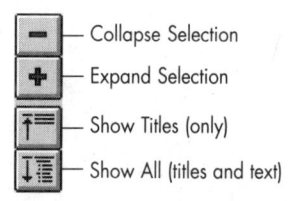

- — Collapse Selection
+ — Expand Selection
- Show Titles (only)
- Show All (titles and text)

Figure 8. The Outlining toolbar

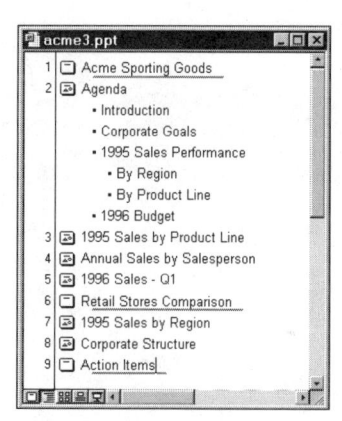

```
acme3.ppt
1  Acme Sporting Goods
2  Agenda
     • Introduction
     • Corporate Goals
     • 1995 Sales Performance
         • By Region
         • By Product Line
     • 1996 Budget
3  1995 Sales by Product Line
4  Annual Sales by Salesperson
5  1996 Sales - Q1
6  Retail Stores Comparison
7  1995 Sales by Region
8  Corporate Structure
9  Action Items
```

Figure 9. The text in Slide 2 is expanded; the text in Slides 1, 6, and 9 is collapsed.

Collapsing and Expanding the Outline

You can get a better picture of your presentation's structure by hiding the main text on your slides, and displaying only the slide titles (Figure 7). This way, you can get an idea of how the information flows. Furthermore, when text is hidden, you can see more slides in the window. When you hide text, you are *collapsing* the outline.

Use the Show Titles button to collapse the entire outline so that only the slide titles are displayed. Use the Show All button to display *(expand)* all the text again (Figure 8).

PowerPoint also allows you to selectively collapse and expand parts of the outline (Figure 9). This capability is useful if you want to see the text on some slides but not on others. To expand or collapse parts of your outline, follow these steps

1. Click anywhere in the slide whose text you want to expand or collapse.

    or

    Drag over several slides.

2. Click the Collapse Selection button to hide or the Expand Selection button to redisplay (Figure 8).

■ Tips

✓ Suppose you want to collapse all text in the outline except the text on one slide. First, use the Show Titles button to hide all the main text. Then click the slide whose text you want to show, and use the Expand Selection button.

✓ Here are some keyboard shortcuts:

    Alt+Shift+1   Show Titles
    Alt+Shift+A   Show All
    Alt+Shift+Plus   Expand Selection
    Alt+Shift+Minus   Collapse Selection

161

Creating Bulleted Lists

Typing bulleted lists is simple in Outline view. Keyboard shortcuts make it easy to enter and arrange bullet items, as well as create new slides.

1. Click anywhere on an existing slide and then click the New Slide button at the bottom of the PowerPoint window.

   or

   Click at the beginning of an existing slide and press Enter.

   A new slide appears before the current one.

2. Type the slide title and press Enter.
3. Press Tab to insert a bullet (Figure 10).
4. Type the bullet item and press Enter.
5. Continue typing bullet items, following the same rules you do in Slide view:
   - Press Enter to type another bullet.
   - Press Tab to indent the current line.
   - Press Shift+Tab to outdent the current line.
6. To create another slide, press Ctrl+Enter after the last bullet in the list.
7. Repeat steps 2 through 6 for each Bulleted List.

■ Tips

✓ To create a two-line title (such as the one in Slide 2 in Figure 10), press Shift+Enter after the first line.

✓ If you inadvertently type an item at the wrong level, use the Promote or Demote buttons (Figure 11) to change the indent level of the current line.

✓ To move a bullet item up or down in a list, click the item and then click the Move Up or Move Down button (Figure 11) until the item is in position.

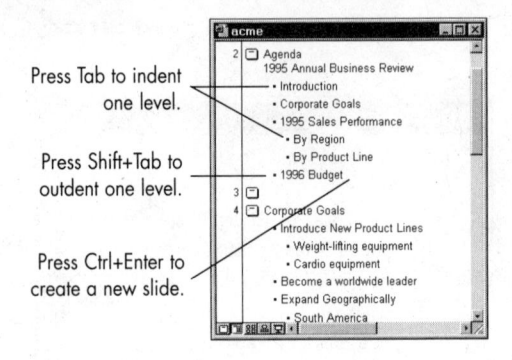

Figure 10. Typing Bulleted Lists in Outline view

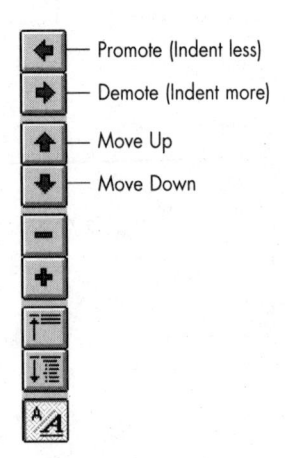

Figure 11. Outlining toolbar

WORKING IN OUTLINE VIEW

Reordering the Slides

Because you can see many slides at once in Outline view, it is ideal for repositioning slides in a presentation. PowerPoint offers three ways to move slides: the Move buttons, the drag-and-drop technique, and the cut-and-paste technique.

The Move Buttons

1. Click the Show Titles button (Figure 12) so that only slide titles are displayed (Figure 13).
2. Click anywhere in the title of the slide you want to move.
3. Click either the Move Up or Move Down button (Figure 12) until the slide is in position.

The Drag-and-Drop Technique

1. Click the Show Titles button so that only slide titles are displayed.
2. Drag the slide icon for the slide you want to move (Figure 14). A horizontal line indicates where the slide will be inserted.
3. When the horizontal line is in position, release the mouse button.

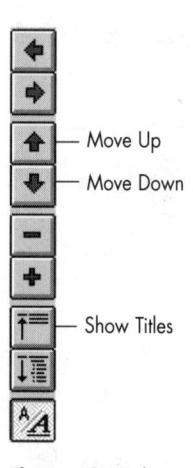

Figure 12. Outlining toolbar

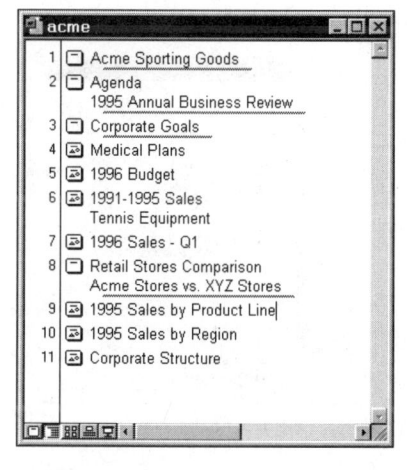

Figure 13. Reordering slides is easier if only the slide titles are displayed.

Drag the slide icon.

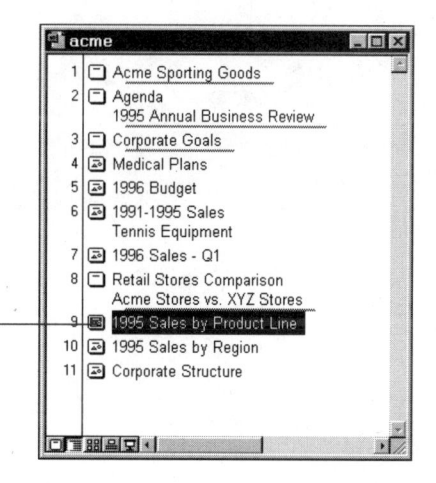

Figure 14. Using the drag-and-drop technique

163

CHAPTER 12

Reordering the Slides (cont'd)

The Cut-and-Paste Technique

1. Click the slide icon for the slide you want to move (Figure 15); this selects the entire slide.
2. Click the Cut button (Figure 16).
3. Position the cursor at the slide's new destination (Figure 17). Be sure to place the cursor at the beginning of a slide title.
4. Click the Paste button (Figure 16). The slide is inserted *above* the cursor. Figure 18 shows the results.

■ **Tip**

✓ The Move Up and Move Down buttons and the drag-and-drop technique are best for short distance moves. The cut-and-paste technique works well when the target location has scrolled off the screen.

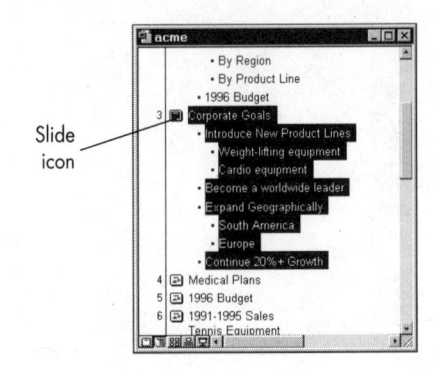

Figure 15. Select a slide before cutting it.

Figure 16. The Standard toolbar

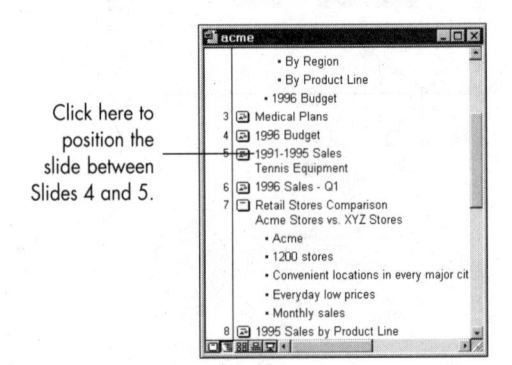

Figure 17. Position the cursor before pasting the slide.

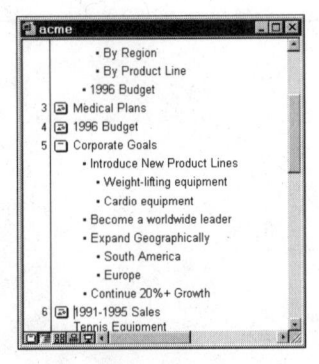

Figure 18. The pasted slide

Working in Outline View

164

WORKING IN OUTLINE VIEW

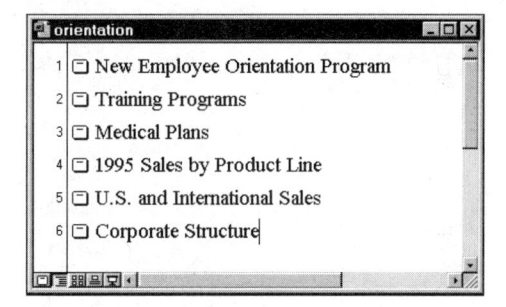

Figure 19. Typing an outline in Outline view

General tab
Presentation Designs tab

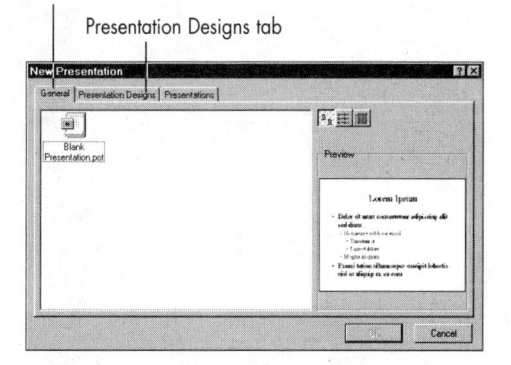

Figure 20. Creating a new presentation

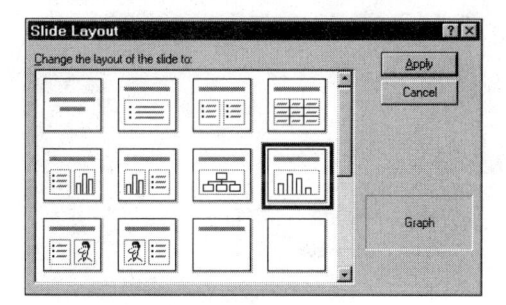

Figure 21. This dialog box lets you choose a layout for the current slide.

Outlining a Presentation

When initially creating a presentation, you may want to focus on developing the overall content and structure rather than on creating individual slides. You can do this by typing slide titles in Outline view (Figure 19).

Once you have typed your outline, you can go back to Slide view and complete each slide by choosing a type, and adding other elements.

Here are the specific steps for creating a new outline:

1. Select File/New to create a new presentation.
2. Click the General tab, and double-click Blank Presentation (Figure 20).

   or

   Click the Presentation Designs tab and choose a template.
3. Click the Outline View button.
4. For each slide, type the title and press Enter.
5. When finished, press Ctrl+Home to move the cursor to the first slide.
6. Click the Slide View button.
7. To change the layout for a particular slide, go to that slide and click the Slide Layout button at the bottom of the PowerPoint window. Choose the appropriate AutoLayout for the current slide (Figure 21) and click OK.
8. Complete the slide—for example, add a graph, table, or org chart.
9. Go to the next slide and repeat steps 7 and 8.

■ Tip

✓ As you are creating your outline, it's a good time to type any bulleted lists.
See Creating Bulleted Lists on page 162.

CHAPTER 12

Importing an Outline

If you have created an outline in your word processor (Figure 22), you can import it into an existing PowerPoint presentation, or simply open it to create a new presentation.

If you intend to import an outline into PowerPoint, you need to follow a few simple rules when typing the outline in your word processor:

- Type each slide title in a separate paragraph (that is, press Enter after each title).
- For a two-line slide title, press Shift+Enter between lines.
- Press Tab to indent bullet items (but don't insert any bullet symbols).

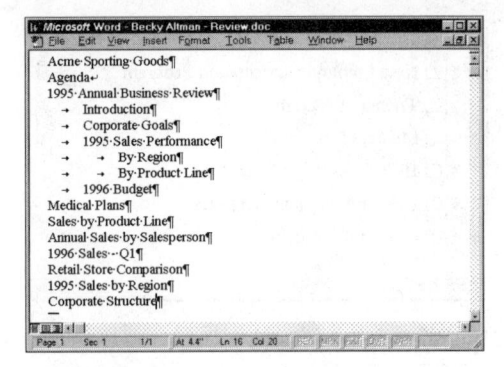

Figure 22. An outline created in Word for Windows

Inserting an Outline into an Existing Presentation

1. Select Insert/Slides from Outline. The Insert Outline dialog box appears (Figure 23).
2. Navigate to the folder in which your outline is stored.
3. Click the name of the outline file to import.
4. Click Insert.

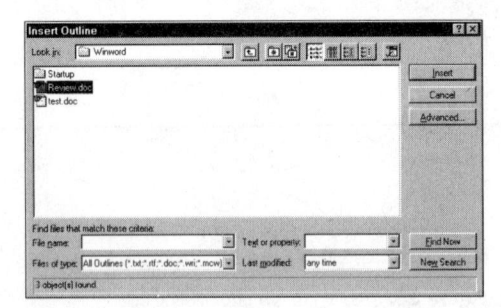

Figure 23. Inserting an outline into an existing presentation

Creating a New Presentation by Opening an Outline

1. Select File/Open.
2. In the Files of Type field, choose All Outlines (Figure 24).
3. Navigate to the folder in which your outline is stored.
4. Click the name of the outline file.
5. Click Open.

■ **Tip**

✓ PowerPoint can import outlines from a variety of word processing and spreadsheet programs; your choices depend on which import filters you selected during installation.

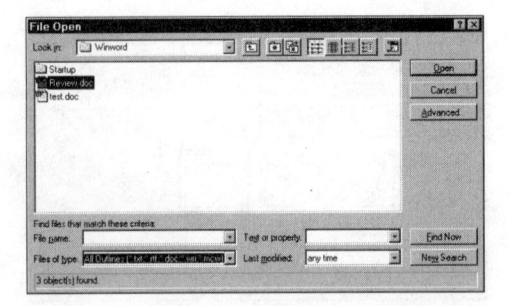

Figure 24. By opening an outline file, a new presentation is automatically created from that outline.

WORKING IN OUTLINE VIEW

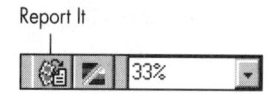

Report It

Figure 25. The Standard toolbar

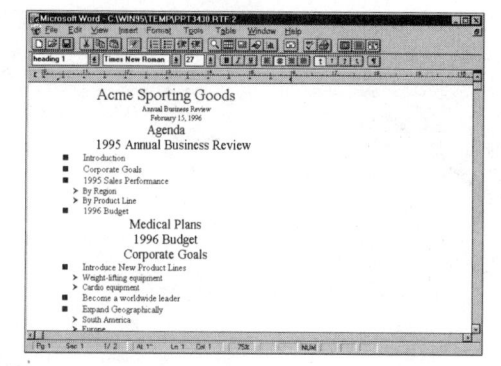

Figure 26. After you click the Report It button, the outline appears in Word for Windows 95.

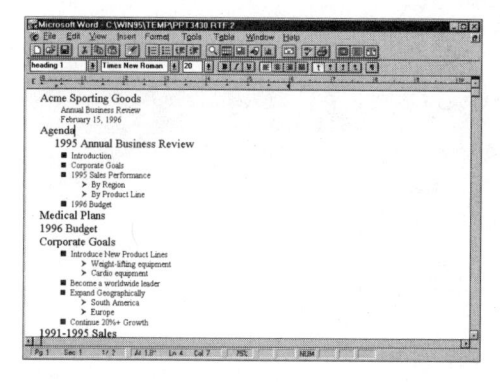

Figure 27. The formatted outline in Word for Windows

Editing an Outline in Word

If you have Microsoft Word for Windows 95, you can easily bring in a presentation's outline to edit, format, and print. You might want to do this if you want your outline to have a special format for audience handouts. Note that the changes you make to the outline do not affect your PowerPoint presentation.

1. Click the Report It button (Figure 25). The outline appears in Microsoft Word (Figure 26).
2. Edit the outline as needed (Figure 27), and print it if you like.
3. Save your changes.
4. Select File/Exit to return to PowerPoint.

■ Tips

✓ When the outline is brought into Word, each paragraph is assigned an appropriate style: Heading 1 (for slide titles), Heading 2 (for first-level bullets), Heading 3 (for second-level bullets), and so forth. By editing the styles, you can quickly reformat the entire outline.

✓ You can use Outline view in Word to reorganize, collapse, and expand the outline.

✓ Unless you specify otherwise, Word saves the outline as an .RTF (Rich Text Format) file. To save it as a Word .DOC file, use File/Save As.

167

WORKING IN SLIDE SORTER VIEW 13

Slide Sorter toolbar

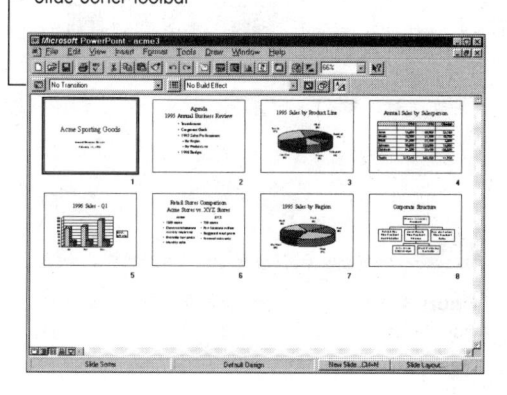

Figure 1. Slide Sorter view

Slide Sorter View

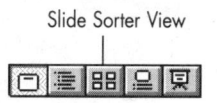

Figure 2. The View buttons

Show Formatting button

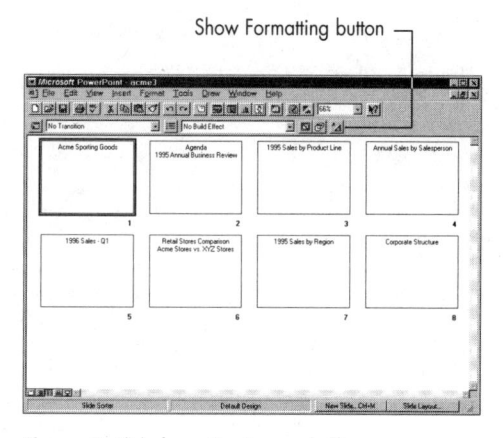

Figure 3. Slide formatting is turned off.

Introducing Slide Sorter View

Slide Sorter view shows miniatures of each slide in your presentation (Figure 1). It's similar to Outline view in that you see many slides at once, but in Slide Sorter view you have the advantage of seeing the actual slide image, including objects (graphs, tables, and so forth).

Slide Sorter view lets you observe the flow of your presentation, and reorder your slides if necessary. You can easily copy and delete slides as well. This view is also useful for copying and moving slides to other presentations. In Chapter 14, you'll see how to use Slide Sorter view to add transitions to your slide shows.

See Adding a Transition Effect to a Slide on page 184.

Switch to Slide Sorter view by clicking the Slide Sorter View button (Figure 2) or by selecting the View/Slide Sorter command. Note that Slide Sorter view has its own toolbar (Figure 1).

■ Tips

- ✓ Use Slide Sorter view when making global changes to your presentation (applying a template, changing the color scheme, etc.) so that you can instantly see the effect on all the slides.

  See Chapter 11, starting on page 147, for information on making global changes.

- ✓ Double-click a slide to jump to it in Slide view.

- ✓ Slide Sorter view runs a little faster when you don't display the slide formatting and objects (Figure 3). The Show Formatting button toggles formatting on and off.

Working in Slide Sorter View

169

CHAPTER 13

Zooming In and Out

You can control the number of slides you see in Slide Sorter view, as well as the level of detail, by zooming in and out. To see more slides, zoom out (Figure 4). To see more detail, zoom in (Figure 5).

There are three ways to zoom in and out:

- Click the arrow in the Zoom Control field (Figure 6) to display a list of zoom percentages. Then click the desired number.

    or

- Click the percentage in the Zoom Control field, type a number between 10 and 400, and press Enter.

    or

- Select View/Zoom and choose the desired zoom percentage in the Zoom dialog box (Figure 7).

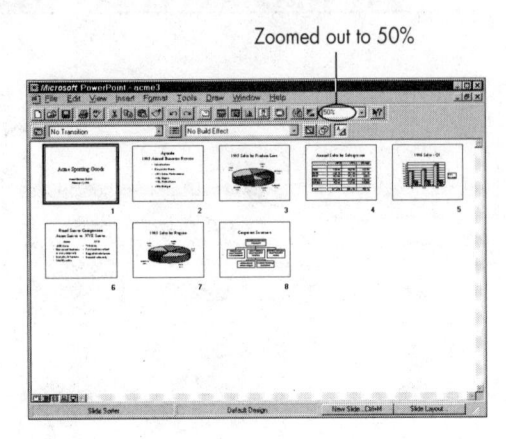

Figure 4. When you zoom out to 50%, you can see more slides at once.

Zoomed out to 50%

Zoom Control — Click here to display a list of zoom percentages.

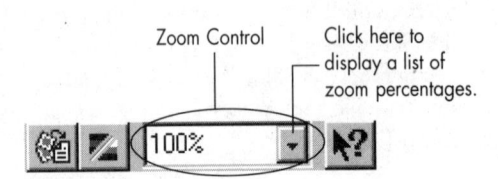

Figure 6. The Standard toolbar

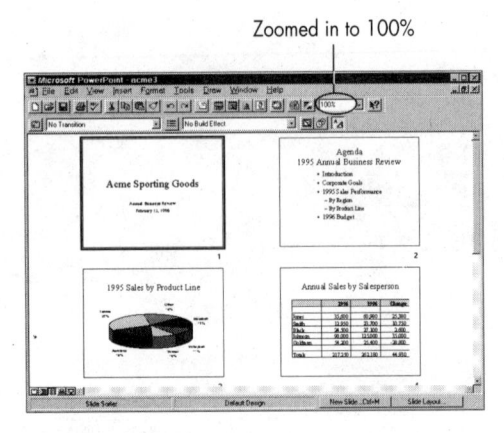

Figure 5. When you zoom in to 100%, you can see more detail on the slides.

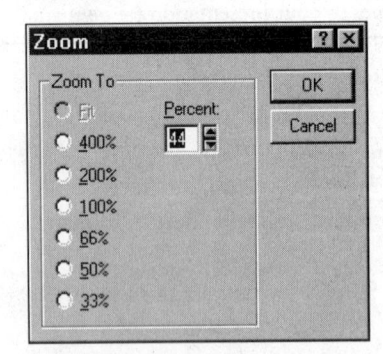

Zoomed in to 100%

Figure 7. Choose a zoom percentage, or enter any value between 10 and 400 in the Percent field.

Working in Slide Sorter View

170

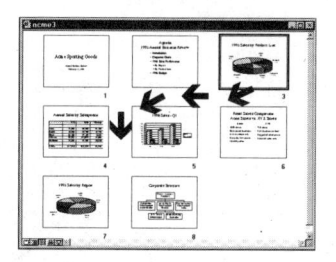

WORKING IN SLIDE SORTER VIEW

Figure 8. Using the drag-and-drop technique to move a slide

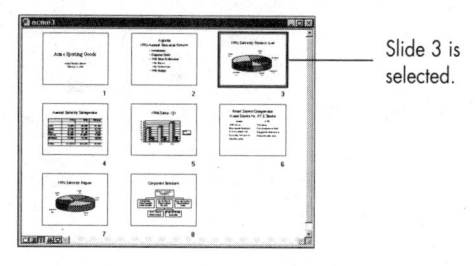

Drag slide 3 between slides 4 and 5.

Figure 9. Select a slide before cutting it.

Slide 3 is selected.

Figure 10. The Standard toolbar

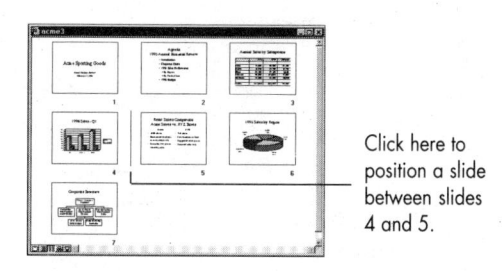

Cut   Paste

Figure 11. Position the cursor before pasting the slide.

Click here to position a slide between slides 4 and 5.

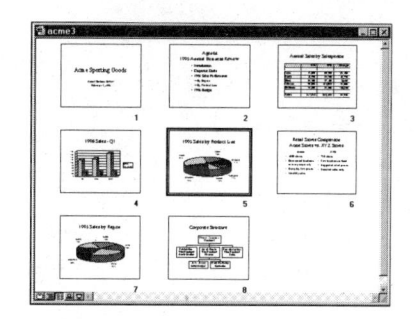

Figure 12. The pasted slide

Reordering the Slides

Because you can see many slides at once in Slide Sorter view, it is ideal for rearranging your presentation. PowerPoint offers two ways to move slides in this view.

The Drag-and-Drop Technique

1. Zoom out until you can see the slide you want to move as well as the destination.
2. Drag the slide you want to move (Figure 8). A vertical slide follows the mouse pointer to indicate where the slide will be inserted.
3. When the vertical line is in position, release the mouse button.

The Cut-and-Paste Technique

1. Click the slide you want to move (Figure 9). When a slide is selected, it is surrounded by a thick border.
2. Click the Cut button (Figure 10). The slide disappears.
3. Click between two slides where you want to move the cut slide (Figure 11). A tall cursor (the height of a slide) indicates where the slide will be inserted.
4. Click the Paste button (Figure 10) to insert the slide (Figure 12).

■ **Tip**

✓ When you reorder, the slides are renumbered automatically.

Working in Slide Sorter View

171

CHAPTER 13

Copying Slides

Sometimes you may want to create a slide that is similar to an existing one. Rather than creating the new slide from scratch, you can create a copy of the existing slide, and then make any necessary revisions.

There are three ways to copy slides.

The Drag-and-Drop Technique

1. Zoom out until you can see the slide you want to copy as well as the destination.
2. Hold down Ctrl and drag the slide you want to copy (Figure 13). A vertical line follows the pointer to indicate where the copy will be inserted.
3. When the vertical line is in position, release the mouse button.

The Duplicate Technique

1. Select the slide to be copied.
2. Select Edit/Duplicate or press Ctrl+D. A copy appears to the right of the original.
3. Drag the copy into place, if necessary.

The Copy-and-Paste Technique

1. Click the slide to be copied (Figure 14).
2. Click the Copy button (Figure 15).
3. Click where you want to insert the copy (Figure 16). A tall cursor indicates where the slide will be inserted.
4. Click the Paste button (Figure 15) to insert a copy of the slide (Figure 17).

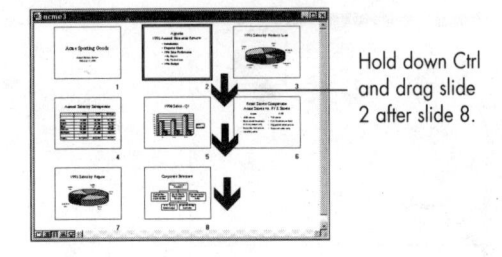

Figure 13. Copying with the drag-and-drop technique

Hold down Ctrl and drag slide 2 after slide 8.

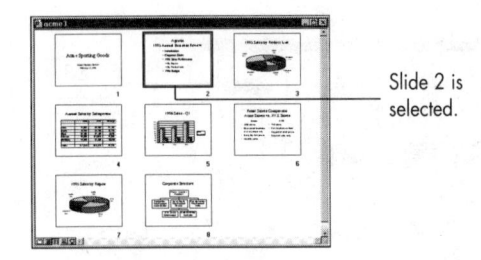

Figure 14. Select a slide before copying it.

Slide 2 is selected.

Figure 15. The Standard toolbar

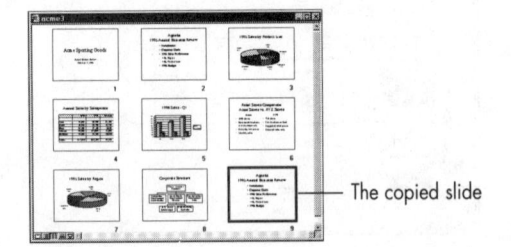

Copy
Paste

Figure 17. After pasting the copied slide

The copied slide

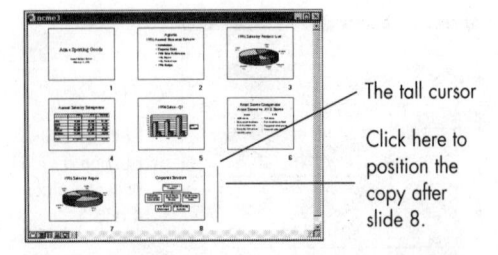

Figure 16. Position the cursor before pasting the slide.

The tall cursor

Click here to position the copy after slide 8.

Working in Slide Sorter View

172

WORKING IN SLIDE SORTER VIEW

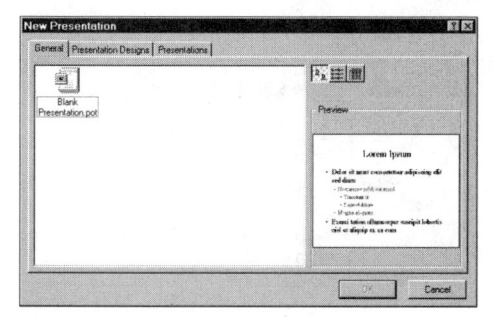

Figure 18. Creating a new presentation

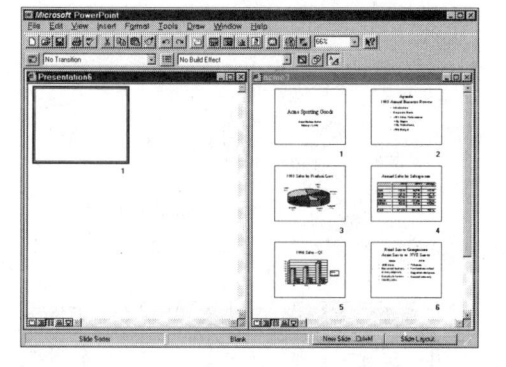

Figure 19. The new presentation is in the left window; the original presentation is in the right window.

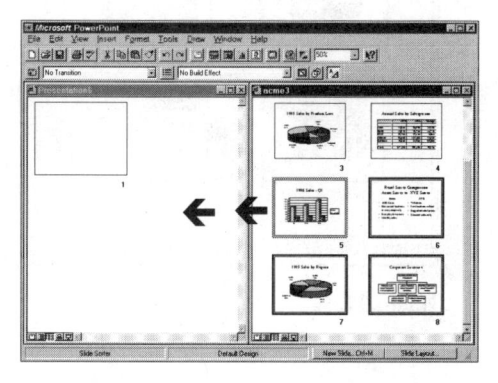

Figure 20. Select all the slides to be moved. Drag one selected slide to the other presentation, and all the others will follow.

Moving Slides Between Presentations

If a presentation gets so large that it becomes unwieldy, you may want to divide it into two or more different files. You can do this by moving some of the slides into a new presentation. Or, you may decide to move your slides into an existing presentation.

1. Open the presentation that needs to be divided, and switch to Slide Sorter view.
2. If you are moving the slides into an existing presentation, open it also.

   or

   If you are moving the slides into a new presentation, select File/New. Click the General tab, and double-click Blank Presentation.pot (Figure 18).
3. Switch the second presentation to Slide Sorter view.
4. Select Window/Arrange All to display the two presentations side by side (Figure 19).
5. Hold down Shift as you click each slide to be moved. A thick border appears around each selected slide.
6. Drag one of the slides you want to move to the other presentation window (Figure 20).
7. Release the mouse button. All selected slides are moved.

■ Tips

✓ You'll probably want the new presentation to have the same format as the original one. In the new presentation, select Format/Apply Design Template, navigate to the folder containing the original presentation file, and choose this file. The new presentation will then have the same Masters, background, and color scheme as the original.

✓ Another way to move slides between presentations is with the cut-and-paste technique.

Working in Slide Sorter View

173

CHAPTER 13

Copying Slides Between Presentations

Sometimes while working on a presentation you'll realize there are slides in another presentation that you can use in the current one. By having both presentations open at the same time (Figure 21), you can copy slides from one to the other.

1. Open both presentations, and switch to Slide Sorter view in each one.
2. Select Window/Arrange All to display the two presentations side by side.
3. Click the slide to be copied.

    or

    To copy more than one slide, hold down Shift as you click each one. A thick border appears around each selected slide (Figure 22).
4. Hold down Ctrl and drag one of the slides to the other presentation window. When the pointer is between slides, a vertical line indicates where the copies will be inserted.
5. When the vertical line is in position, release the mouse button.

■ Tip

✓ The copied slides adopt the Slide Master and color scheme of the target presentation.

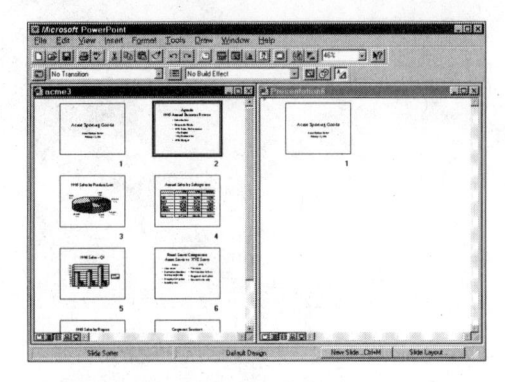

Figure 21. Side-by-side windows make it easy to copy slides between presentations.

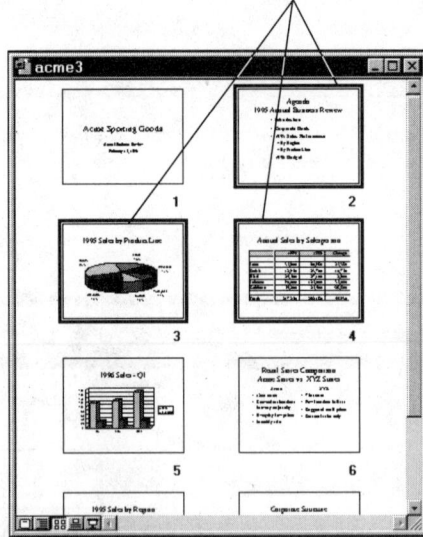

Figure 22. Selecting multiple slides

WORKING IN SLIDE SORTER VIEW

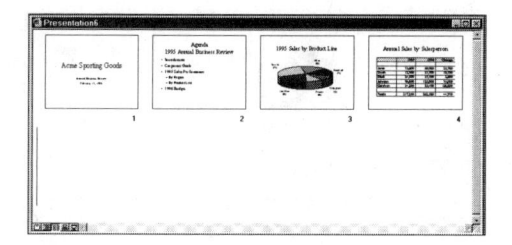

Figure 23. The target presentation currently contains four slides.

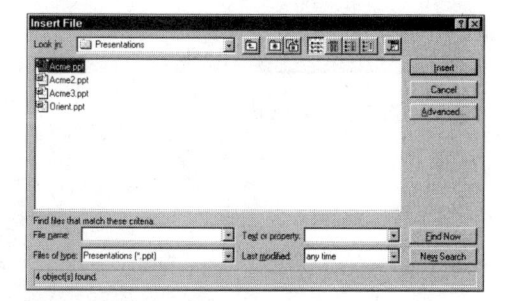

Figure 24. Selecting a presentation file to insert; the selected presentation also contains four slides.

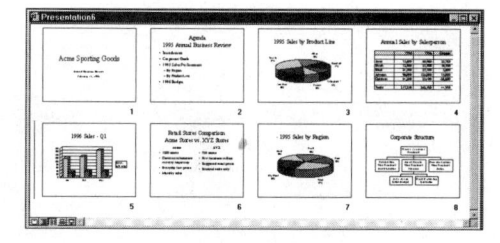

Figure 25. After inserting slides from another file, this presentation contains eight slides.

Inserting an Entire Presentation

PowerPoint offers an easy way to consolidate presentations when you want to copy all the slides from one presentation into another. This is useful when you need to combine the slides created by several individuals, into a single presentation.

1. Open the presentation into which you want to copy the slides (Figure 23).
2. In Slide Sorter view, click where you want the slides to be inserted. A vertical line appears.
3. Select Insert/Slides from File. The Insert File dialog box appears (Figure 24).
4. Navigate to the folder containing the presentation file you want to insert.
5. Select the file and click OK.

All the slides from the selected presentation file are inserted into the target presentation (Figure 25).

■ Tips

✓ The copied slides adopt the Slide Master and color scheme of the target presentation.

✓ The Insert/Slides from File command lets you copy slides from other programs, such as Harvard Graphics and Freelance.

175

CHAPTER 13

Deleting Slides

You can delete slides in any view, but doing it in Slide Sorter offers several advantages. First, you see miniatures of the slides, so you can be sure you are selecting the right ones for deletion. Second, you can delete more than one slide at a time.

1. Click the slide you want to delete.

    or

    To select multiple slides, hold down Shift as you click each one (Figure 26).

2. Press Delete or select Edit/Delete Slide.

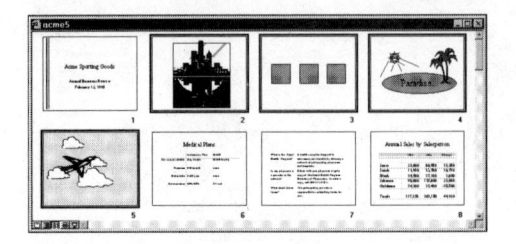

Figure 26. Four slides are selected for deletion.

■ Tip

✓ If you accidentally delete slides, immediately select Edit/Undo or use the Undo button (Figure 27).

Figure 27. The Standard toolbar

PRODUCING A SLIDE SHOW   14

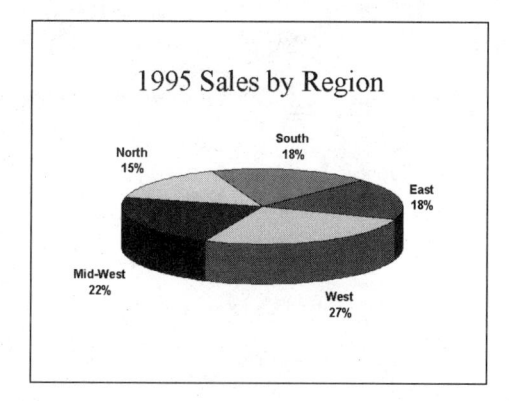

Figure 1. A slide presented full screen in a slide show

About Slide Shows

PowerPoint's *slide show* feature displays one slide at a time, full screen (Figure 1). You can use this feature to show your presentation to an audience, or merely to preview it yourself. Since your computer becomes the equivalent of a slide projector, you can see how your presentation will look to your audience. In this full-screen view, you can concentrate on individual slides, and perhaps spot mistakes you may have missed in the other views. However, you cannot edit slides during a slide show.

When you're ready for an audience, you can present your slide show directly on your monitor with one or two people looking over your shoulder; or, for a larger audience, you will want to project the show onto a big screen. Projection requires special equipment; you will need either an LCD panel and an overhead projector, or an RGB projector. Projecting a slide show in this manner saves you the time and expense of producing 35mm slides and allows you to make last-minute changes.

To spice up your slide show, you may want to add special *transition effects* for drawing slides on the screen. Blinds, checkerboards, fade, and dissolve are a few of these effects.

Because the Slide Sorter toolbar (Figure 2) contains options for slide shows, you will usually want to be in Slide Sorter view when working on your slide show.

See Chapter 13, starting on page 169, for more information on Slide Sorter view.

Figure 2. The Slide Sorter toolbar

177

CHAPTER 14

Organizing a Slide Show

During a slide show, slides are displayed in the order they appear in your presentation. Therefore, before presenting your slide show, you should give some thought to the order of your slides, and rearrange them if necessary.

To change the slide order, move the slides in Outline view (Figure 3) or Slide Sorter view (Figure 4).

See Reordering the Slides on pages 163 and 171.

To move a slide in the outline, drag the slide icon.

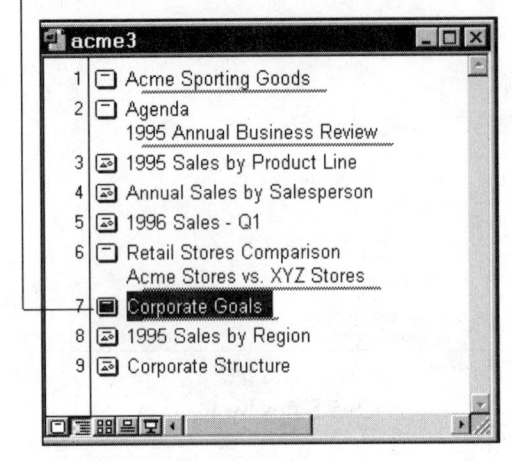

Figure 3. Using the drag-and-drop technique to move a slide in Outline view

Drag the slide to a new location.

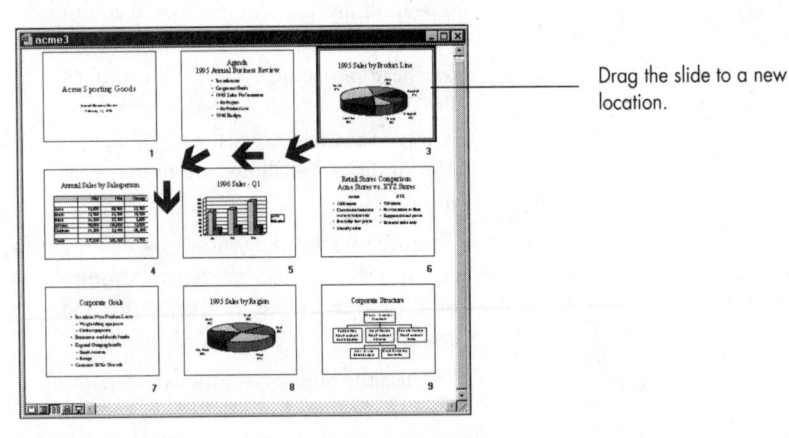

Figure 4. Using the drag-and-drop technique to move a slide in Slide Sorter view

Figure 5. The view buttons

Figure 6. Entering a range of slides to display in a slide show

Navigating a Slide Show	
Next Slide	Left mouse button
	Right Arrow
	Down Arrow
	Page Down
	Spacebar
	N
	Enter
Previous Slide	Left Arrow
	Up Arrow
	Page Up
	Backspace
	P
First Slide	Home
Last Slide	End
Specific Slide	Slide number and press Enter

Displaying a Slide Show

To view the current presentation in a slide show, do the following:

1. In any view, press Ctrl+Home to go to the first slide in the presentation.
2. Click the Slide Show button (Figure 5).
3. Press the left mouse button to view the next slide.
4. Keep pressing the left mouse button until you have viewed all the slides.

To view a range of slides, follow these steps:

1. Select View/Slide Show.
2. In the Slide Show dialog box (Figure 6), click in the From field, enter the first slide number you want to view, press Tab, and then enter the last number in the To field.
3. Click Show.
4. Press the left mouse button to view the next slide.
5. Keep pressing the left mouse button until you have viewed all the slides.

■ Tips

✓ To cancel the slide show while you're viewing it, press Esc.

✓ For a list of ways to navigate a slide show, see the boxed table to the left.

✓ To preview the current slide, just click the Slide Show button. When you're ready, press Esc to cancel the show.

✓ To jump to a specific slide in the show, type the slide number and press Enter. If you don't know the slide number, use the Slide Navigator.

See Using the Slide Navigator on the next page.

CHAPTER 14

Using the Slide Navigator

PowerPoint for Windows 95 comes with a Slide Navigator that allows you to jump to any slide in the presentation during a slide show—without having to know the specific slide number.

1. During a slide show, press the right mouse button to display the shortcut menu (Figure 7).

   or

   Place the mouse pointer in the lower-left corner of the screen and click the icon that appears (Figure 8).

2. Point to Go To and then select Slide Navigator. The Slide Navigator list appears in the middle of the screen (Figure 9).

3. Click the slide you want to view.

4. Choose the Go To button.

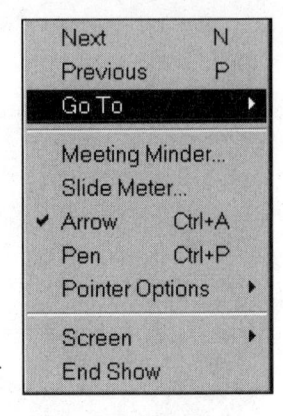

Figure 7. The slide show shortcut menu

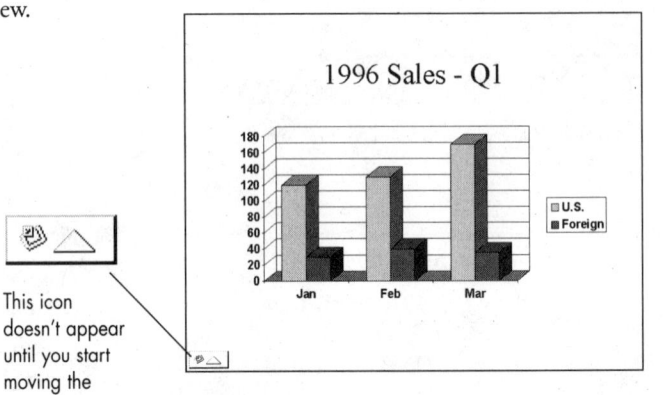

This icon doesn't appear until you start moving the mouse.

Figure 8. Another way to display the shortcut menu is to click the icon in the lower-left corner of the screen.

Click the slide you want to view.

Figure 9. The Slide Navigator

Producing a Slide Show

180

This branch button was drawn with the cube AutoShape.

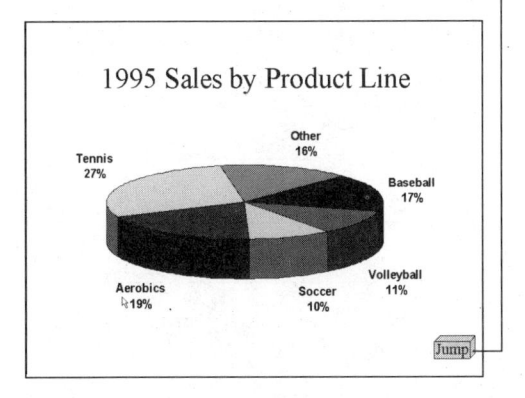

Figure 10. When you click the branch button in a slide show, a particular slide will instantly display.

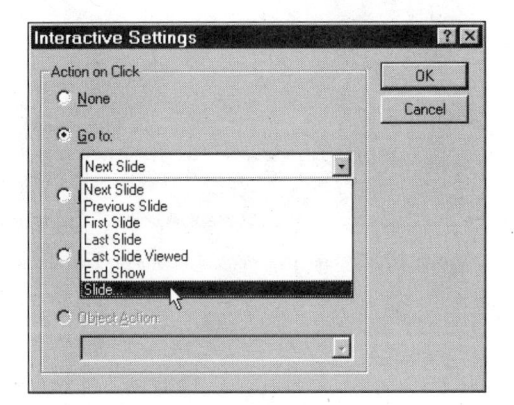

Figure 11. Assigning a destination for the branch button

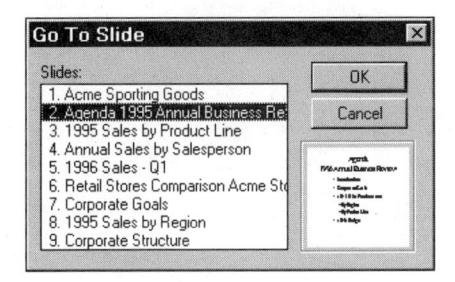

Figure 12. Choosing a slide to branch to.

Branching to Other Slides

In addition to keyboard shortcuts and the Slide Navigator, PowerPoint for Windows 95 offers another way to jump to a slide in a slide show: you can draw a button on a slide, and program it to go to a specific slide when you click on it during a show. This branching is faster and more seamless than the Slide Navigator. Branch buttons are helpful when it's likely you'll want to leap to a particular slide at a certain time during a show.

A branch button can be just about anything on the slide: a slide title, a text placeholder, a graph placeholder, a piece of clip art, or a shape you draw yourself (Figure 10).

1. Decide which object will be your branch button. (Draw one if necessary.)
2. In Slide view, select the object.
3. Select Tools/Interactive Settings.
4. Choose Go To, and display the list (Figure 11).
5. To go to a specific slide, choose Slide on the list and then select the slide title you want to go to (Figure 12). Click OK.
6. Click OK.

■ Tips

✓ During a slide show, you may want to have access to a certain slide, such as an agenda, from any slide in the presentation. An easy way to accomplish this is to create a branch button on one slide, assign the interactive settings, and then copy and paste it on each slide.

✓ The branch button can be a special one that you create specifically for this task or it can be one that is already on the slide (such as a slide title). Though using a slide title might be neater, a labeled button (such as the one in Figure 10) has an obvious purpose, and you're not likely to forget which object is your branch button.

181

Annotating a Slide

During a slide show, you may want to mark up a slide to emphasize an important point. Using your mouse like a pencil, you can draw circles, lines, arrows, and so forth (Figure 13). These annotations are temporary, and as soon as you move on to the next slide in the show, your freehand drawings disappear.

1. Press Ctrl+P to display the pen.
2. Position the pen where you want to begin drawing.
3. To draw, hold down the left mouse button and drag.
4. To turn off Annotation mode, you have three alternatives: press Esc, Ctrl+A (to see the pointer arrow), or Ctrl+H (to hide the pen or pointer).

■ Tips

✓ To erase the annotations on the slide, press E.

✓ To draw straight lines, hold down Shift as you drag.

✓ While you're in Annotation mode, you won't be able to use the mouse button to continue the slide show. Keyboard navigation keys such as the arrow keys, however, will still operate.

✓ If you're having trouble seeing your pen markings, you can choose a different pen color. During the show, click the right mouse button, point to Pointer Options, click Pen Color, and then choose a color (Figure 14).

Figure 13. The circle is an annotation that was drawn during a slide show.

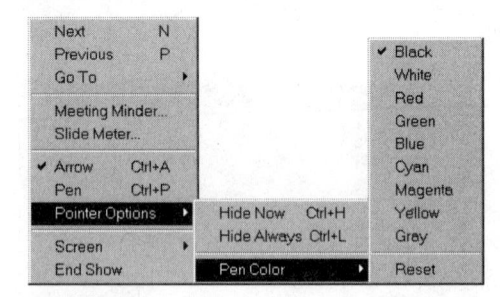

Figure 14. Changing the pen color during a slide show

PRODUCING A SLIDE SHOW

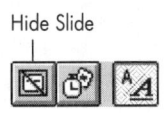

Figure 15. The Slide Sorter toolbar

Figure 16. Slide 5 is hidden.

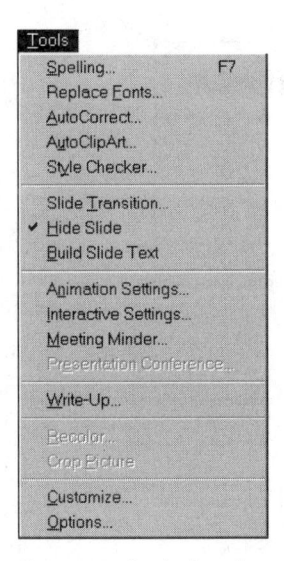

Figure 17. The check mark next to Hide Slide indicates the current slide is hidden.

Hiding a Slide

If you have a slide that you want to keep in your presentation but omit from a slide show, you can *hide* it. Hidden slides still appear in all views in your presentation, but they are skipped during a slide show.

1. In Slide Sorter view, click the slide you want to hide.

   or

   To select more than one slide, hold down Shift as you click each slide.

2. Click the Hide Slide button (Figure 15).

The slide number of a hidden slide has a slash through it (Figure 16).

■ Tips

- ✓ To redisplay a hidden slide, select the slide, and click the Hide Slide button again.
- ✓ You can hide slides in any view using the Tools/Hide Slide command. However, Outline and Slide view don't have an immediate way to tell that a slide is hidden. However, you can look for a check mark next to Hide Slide in the Tools menu (Figure 17).
- ✓ Another way to hide a slide is to right-click it in Slide Sorter view and choose Hide Slide from the shortcut menu.

183

CHAPTER 14

Adding a Transition Effect to a Slide

Transition effects control how slides are drawn on the screen during a slide show. Transition effects not only hold your audience's attention, but it also adds a professional touch.

1. Switch to Slide Sorter view (Figure 18).
2. Click the slide for which you want to add a transition effect (Figure 19).

   or

   To add the same transition effect to multiple slides, hold down Shift as you click each slide.
3. In the Slide Sorter toolbar, click the Slide Transition Effects field (Figure 19) to display the list of effects (Figure 20).
4. Click the desired transition effect.

Immediately after you choose an effect, the first selected slide is drawn with that effect, to give you an idea of what it looks like.

5. Repeat the above steps until all your slides have transition effects.
6. To see the effects during a slide show, press Ctrl+Home and then click the Slide Show button (Figure 18).

■ Tips

✓ To preview the effect chosen for a slide, click the transition icon beneath the slide in Slide Sorter view (Figure 21). When the slide is selected, the name of the effect appears in the Slide Transition Effects field in the Slide Sorter toolbar.

✓ For consistency, don't use too many different transition effects in one show. Stick with a conservative transition effect for most slides, and, if you like, emphasize certain slides with a special effect (such as a fade).

See the next page for another way to specify transition effects.

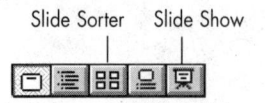

Figure 18. The view buttons

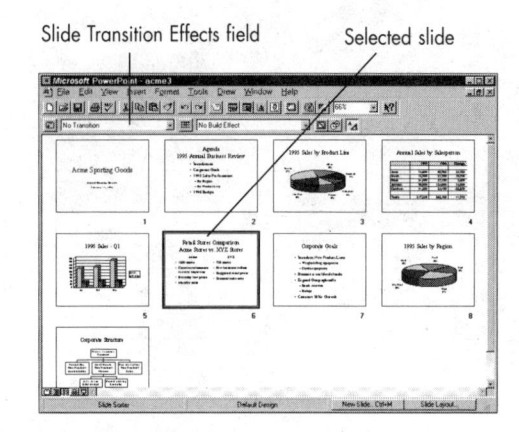

Figure 19. In Slide Sorter view, select the slide(s) and then choose a transition effect.

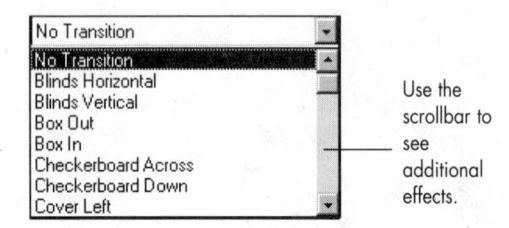

Figure 20. The list of transition effects

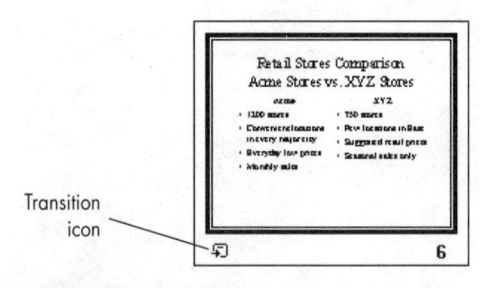

Figure 21. To preview the effect, click the transition icon.

PRODUCING A SLIDE SHOW

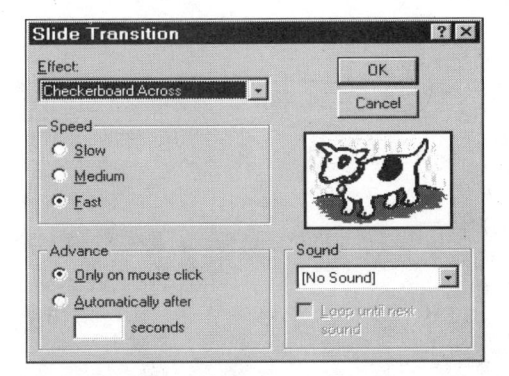

Figure 22. The Transition dialog box is another way to specify a transition effect.

Slide Transition

Figure 23. The Slide Sorter toolbar

Click here to display a list of effects.

Watch a preview of the selected transition here.

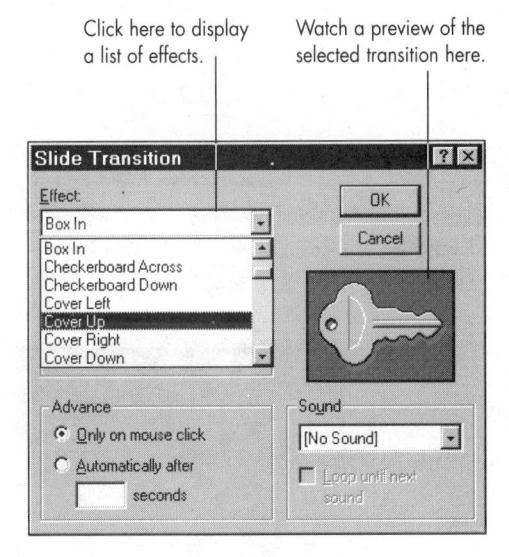

Figure 24. Choosing and previewing a transition

Adding a Transition Effect to a Slide (cont'd)

Another way to choose a transition effect is in the Slide Transition dialog box (Figure 22). This way offers two advantages: You can do it from any view (not just Slide Sorter), and you can designate a speed at which the effect is drawn on the screen.

1. In any view, select the slide(s) to which you want to add a transition effect.
2. Select Tools/Slide Transition, or in Slide Sorter view, click the Slide Transition button (Figure 23).
3. Click the Effect field to display a list of effects (Figure 24).
4. Click the desired transition effect. The preview box shows an example of how the effect looks.
5. You can click the preview box to see the effect again. If you don't like it, pick another one.
6. Choose a speed: Slow, Medium, or Fast.
7. Click OK.
8. Repeat the above steps until you have specified transition effects for all slides.
9. To see the effects during a slide show, press Ctrl+Home and then click the Slide Show button.

■ Tips

✓ To choose a single transition effect for the entire presentation, press Ctrl+A to select all the slides. Then choose a transition.

✓ It's nice to be able to control the rate at which slides are drawn on the screen during a slide show because some effects draw more slowly than others. Furthermore, the speed of your computer influences the pace as well, so you may want to slow down or accelerate the transitions.

185

CHAPTER 14

Creating a Self-Running Slide Show

If you want to sit back and watch your slide show without having to click the mouse or press keys, you can tell PowerPoint to automatically advance each slide after a certain number of seconds. Self-running slide shows are useful during trade shows, for instance.

1. In Slide Sorter view, press Ctrl+A to select all slides.
2. Click the Slide Transition button (Figure 25). The Slide Transition dialog box appears (Figure 26).
3. In the Automatically After ___ Seconds field, enter the number of seconds you want the slide to remain on the screen before the next slide is displayed.
4. Click OK. The time is indicated beneath each slide (Figure 27).
5. If you want a particular slide to remain on screen for a longer or shorter time, select it and repeat steps 2 through 4.
6. Select View/Slide Show.
7. In the Slide Show dialog box (Figure 28), choose Use Slide Timings and click Show.

■ Tips

✓ To temporarily suspend a self-running slide show, press S or the plus key (+). To continue with the show, press any key or click the left mouse button.

✓ You can always advance a slide before the specified time has passed, by clicking the left mouse button, pressing the right arrow key, etc.

✓ Choose the Manual Advance option in the Slide Show dialog box to return to the manual method of advancing slides.

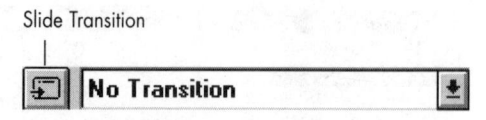

Figure 25. The Slide Sorter toolbar

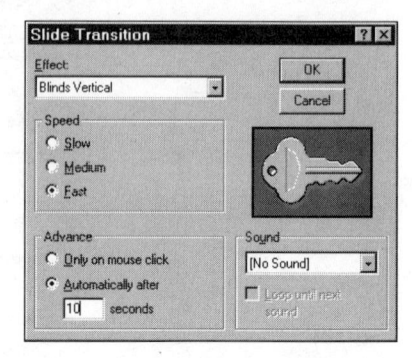

Figure 26. With these transition settings, slides will automatically advance every 10 seconds.

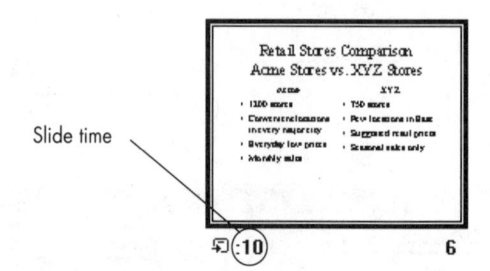

Figure 27. In Slide Sorter view, the slide time is displayed beneath each slide.

Figure 28. Starting a self-running slide show

PRODUCING A SLIDE SHOW

Rehearse Timings

Figure 29. The Slide Sorter toolbar

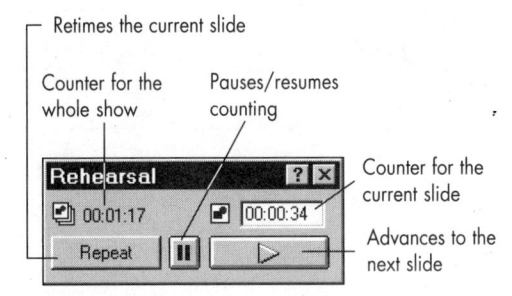

- Retimes the current slide
- Counter for the whole show
- Pauses/resumes counting
- Counter for the current slide
- Advances to the next slide

Figure 30. The Rehearsal dialog box

- Records slide timings and creates a self-running slide show

The total time for the slide show was 09:08 minutes. Record the new slide timings to see them in Slide Sorter view?

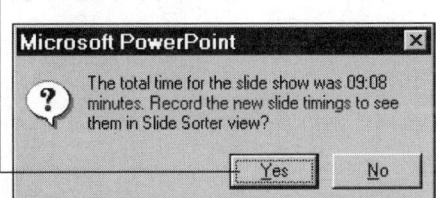

Figure 31. This dialog box lets you know the total time of your slide show rehearsal.

Rehearsing the Slide Show

To make sure your slide show is timed properly, you can have PowerPoint time your show as you rehearse it.

1. In Slide Sorter view, click the Rehearse Timings button (Figure 29). The first slide in the show appears, and the Rehearsal dialog box displays in the corner of the screen (Figure 30).
2. Either aloud or in your head, rehearse what you want to say when the slide is displayed.
3. When you are ready to advance to the next slide, click the advance button in the Rehearsal dialog box (Figure 30).
4. Repeat steps 2 and 3 for each slide.
5. When you are finished, PowerPoint displays the total time for the slide show (Figure 31) and asks if you want the slide times to be displayed in Slide Sorter view.
6. Select Yes to record the slide times or No if you don't want to record them. If you record the times, they display underneath each slide.

After recording the slide times, you have essentially created a self-running slide show. If you choose Use Slide Timings in the Slide Show dialog box when you run the show, each slide is automatically advanced after the indicated time has elapsed.

See Creating a Self-Running Slide Show on the previous page.

■ Tip

✓ On the average, two to three minutes per slide is a good pace and will keep the audience's attention. Slides that have more than three minutes worth of material can be broken up into several slides.

187

Creating a Build for a Bullet Slide

During a slide show, a *build* reveals bullet items progressively in a Bulleted List slide. By using a build, you can display each successive bullet item when you are ready to discuss it. Optionally, you can dim previous items so the current item stands out. Figures 32 through 34 show a build in progress.

1. In Slide Sorter view, select the Bulleted List slide for which you want to create a build, and choose Tools/Build Slide Text/Other.

   or

   In Slide view, select the bullet placeholder and choose Tools/Animation Settings.

2. In the Animation Settings dialog box (Figure 35), choose one of the Build Options (such as By 1st Level Paragraphs).

3. Click the arrow in the Effects field to display a list (Figure 36), and choose an effect for bullet items.

4. If you would like previous text to dim when new text appears, choose a color for dimmed text in the After Build Step field (Figure 37).

5. Click OK.

6. Click the Slide Show button. Only the slide title is displayed. To build successive bullet items, click the left mouse button.

■ Tips

✓ Another way to create or modify a build is with the Text Build Effects field (Figure 38). In this field, you can only choose an effect; you can't specify that you want to dim previous points.

✓ Use the View/Toolbars command to display the Animation Effects toolbar (Figure 39). You can then select a bullet text placeholder in Slide view, and try some of the special effects available on this toolbar. (They even include sound effects!)

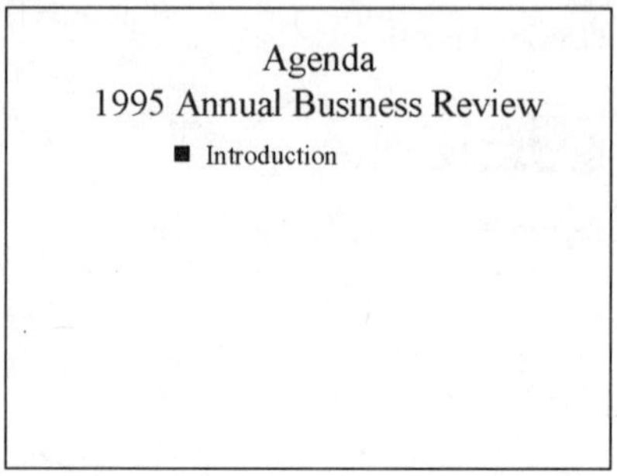

Figure 32. After the first mouse click, the first bullet item is displayed.

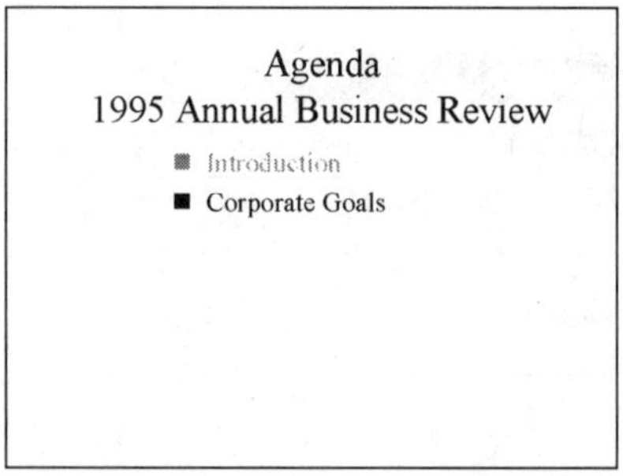

Figure 33. After the next mouse click, the first item is dimmed and the next item is displayed.

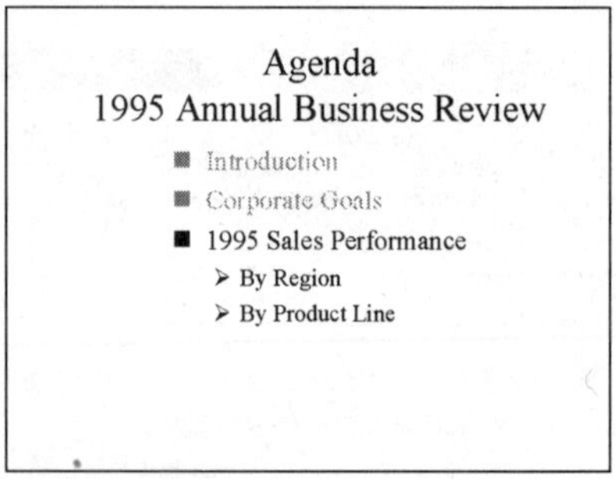

Figure 34. After the next mouse click, the previous two items are dimmed and the next bullet item is displayed.

PRODUCING A SLIDE SHOW

Creating a Build for a Bullet Slide (cont'd)

Click here to display a list of build options.

Figure 35. Creating a build

Click here to display a list of effects.

Choose an effect.

Figure 36. Choosing an effect for the build

Click here to choose a color for dimmed text.

For additional color choices, click here.

Figure 37. Choosing a color for dimmed text

Text Build Effects

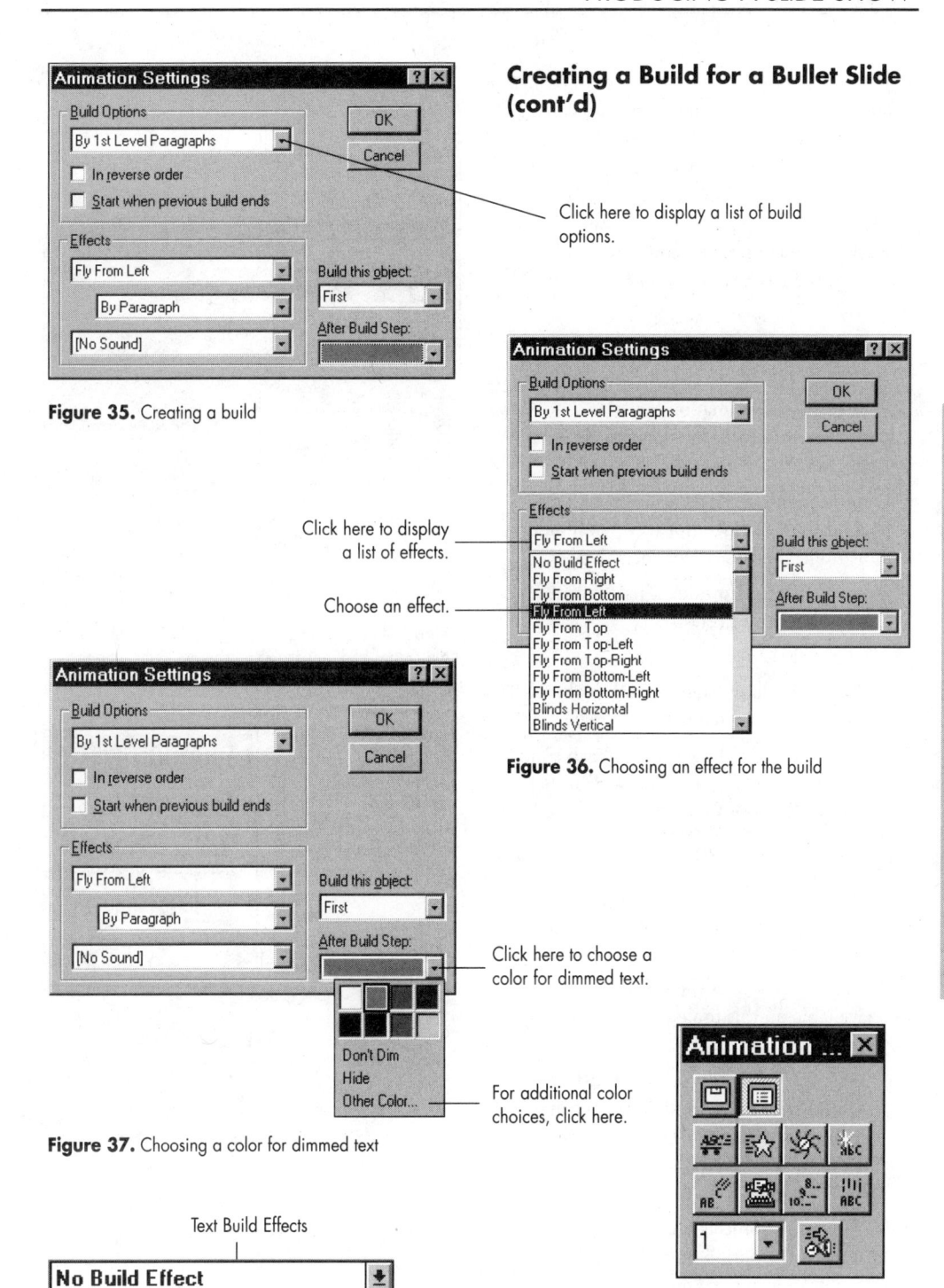

Figure 38. The Slide Sorter toolbar

Figure 39. The Animation Effects toolbar

189

CHAPTER 14

Animating Objects

Bullet lists are not the only thing you can build in PowerPoint for Windows 95. You can add a special effect to any object, achieving the appearance of animation during a slide show. Any slide object (the title, graph placeholder, pictures, and so forth) can have an effect, such as a banner flying across the screen.

1. In Slide view, select the first object you want to animate.
2. Select Tools/Animation Settings. The Animation Settings dialog box appears (Figure 40).
3. In the Build Options drop-down list, choose All at Once (for text placeholders) or Build (for other types of objects).
4. In the Effects drop-down list, choose an effect for the object.
5. Click OK.
6. Repeat the above steps for other objects you want to animate.
7. Click the Slide Show button. Each time you click the left mouse button, an animated object flies onto the screen.

■ Tips

✓ Use the View/Toolbars command to display the Animation Effects toolbar (Figure 41). You can then select an object and choose one of the special effects available on this toolbar

✓ Use the Animation Order field in the toolbar (Figure 41) or the Build/Play Object field in the Animation Settings dialog box (Figure 40) to control the order the animated objects are displayed on the screen.

✓ To have the objects build automatically, turn on the option Start When Previous Build Ends in the Animation Settings dialog box. (Do this for each object.)

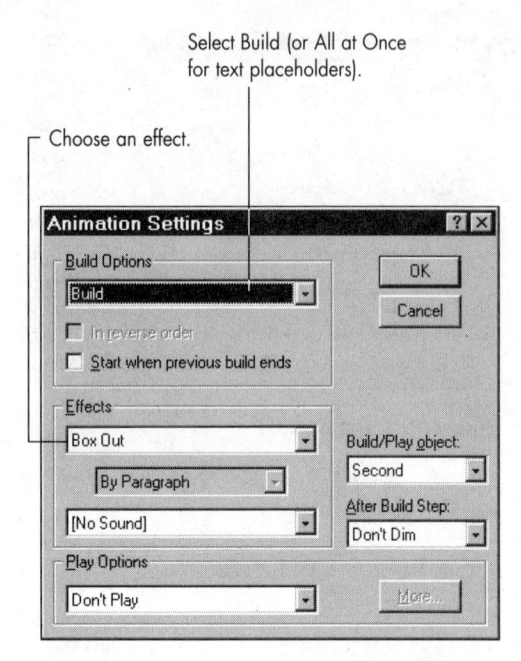

Figure 40. Choosing animation settings (Note: this dialog box changes slightly according to the type of object you have selected)

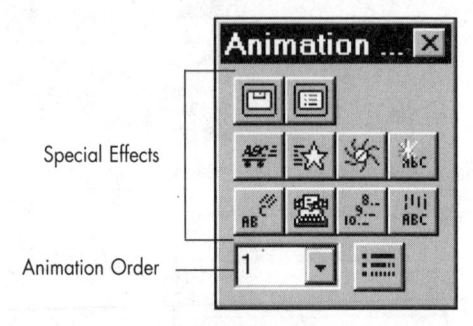

Figure 41. The Animation Effects toolbar

PRODUCING A SLIDE SHOW

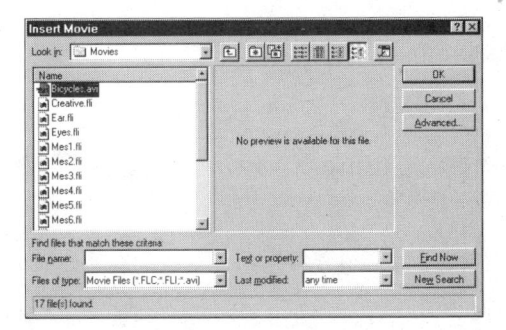

Figure 42. Choosing a movie file

Drag a selection handle to resize the movie.

Figure 43. The first frame of an inserted movie file

Figure 44. A movie playing during a slide show

Click in here to begin playing

Stops movie
Pauses movie
Drag slider to rewind or advance.

Inserting Movie Clips

PowerPoint for Windows 95 can insert movies in the Video for Windows (.AVI) format as well as the AutoDesk Animator (.FLC and .FLI) format.

1. In Slide view, go to the slide on which you want to insert a movie (or insert a blank slide).
2. Select Insert/Movie (Figure 42).
3. Navigate to the folder containing your movie file.
4. Select the movie file and click OK. The first frame of the movie appears in the center of the slide.
5. Drag and resize the movie object, as necessary (Figure 43).

To play the movie during a slide show, just click inside the movie frame (Figure 44). If you want the movie to play automatically when the slide is displayed in a slide show, follow the steps below.

1. In Slide view, click the movie object.
2. Select Tools/Animation Settings. The Animation Settings dialog box appears.
3. From the Play Options drop-down list, choose Play.
4. Click the More button. The More Play Options dialog box appears.
5. Choose Automatically.
6. Close the dialog boxes.

■ Tips

✓ If you need to edit the movie clip (for instance, to play just part of the clip), right-click the movie object and choose Edit Video Clip Object from the shortcut menu. This will launch Microsoft Media Player where you can edit the clip.

✓ Another way to insert a movie clip is by choosing the Media Clip & Text AutoLayout when you insert a new slide.

CHAPTER 14

Adding Sound

There are two ways you can add sound to your presentation. You can either insert a sound object (described below) or you can associate a sound with an existing object (explained on the next page).

Inserting a Sound Object

1. In Slide view, go to the slide to which you want to add a sound.
2. Select Insert/Sound.
3. Navigate to the folder containing your sound files (such as, c:\msoffice\sounds).
4. Select the .WAV file and click OK. A sound object appears in the center of the slide (Figure 45).
5. Drag the sound object to an empty area of the slide (such as a corner).

If you want the sound to play automatically when the slide appears, and if you want to hide the sound object during the slide show, follow these steps:

1. Make sure the sound object is selected, and select Tools/Animation Settings. The Animation Settings dialog box appears (Figure 46).
2. From the Play Options drop-down list, choose Play.
3. In the Build/Play Object field, select First.
4. Click the More button. The More Play Options dialog box appears (Figure 47).
5. Choose Automatically.
6. Turn on the Hide While Not Playing check box.
7. Close the dialog boxes.

■ Tip

✓ If you don't adjust the animation settings as described above, the sound will play only if you click the sound object during the slide show.

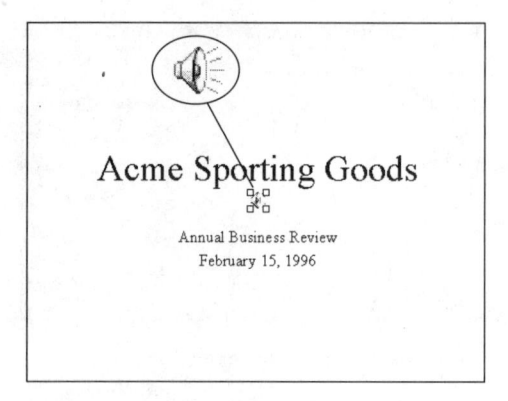

Figure 45. An inserted sound file

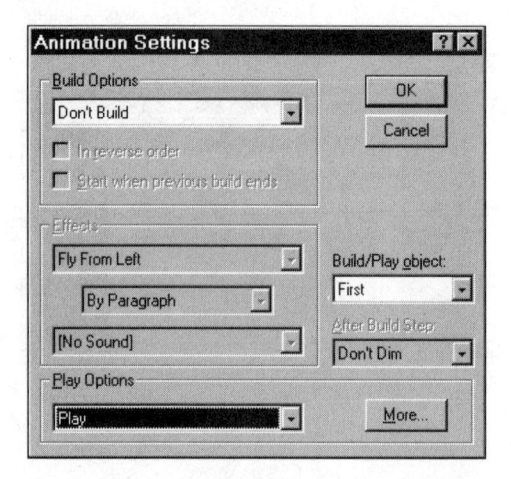

Figure 46. Specifying options for how the sound file is to be played

Figure 47. Automating the playing of a sound file

PRODUCING A SLIDE SHOW

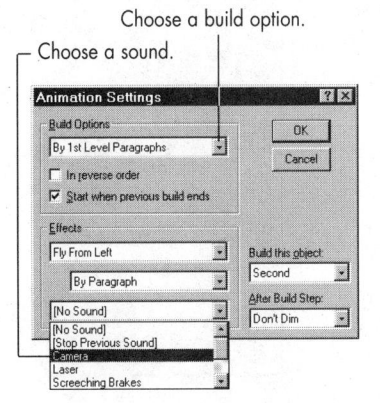

Choose a build option.
Choose a sound.

Figure 48. Adding sound to a build object

Navigate to the Sounds folder.

Figure 49. Choosing a sound file

Adding Sound (cont'd)

Another way to add sound to your slide show is during a build. For example, you can play a whoosh sound as each bullet item flies onto the screen. Or, you could play a clapping sound as a sales graph appears.

Building with Sound

1. Select an object on the slide (such as a text or graph placeholder).

2. Select Tools/Animation Settings. The Animation Settings dialog box appears (Figure 48).

3. In the Build Options drop-down list, choose the appropriate option. For bulleted text you might want 1st Level, for titles you might want All at Once, and for other objects choose Build.

4. Click the field that says [No Sound] and choose one of the sounds listed, or choose Other Sound (at the bottom of the list) to see the Add Sound dialog box (Figure 49).

5. Navigate to the folder containing your sound files.

6. Select the desired .WAV file and click OK.

7. Click OK.

During a slide show, the sound plays each time you click to build the selected object.

193

CHAPTER 14

Creating Meeting Minutes

During a slide show, you can record minutes of your meeting and then print them out.

Recording Meeting Minutes

1. During a slide show, click the right mouse button to display the shortcut menu (Figure 50).
2. Choose Meeting Minder. The Meeting Minder dialog box appears (Figure 51).
3. Make sure the Meeting Minutes page is displayed. If it's not, click the the Meeting Minutes tab.
4. Type the minutes for the current slide and click OK.
5. Repeat the above steps for each slide in your show.

Printing Meeting Minutes

If you like, you can export the minutes to a Microsoft Word file and then print them out.

1. In Slide view, display any slide for which you recorded minutes and select Tools/Meeting Minder. The minutes for the current slide appear.

   or

   During a slide show, go to Meeting Minder.
2. Click the Export button.
3. Make sure the option Send Meeting Minutes and Action Items to Microsoft Word is turned on.
4. Click Export Now. After a moment, you will see your minutes typed up and formatted in Microsoft Word (Figure 52).
5. Select File/Print and click OK.

■ Tip

✓ The Meeting Minder dialog box also has a page for your speaker notes, allowing you to refer to or edit your notes as you are giving the presentation.

See Adding Notes on page 206.

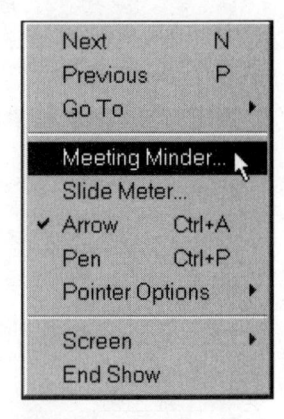

Figure 50. The slide show shortcut menu

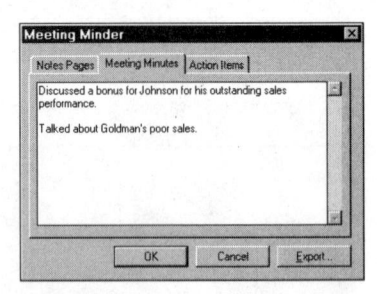

Figure 51. Recording meeting minutes

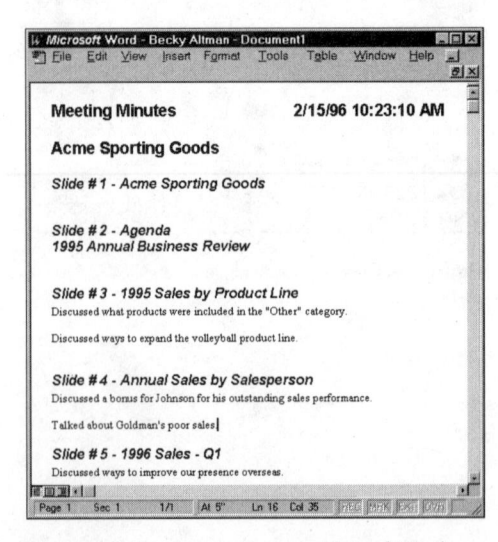

Figure 52. The meeting minutes in Microsoft Word

PRODUCING A SLIDE SHOW

Action Items tab

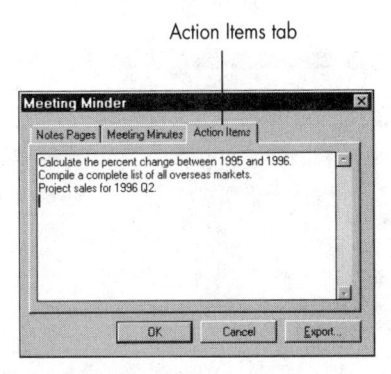

Figure 53. Create a to-do list on the Action Items page of the Meeting Minder dialog box.

Creating an Action Item List

As you are giving a slide show, you and your audience will sometimes come up ideas that need to be followed up on in the future. Using PowerPoint's new action item feature, you can create a to-do list during a show and then print it out along with your meeting minutes.

1. During the slide show, click the right mouse button to display the shortcut menu (Figure 50 on the previous page).
2. Choose Meeting Minder. The Meeting Minder dialog box appears.
3. Click the the Action Items tab (Figure 53).
4. Type the action item and click OK.
5. Repeat the above steps for each action item.

■ Tips

✓ Unlike meeting minutes, there is only one action item page for the entire presentation. However, you can add to this page or edit it at any time.

✓ PowerPoint automatically creates a Bulleted List slide of your action items and puts it at the end of your presentation (Figure 54). This slide is continually updated as you add to your action item list.

✓ Action items are printed at the end of your meeting minutes.

See the previous page for steps on printing.

Action Items

- Calculate the percent change between 1995 and 1996.
- Compile a complete list of all overseas markets.
- Project sales for 1996 Q2.

Figure 54. PowerPoint automatically creates a Bulleted List slide of your action items.

Producing a Slide Show

195

CHAPTER 14

Giving Your Presentation on Another Computer

Using PowerPoint's *Pack and Go Wizard*, you can easily copy to a floppy disk all the files that you need to run a slide show on another computer—even one that doesn't have PowerPoint. Specifically, Pack and Go Wizard copies your presentation and optionally copies *PowerPoint Viewer*, a handy utility for viewing slide shows.

1. Open the presentation you want to package.
2. Insert a formatted floppy disk in your A: or B: drive.
3. Select File/Pack And Go.
4. Follow the onscreen instructions, clicking the Next button to continue to the next step. Figure 55 shows an example of one of these dialog boxes.
5. When you've finished answering all of the wizard's questions, click Finish.

See the next page for details on showing the packaged presentation on another computer.

Click Next after answering each question.

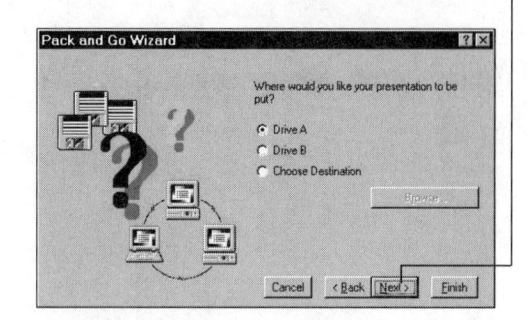

Figure 55. The Pack and Go Wizard

■ Tips

✓ In order to package the Viewer with your presentation, you need to have installed PowerPoint Viewer during setup.

✓ If you change your presentation after you package it, you will need to run the Pack and Go Wizard again.

✓ If your presentation includes linked files or TrueType fonts, and the destination computer does not have them, you can ask Pack and Go to embed them in your package.

Producing a Slide Show

PRODUCING A SLIDE SHOW

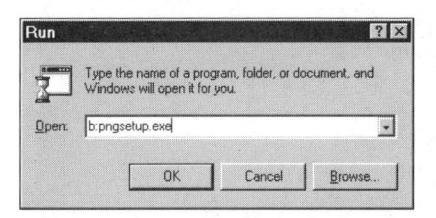

Figure 56. Running the pngsetup.exe file copies the presentation and Viewer files to another computer.

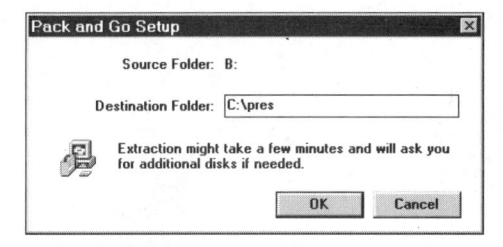

Figure 57. The destination folder can be a new or existing foler on the computer on which you are delivering your presentation.

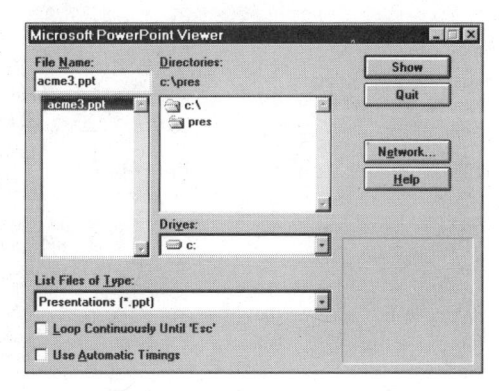

Figure 58. PowerPoint Viewer

Giving Your Presentation on Another Computer (cont'd)

The Pack and Go Wizard creates a file on the floppy disk called PNGSETUP.EXE. Executing this file will copy the necessary files onto the computer you will be using to give the presentation, and give you the opportunity to run the slide show immediately.

Showing the Packaged Presentation

1. Insert the floppy disk in the A: or B: drive.

2. In Windows 95, click the Start button and choose Run (Figure 56).

3. Type A:pngsetup.exe (or B:pngsetup.exe) and click OK.

4. Enter a destination folder for your presentation files—it can be a new one, if you prefer (Figure 57).

5. Click OK.

After the files have been "unpackaged," you'll see a message asking you if you want to run the slide show now.

6. Click Yes to run the slide show.

■ Tips

✓ So that you know everything works properly, you may want to unpackage the files before presenting the slide show to your audience.

✓ To run a slide show after the files have been unpackaged, go to the destination folder and double-click the file PPTVIEW.EXE—this is the PowerPoint Viewer program (Figure 58). Then double-click the presentation file name to begin the show.

CHAPTER 14

Giving a Slide Show: The Easy Way

How would you like to give a slide show without having to launch PowerPoint and open your presentation? There's a real easy way.

1. In My Computer or Windows Explorer, navigate to the folder containing the presentation file you want to show (Figure 59).

2. Right-click the file name and choose Show from the shortcut menu (Figure 60). The slide show begins.

3. Press the left mouse button (or any of the other slide show navigation keys) to advance to the next slide.

■ **Tip**
✓ This technique only works on computers that have PowerPoint.

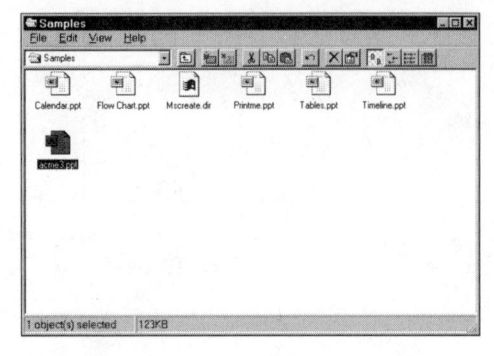

Figure 59. A folder in My Computer that contains PowerPoint presentation files

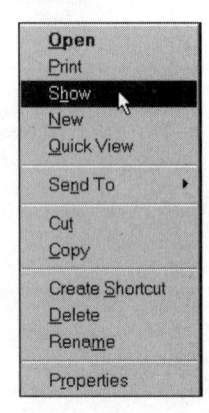

Figure 60. The shortcut menu

PRESENTATION OUTPUT 15

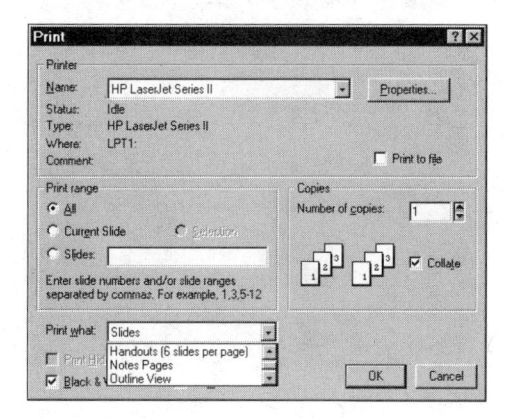

Figure 1. The types of output you can produce with PowerPoint

Types of Output

You can output your presentation to the screen (in the form of a slide show), to a printer (on paper or on overhead transparencies), or to a file (to produce 35mm slides or high-resolution output).

In the Print dialog box (Figure 1), you indicate what you want to print: slides, handouts, speaker notes, or an outline of the presentation.

Handouts are copies of your slides that the audience can use to follow along with your presentation. They can consist of either two, three, or six slides per page. Handouts are formatted on the *Handout Master* (Figure 2), where you can enter text or add background objects.

Each *notes page* contains a slide on top and notes at the bottom. Notes pages can be used to aid the speaker during a slide show, or to provide further information to the audience. You enter notes in Notes Pages view (Figure 3) and format the text on the *Notes Master*.

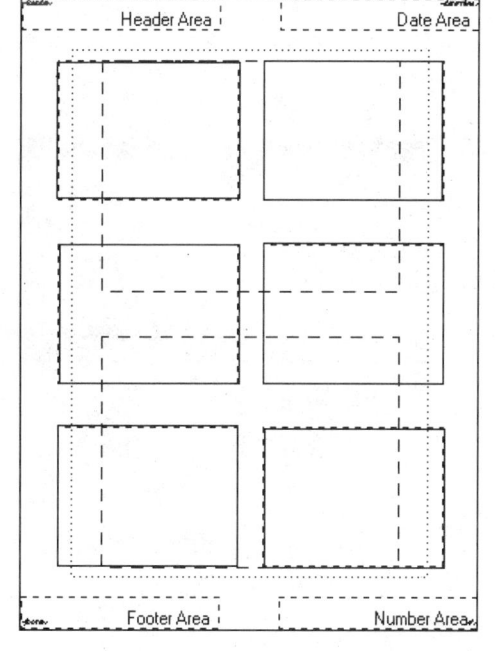

Figure 2. A Handout Master formatted with borders for six slides per page, with placeholders for a header and a footer

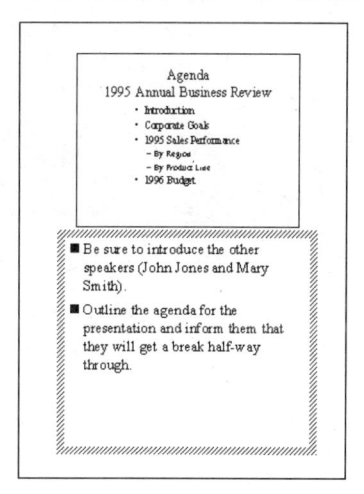

Figure 3. Notes Pages view

199

CHAPTER 15

Selecting a Printer

The Print dialog box (Figure 4) indicates the current printer. If you are connected to more than one printer and would like to specify a different one, follow these steps.

1. Select File/Print or press Ctrl+P.
2. In the Name list, choose the printer you want to use.
3. Finish filling in the Print dialog box and click OK to begin printing.

■ Tip

✓ To set printer-specific options (such as paper size), click the Properties button in the Print dialog box.

Setting the Slide Size for Printing

Before printing, make sure that your slides are set to the desired size.

1. Select File/Slide Setup. The Slide Setup dialog box appears (Figure 5).
2. In the Slides Sized For list, select Letter Paper (8.5x11 in), A4 Paper (210x297 mm), Overhead, or Custom (for other paper sizes).
3. If necessary, adjust the dimensions of the printed size in the Width and Height boxes. (Be sure to leave room for the margins on the paper.)
4. Click OK.

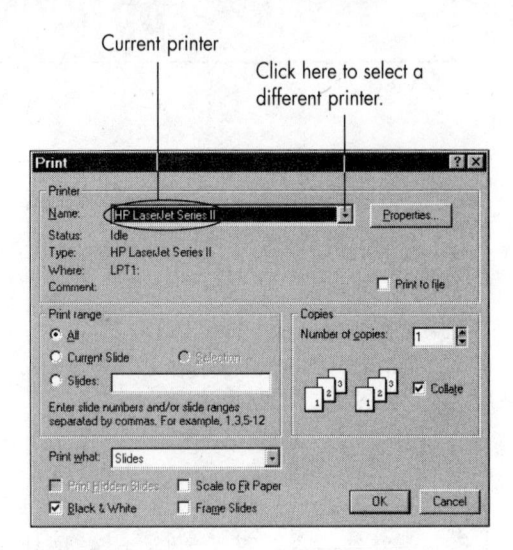

Figure 4. Choosing another printer

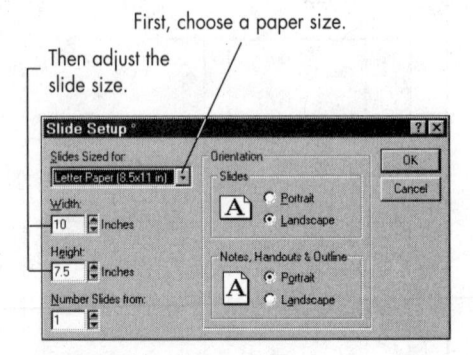

Figure 5. Setting the slide size

PRESENTATION OUTPUT

Figure 6. The Standard toolbar (B&W View indicated on the Standard toolbar)

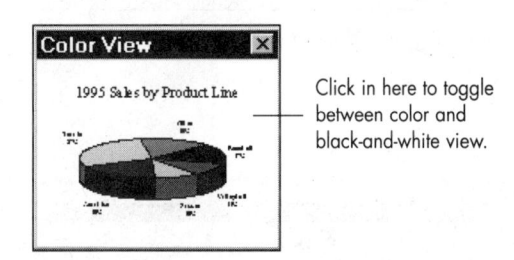

Figure 7. A slide miniature — Click in here to toggle between color and black-and-white view.

Previewing Slides in Black and White

If you are going to be printing your slides on a monochrome printer, you may want to preview them in black and white before printing. PowerPoint for Windows 95 offers an easy way to do this.

1. Select View/Black and White.

    or

    Click the B&W View button on the Standard toolbar (Figure 6).

A check mark next to Black and White on the View menu indicates this view is currently turned on.

■ Tips

- ✓ To preview your slides in color, select View/Black and White again or click the B&W View button.

- ✓ When you turn on black-and-white view, a color slide miniature (Figure 7) is automatically displayed.

- ✓ To control the gray scaling of a particular object, right-click the object and choose Black and White from the shortcut menu. Then choose one of the options (such as Light Grayscale) on the Black and White menu.

CHAPTER 15

Printing Slides

Probably the most common type of printing is full-page slides on either paper or overhead transparencies.

1. Select File/Print or press Ctrl+P to display the Print dialog box (Figure 8).

   To choose a different printer, see Selecting a Printer on page 200.

2. Under Print Range, choose All to print the entire presentation.

   or

   To print certain slides, choose Slides and then enter the range of slides you want to print. Use a dash to indicate a range of slides (as in 1-5), and a comma to indicate non-consecutive slides (as in 1-5, 7, 10).

3. In the Print What list box, choose Slides. If your presentation contains builds, choose either Slides (without Builds) or Slides (with Builds). To ignore builds during printing, choose Slides (without Builds).

4. Make sure your paper or overhead transparencies are loaded in the printer and click OK.

■ Tips

✓ Another way to specify a range of slides is by first selecting them in Slide Sorter view. Then, in the Print dialog box, choose Selection as the Print Range (Figure 9).

✓ The Print button (Figure 10) is another way to print. However, this button does not display the Print dialog box—it immediately prints the range last specified.

✓ When you print a color presentation on a black-and-white printer, PowerPoint automatically converts the colors to shades of gray.

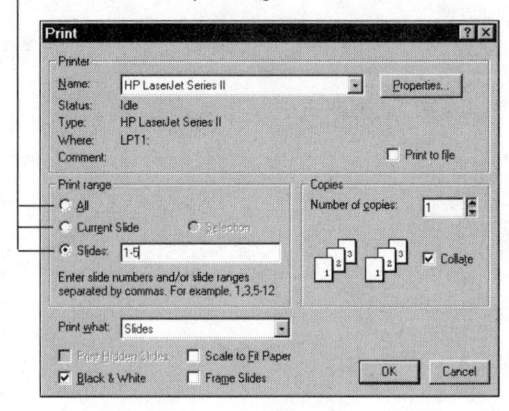

Figure 8. To display the Print dialog box, choose File/Print.

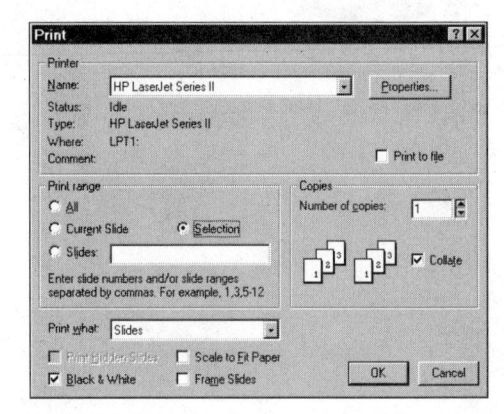

Figure 9. Choose Selection to print the slides you have selected in Slide Sorter view.

Figure 10. The Standard toolbar

PRESENTATION OUTPUT

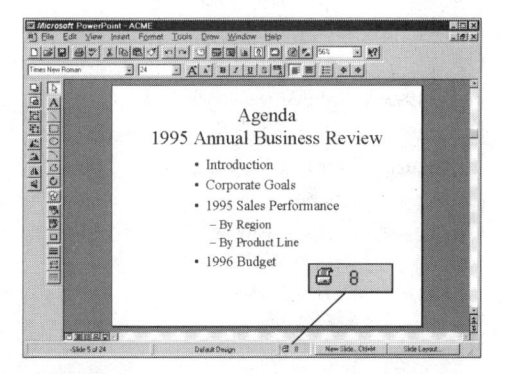

Figure 11. While the presentation is being sent to the printer, you'll see a printer icon on the status bar.

Figure 12. To stop printing while the presentation is still spooling, choose File/Print.

Double-clicking the printer icon on the taskbar displays the print queue.

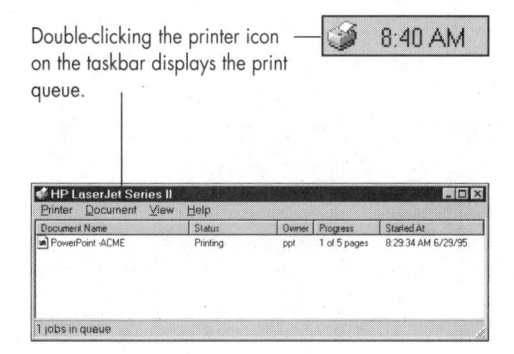

Figure 13. The print queue

Stopping a Print Job

There are two ways to cancel a print job in PowerPoint for Windows 95, depending on whether the presentation is still *spooling* (being sent to the print queue).

Canceling a Spooling Print Job

As PowerPoint spools your presentation, the status bar displays a printer icon along with the slide number that is currently spooling (Figure 11).

The easiest way to stop printing a spooling presentation is directly in PowerPoint.

1. Select File/Print (Figure 12).
2. Choose Stop Print.

Canceling a Spooled Print Job

If PowerPoint has finished spooling your presentation, you can't cancel the print job in PowerPoint—you must delete the job from the print queue.

1. Double-click the printer icon on the taskbar (next to the clock) to display the print queue (Figure 13).
2. Click the document name.
3. Press Delete.

   or

   Select Document/Cancel Printing.
4. Close the print queue window.

■ Tip

✓ Another way to cancel a spooling print job is to double-click the printer icon at the bottom of the PowerPoint window (Figure 11).

203

CHAPTER 15

Printing the Outline

You can print your presentation's outline exactly as it appears in Outline view. For instance, if only the slide titles are displayed in Outline view, only the slide titles are printed (Figure 14). Or, if the outline is completely expanded, all the slide titles and bullet items are printed (Figure 15). In addition, if formatting is hidden, the text and bullets are not formatted (Figure 16).

To get the results you want, go into Outline view and set your options—before printing your outline.

1. Switch to Outline view (Figure 17).
2. Make any of the following changes:
   - To display only the slide titles, click the Show Titles button (Figure 18). *See Collapsing and Expanding the Outline on page 161.*
   - To display the entire outline, click the Show All button (Figure 18).
   - To hide or display formatting, click the Show Formatting button (Figure 18). *See Hiding Text Formatting on page 160.*
3. Select File/Print or press Ctrl+P to display the Print dialog box.
   To choose a different printer, see Selecting a Printer on page 200.
4. In the Print What list box, choose Outline View (Figure 19).
5. Click OK to begin printing.

Figure 14. A printed outline of slide titles only

Figure 15. A printed outline of slide titles and bullet items

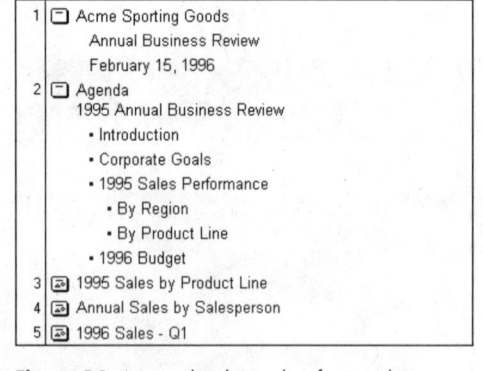

Figure 16. A printed outline with unformatted text

PRESENTATION OUTPUT

Outline View

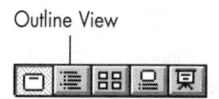

Figure 17. The view buttons

- Show Titles
- Show All
- Show Formatting

Figure 18. Outlining toolbar

Printing the Outline (cont'd)

■ Tip

✓ Another way to print the outline is to click the Print button on the Standard toolbar while you're in Outline view. (PowerPoint assumes you want to print the outline when you print from Outline view.)

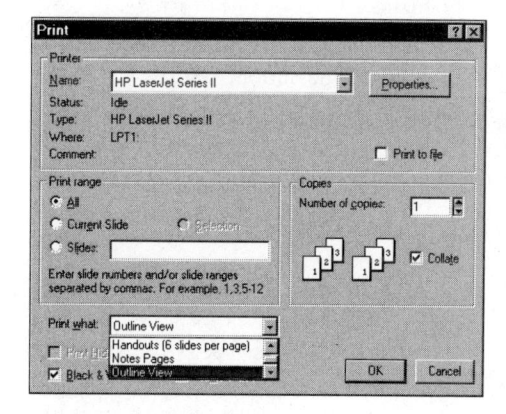

Figure 19. Printing the outline

205

CHAPTER 15

Adding Notes

To help remind yourself of what to say when you present each slide during a slide show, you can refer to *notes pages*. Each page of notes consists of a half-page slide along with the remarks you want to make when presenting that slide.

You enter your remarks in Notes Pages view (Figure 20).

1. Go to the slide for which you want to type notes.
2. Click the Notes Pages View button.
3. Click the text placeholder, and type your remarks.
4. To enter remarks for the next slide, click the Next Slide button.
5. Repeat steps 3 and 4 for each slide.

■ Tips

✓ To enlarge your text on the screen so that you can read it easily, choose a higher zoom percentage in the Zoom Control field.

✓ The default font size for note text is 12 points. You may want to choose a bigger size for easier reading in a dimly lit room during your slide show.

✓ You can view your notes pages during a slide show using Meeting Minder.
See Creating Meeting Minutes on page 194.

✓ You can also use notes pages as handouts for your audience, giving them pertinent information, with perhaps extra room to write their own notes. Or, you can add your notes to handouts pages.
See Creating Handouts with Notes on page 211.

See also Editing the Notes Master and Printing Notes Pages on the following pages.

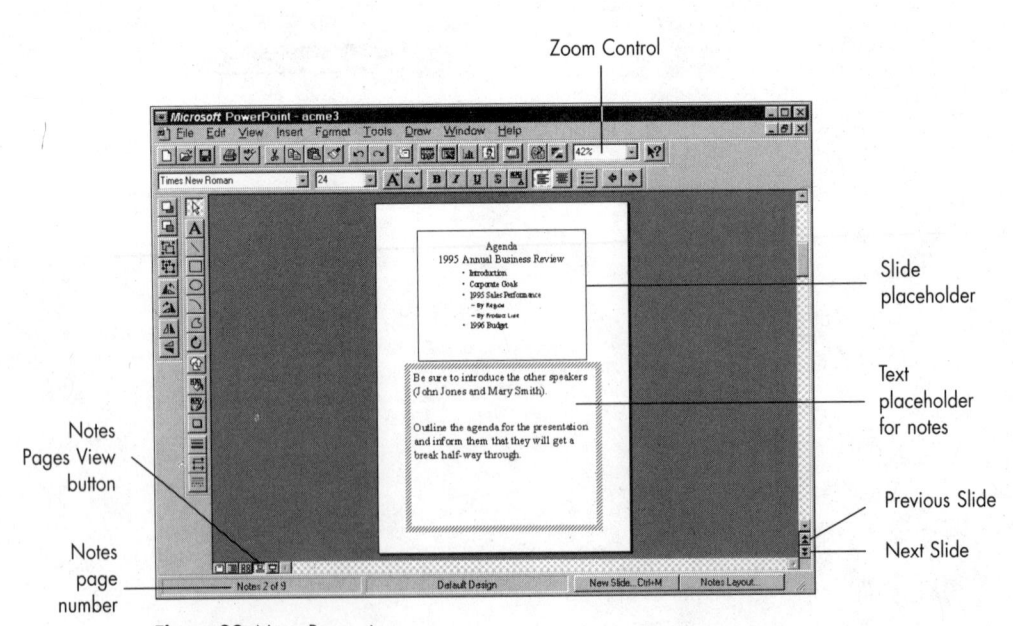

Figure 20. Notes Pages view

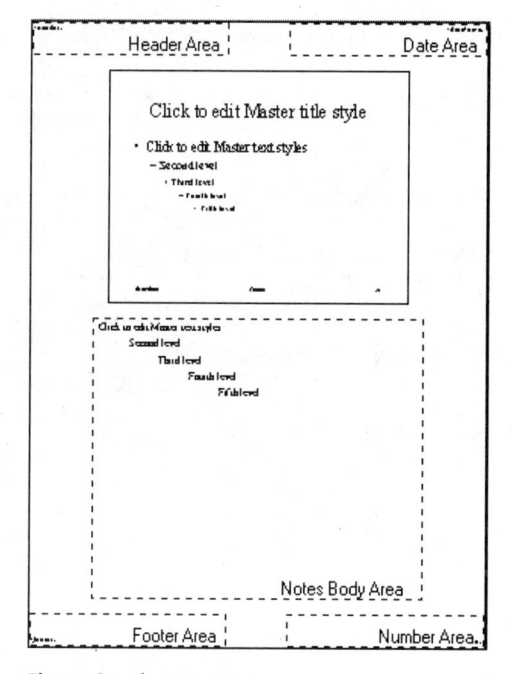

Figure 21. The Notes Master

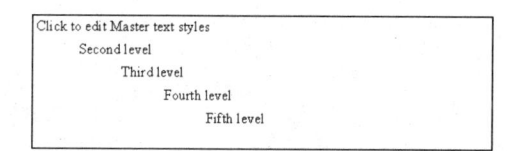

Figure 22. Zooming in on the notes area

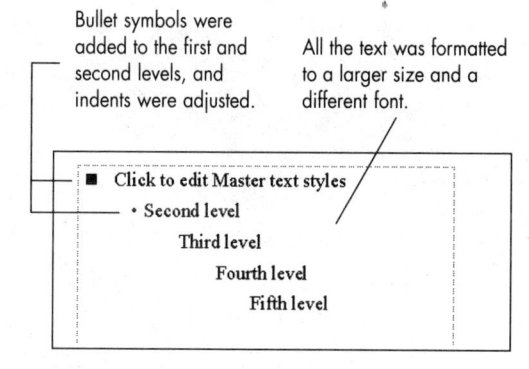

Bullet symbols were added to the first and second levels, and indents were adjusted.

All the text was formatted to a larger size and a different font.

Figure 23. A formatted notes area

Editing the Notes Master

You can perform global formatting of your notes pages on the Notes Master. (It works just like the Slide Master discussed in Chapter 11.) For instance, by editing the Notes Master, you can have bullet symbols automatically appear when you enter your notes on all notes pages. You might also want to add a page number, format the text in a different font, or resize the slide or text placeholders.

1. Select View/Master/Notes Master or hold down Shift as you click the Notes Pages View button. The Notes Master appears (Figure 21).

2. You may want to zoom in so that you can clearly see the notes area (Figure 22).

3. Make any of the following changes:

   - Adjust the size and position of the slide or text placeholders.
   See Manipulating Text Placeholders on page 33.

   - Format the text as desired—add bullet symbols, adjust indents, change the font, and so forth. Figure 23 shows the text placeholder after formatting.
   See pages 41-45 for more information on formatting text.

   - To add text that you want to appear on each page (such as the page number or presentation title), use the View/Header and Footer command.

   - Add any background graphics.
   See Chapter 9, starting on page 117, for information on adding graphic objects.

4. When finished, click the Notes Pages View button.

■ **Tip**

✓ The headers and footers you specify in the Header and Footer dialog box do not display on the Notes Master; however, you will see them in Notes Pages view.

Printing Notes Pages

Once you have typed your notes and formatted the Notes Master, you are ready to print the notes pages.

1. Select File/Print or press Ctrl+P to display the Print dialog box (Figure 24).

   To choose a different printer, see Selecting a Printer on page 200.

2. Choose All for the Print Range.

   or

   To print certain notes pages, choose Slides and then enter the range of pages you want to print. Use a dash to indicate a range of slides (as in 1-5), and a comma to indicate non-consecutive slides (as in 1-5, 7, 10).

3. In the Print What list box, choose Notes Pages.

4. Click OK.

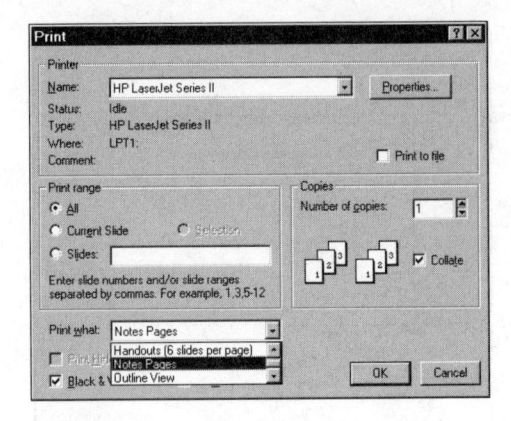

Figure 24. Printing notes pages

■ Tip

✓ You can also print your notes pages by clicking the Print button on the Standard toolbar, while in Notes Pages view. (PowerPoint assumes you want to print your notes when you print from Notes Pages view.)

Formatting Handout Pages

Handout pages are smaller, printed versions of your slides, used to help the audience follow along in your presentation. They can consist of 2, 3, or 6 slides per page. Before printing them, you may want to add titles, page numbers, or borders. You can perform all these tasks on the Handout Master.

1. Select View/Master/Handout Master or hold down Shift as you click the Slide Sorter View button. The Handout Master appears (Figure 25).

2. Make any of the following changes:
   - To add text that you want to appear on each page (such as the presentation title or page number), use the View/ Header and Footer command (Figure 26).
   - Add any desired background graphics. *See Chapter 9, starting on page 117, for information on adding graphic objects.*

3. When finished, go to a view of your choosing.

■ Tips

✓ To place borders around each slide, enable the Frame Slides check box in the Print dialog box.

✓ The headers and footers you specify in the Header and Footer dialog box do not appear on the Handout Master; you see them only on the printed handout page.

To print handout pages, see the next page.

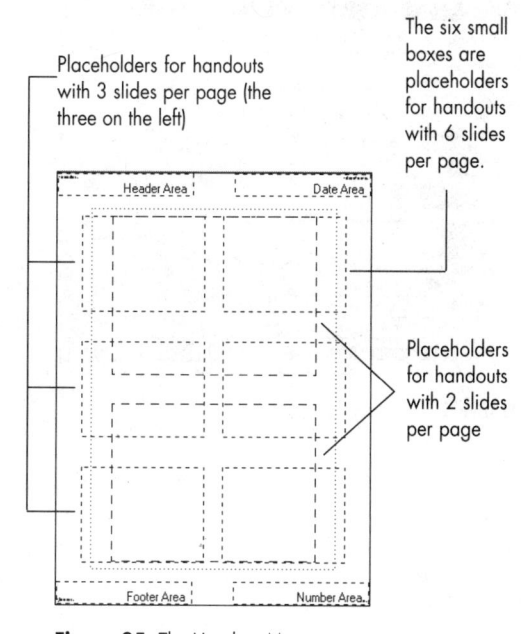

Figure 25. The Handout Master

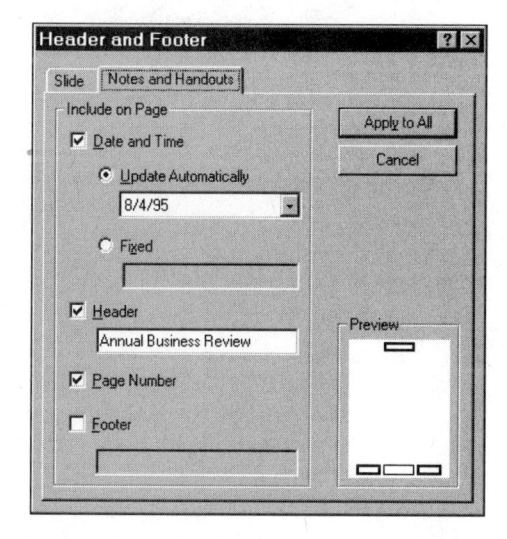

Figure 26. Specifying headers and footers on handout pages.

Printing Handouts

After formatting the Handout Master (described on the previous page), you are ready to print your handouts.

1. Select File/Print or press Ctrl+P. Figure 27 shows the Print dialog box.

   To choose a different printer, see Selecting a Printer on page 200.

2. Under Print Range, choose All to print handouts for all the slides.

   or

   To print certain slides, choose Slides and then enter the range of slides you want to print. Use a dash to indicate a range of slides (as in 1-5), and a comma to indicate non-consecutive slides (as in 1-5, 7, 10).

3. In the Print What list box, choose one of the Handouts options.

4. Click OK.

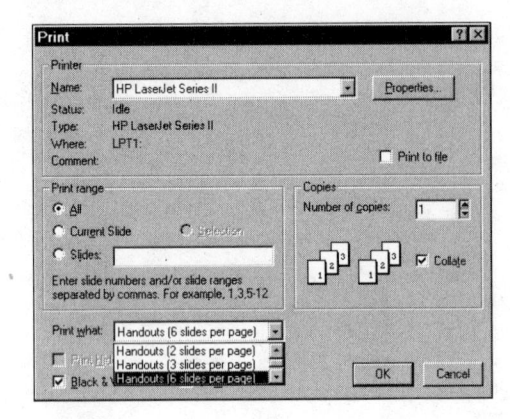

Figure 27. Printing handouts

■ Tip

✓ Don't use the Print button on the Standard toolbar, as this doesn't give you a chance to specify the handout layout (such as 3 slides per page).

PRESENTATION OUTPUT

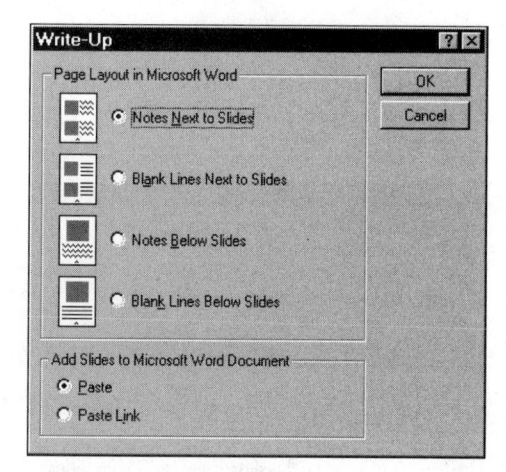

Figure 28. Decide whether you want notes or blank lines, and where they should go.

Creating Handouts with Notes

With a new feature in PowerPoint for Windows 95, you can create handouts that include your speaker notes or blank lines for note-taking.

1. Select Tools/Write-Up.
2. Choose the appropriate option in the Write-Up dialog box (Figure 28).
3. Click OK.

After a moment, your handouts will appear in Microsoft Word (Figure 29). You can format the text if you like, and then print the handouts with the File/Print command.

■ Tips

✓ You must have Microsoft Word in order to use the Write-Up command.

✓ If you want separating lines to print between the slides, select the entire table and use the Format/Borders and Shading command in Word.

These gridlines do not print.

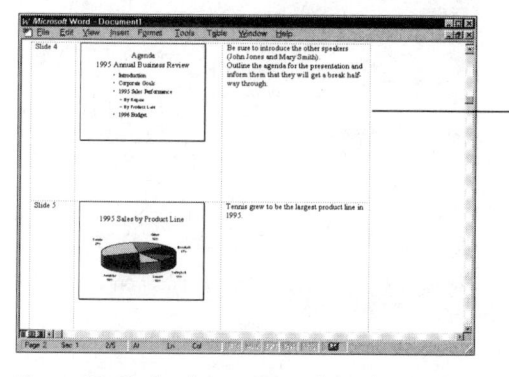

Figure 29. The handouts in Microsoft Word, using the Speaker's Notes to the Side option

211

CHAPTER 15

Producing 35mm Slides

To produce 35mm slides of your presentation, you need to specify the proper slide dimension, and then create an output file that can be used by a service bureau.

Since 35mm slides have a slightly different dimension than printed slides, you will need to change the slide size.

1. Select File/Slide Setup. The Slide Setup dialog box appears (Figure 30).
2. In the Slides Sized For list, select 35mm Slides.
3. Click OK.

PowerPoint automatically scales your slides to fit the new format.

■ Tips

✓ For highest legibility on 35mm slides, choose a dark background with a contrasting color for text.

See Changing the Default Colors in a Presentation on page 148.

✓ If you want to print the slides on paper, you don't need to change the setup again. Just enable the Scale to Fit Paper option in the Print dialog box (Figure 31).

Once your slides are ready for production, refer to the next page to learn how to prepare them for a service bureau.

When you choose 35mm Slides for the size...

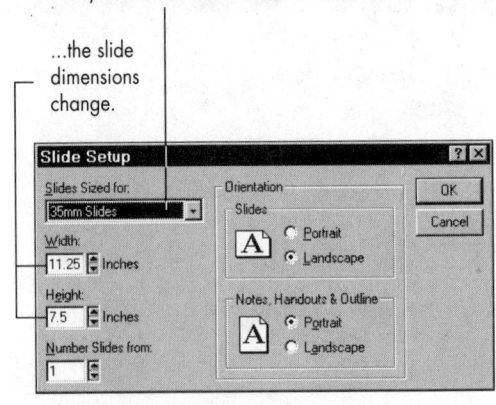

...the slide dimensions change.

Figure 30. Changing the slide setup for 35mm slides

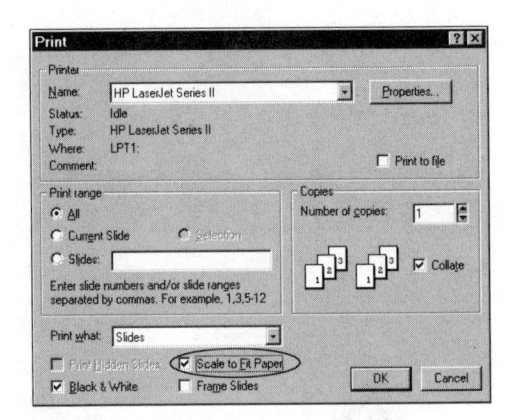

Figure 31. Enable the Scale to Fit Paper option.

PRESENTATION OUTPUT

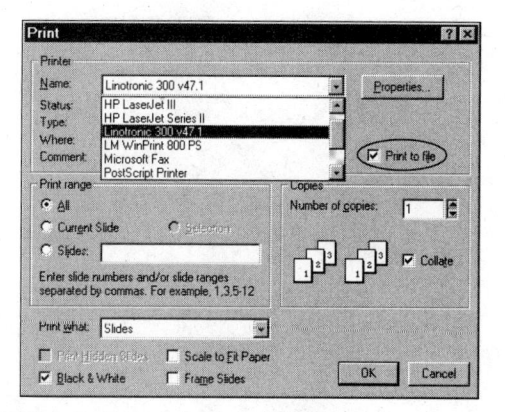

Figure 32. Select your PostScript driver and enable the Print to File check box.

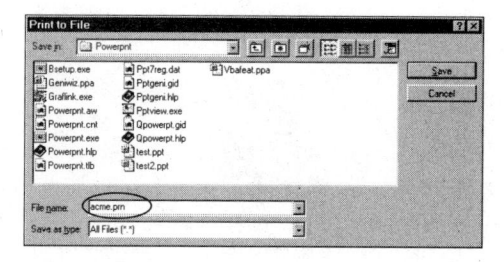

Figure 33. Enter a name for the PostScript file.

Producing 35mm Slides (cont'd)

The second step to producing 35mm slides is creating a PostScript file for a *service bureau* (a business that specializes in high-resolution production work).

You don't need a PostScript printer to create a PostScript file—you just need a PostScript driver. Your service bureau may give you a driver you can use, or you can use one of the ones included with Windows (such as a Linotronic driver). Once you have installed the driver in Windows, follow the steps below to create a PostScript file of the slides in your presentation.

1. Select File/Print or press Ctrl+P.
2. In the Name list, click your PostScript driver (Figure 32).
3. Enable the Print to File check box.
4. Click OK. You are then prompted for a file name (Figure 33).
5. Enter a file name. (If you don't type an extension, PRN is added.)
6. Click Save.

You can then copy this file to a floppy disk and take it to your local service bureau.

■ Tip

✓ To install a printer driver, go to Control Panel and double-click the Printers icon.

See the next page for information on sending your slides to a service bureau called Genigraphics.

213

CHAPTER 15

Sending Slides to Genigraphics

Included with PowerPoint for Windows 95 is a wizard that allows you to send your slides by modem to a service bureau called *Genigraphics*. This wizard not only sends your file, but it also displays order forms for your print job and generates an electronic report to accompany your presentation.

1. Open the presentation you want to send to Genigraphics.
2. Select File/Send to Genigraphics.
3. Follow the Genigraphics Wizard instructions, clicking Next after each step (Figure 34).

■ Tip

✓ Your presentation is transmitted using the GraphicsLink program (Figure 35). If you encounter trouble during data transmission, you can adjust your communication settings (COM port, baud rate, etc.) with the Edit/Communication Options command. You can then use the Connect button to retransmit.

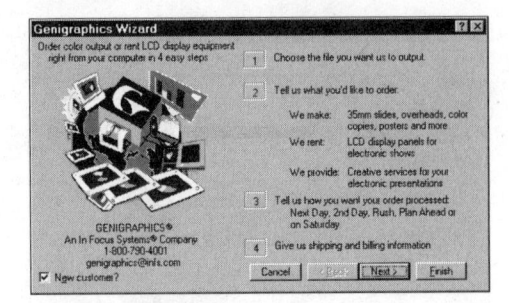

Figure 34. The Genigraphics Wizard

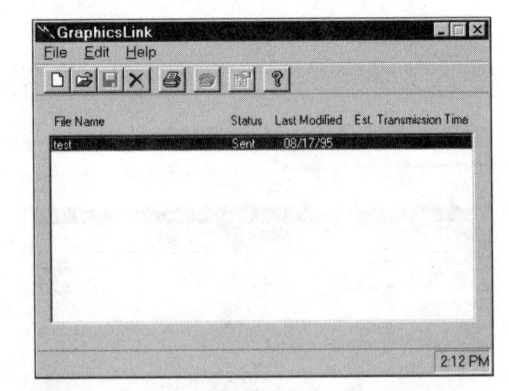

Figure 35. The GraphicsLink communications program is used to transmit your presentation to Genigraphics.

Index

Symbols

2-D charts 22, 53
3-D charts 22, 53
   formatting 70, 83
35mm slides 212, 213

A

action items 195
adding slides
   graphs 49
   organization charts 88
   pie charts 76
   tables 102
aligning
   objects 138
   text 43, 96
      in a table 114
anchor points 44
animating objects 190
Animation Effects toolbar 188, 190
annotating a slide 182
Apply Object Style command 46
Arc tool 125
arcs
   drawing 125
   filling 122
   reshaping 125
   resizing 125
arrows 119
audience handouts. *See* handouts
AutoClipart 130
AutoCorrect 36
AutoFit
   column widths in a table 106
AutoFormats
   applying built-in 22, 72
   applying custom 74
   for graphs 72
   for tables 115

AutoLayouts. *See also* layout
   choosing 19
   text 30
AutoShapes
   creating 127
   filling 122
   replacing 127
   typing text inside 127
AutoShapes button 127
AutoShapes toolbar 117, 127
axis. *See also* category axis; value axis
   adding tick marks 66
   scaling 67

B

backgrounds
   adding background items 156
   choosing a color 148
   creating a shade 150, 151
black-and-white preview 137, 201
bold 41, 69, 79, 96, 111
borders
   on a table 112, 115
   on organization chart boxes 97
branches. *See* organization charts: branches
Bring Forward command 144
Bring to Front command 144
Build Effects field 188
builds 188, 189, 190, 193
bullet items
   moving 34, 162
   selecting 34
   typing 20
Bulleted List slides
   creating in Outline view 162
   creating in Slide view 20
bullets
   changing 39
      for all slides 39, 155
   placement 40
   removing 39
By Column button 77
By Row button 77

INDEX

C

canceling
   print jobs 203
   slide shows 28, 179
case
   changing 37, 38
   sentence case 37
   title case 37
   toggle case 36, 37
category axis
   defined 48
   scaling 67
cells
   defined 50, 103
   editing 56
   selecting 105
centering
   objects 138
   text 43
Change Case command 37
chart
   depth 70
   dimension 53, 76, 85
chart type
   button 53
   choosing 22, 53, 85
   pie charts 76
Chart Type command 22, 53
ChartWizard 52
circles. *See* ellipses
clip art
   inserting 128, 130
   moving 128
   placeholder 128
   resizing 128
   searching 129, 130
ClipArt Gallery
   launching 128
closing presentations 24
co-managers. *See* organization charts: co-managers
co-workers. *See* organization charts: co-workers
Collapse Selection button 161
collapsing an outline 161
color
   changing the defaults 148
   data series 62
   fills 148
   lines 119, 148
   objects 122
   organization chart boxes 97, 98
   palette 42, 62, 81, 122, 148
   pie slices 81
   replacing 141
   scheme 148, 149, 158
   shadow 148
   slide background 148
   text 42, 148
   titles 148
Colors and Lines dialog box 119, 122
columns
   adjusting widths in a table 106
   deleting in a table 110
   inserting in a table 109
   specifying in a table 102
Copy button 172
copy-and-paste technique 172
copying
   formatting attributes 46, 140
   graph placeholders 57
   slides 172
   slides between presentations 174, 175
   text placeholders 33
creating new presentations 18, 158, 165, 173
cropping 143
Current Slide indicator 5, 23
cursor movement 31
custom AutoFormats
   applying 74
   creating 73
Cut button 164, 171
cut-and-paste technique 34, 164, 171

D

data labels
   inserting 55
      on pie charts 78
   moving 55
data markers
   formatting 63
data points
   changing the symbols 63
   defined 48
data series
   changing the color 62, 81
   changing the pattern 81

INDEX

defined 48
in columns versus rows 77
datasheet
   closing 21, 50
   displaying 21, 50, 77
   editing cells 56
   entering data 21, 50
   entering pie data 77
   erasing sample data 21, 50, 77
deleting
   boxes in organization charts 90
   rows and columns in a table 110
   slides 176
   text 31
   text placeholders 33
Demote button 162
dialog boxes
   explained 15
dimension. *See* chart: dimension
doughnut charts
   creating 85
   sizing the hole 85
drag-and-drop technique 34, 163, 171, 172
Draw menu 13
Draw/Align command 138
Draw/Group command 139
Draw/Scale command 142
Draw/Snap to Grid command 135
drawing
   arcs 125
   ellipses 121
   freehand 126
   lines 118
   polygons 126
   rectangles 120
Drawing toolbar
   4, 5, 16, 117, 118, 120, 121, 123, 125, 126, 127
Drawing+ toolbar 119, 139, 144, 145, 146
drop shadows. *See* shadow
duplicating slides 172

E

Edit menu 10
Edit/Duplicate command 172
editing
   graphs 56, 57
   tables 104
   text 31

editing cells
   in a datasheet 56
elevation of 3-D charts 70, 83
Ellipse tool 121
ellipses
   changing the size 120
   drawing 121
   filling 122
   moving 120
   typing text inside 121
embedded objects 132
emboss 42
ending slide shows 28, 179
Exclude Row/Col command 50
Expand Selection button 161
expanding an outline 161
exploding pie slices 80

F

File menu 9
File/Slide Setup command 200, 212
files
   closing 24
   creating 173
   opening 24
   printing 25
   saving 24
filling an object 122
   changing the default color 148
   removing a fill 122
first slide
   going to 23
Flip Horizontal button 146
Flip Vertical button 146
flipping objects 146
font
   changing 41
      in a graph 69, 79
      in a table 111
      in an org chart 96
   changing the default 155
   replacing 152
   size 41, 69, 79, 96, 111
   style 41, 69, 79, 96, 111
footers
   Handout Master 209
   Notes Master 207
   Slide Master 157

INDEX

Format menu 12
Format Painter 46, 140
Format Painter button 46, 140
Format/Apply Design Template command 158, 173
Format/Colors and Lines command 156
Format/Custom Background command 150, 151
Format/Shadow command 124
Format/Slide Color Scheme command 148, 149
formatting
   axis numbers 68
   copying 46
   data markers 63
   data series 62
   graph text 69
   graphs 59
   gridlines 65
   legends 60
   plot area 71
   tick marks 66
Formatting toolbar 4, 5, 16, 41, 43
formulas in a table 116
Free Rotate tool 145
freeform objects
   filling 122
Freeform tool 126
freehand drawing 126

G

gap depth 70
gap width 70
Genigraphics 214
gradient. *See* shaded background
Graph. *See* Microsoft Graph
Graph toolbar 47, 50, 51, 53, 56, 64, 77
graphic images
   inserting 131
   moving 131
   pasting 132
   resizing 131
graphs
   autoformatting 22
   creating two on a slide 57, 86
   entering data 21, 50
   formatting 22, 59
   formatting automatically 72
   inserting 21, 47, 49
   inserting titles 54

placeholders 21, 49, 76
   revising 56, 57
grid snap 135
gridlines
   defined 48
   formatting 65
   inserting 64
   removing 64
   table 103
Group button 139
grouping objects 139
   ungrouping 139
groups. *See* organization charts: groups
guides
   displaying 134
   moving 134

H

Handout Master
   defined 199
   editing 209
handouts
   defined 199
   formatting 209
   printing 210
   with speaker notes 211
headers
   Handout Master 209
Help menu 14
hiding
   formatting in an outline 160
   formatting in Slide Sorter view 169
   slides 183
   text in an outline 161
Horizontal Gridlines button 64

I

Import Data command 51
importing
   graph data 51
   outlines 166
increments on an axis scale 67
indent markers
   adjusting 40
indenting
   bullet items 20
   text in a table 114

INDEX

Insert Clip Art button 128
Insert/New Title Master command 154
Insert/Picture command 131
Insert/Slides from File command 175
Insert/Slides from Outline command 166
inserting
   boxes in organization charts 90
   clip art 128
   data labels on a graph 55
   graph titles 54
   graphic files 131
   gridlines 64
   movie clips 191
   page numbers 157, 207, 209
   rows and columns in a table 109
   slides for graphs 49
   slides for organization charts 88
   slides for pie charts 76
   slides for tables 102
   slides from an outline 166
   slides from another file 175
   sound files 192, 193
italic 41, 69, 79, 96, 111

J

justified text. *See* aligning: text

L

labels. *See* data labels
last slide
   going to 23
launching PowerPoint 17
layering objects 144
layout. *See also* AutoLayout
   Bulleted List 20
   button 5
   choosing a different 19, 30, 165
   Clip Art & Text 128
   Graph 21, 49, 76
   Graph & Text 49, 57
   Org Chart 88
   Table 102
   Text & Clip Art 128
   Text & Graph 49, 57
legends
   defined 48
   enlarging 60

   entering legend labels 50
   formatting 60
   placement 61
   removing 78
Line Color button 122
line graphs
   formatting data markers 63
line spacing 45
Line tool 118
lines
   adding arrowheads 119
   adjusting the angle 118
   adjusting the length 118
   changing the default color 148
   connected segments 126
   drawing 118
   formatting 119
   moving 118
   removing 122
linking data 52
logo
   adding to every slide 156

M

major unit on an axis 67
managers. *See* organization charts: managers
maximum axis value 67
Meeting Minder 194, 195
meeting minutes 194
menus
   displaying 7
   shortcut 7
Microsoft ClipArt Gallery. *See* ClipArt Gallery
Microsoft Graph 21, 47
   exiting 21, 47
   formatting in 59
   loading 21, 22, 47
   revising a graph 56
Microsoft Office 17
Microsoft Organization Chart. *See also*
      organization charts
   exiting 87
   loading 87, 88
Microsoft Word 194, 211
   creating tables 101
   editing outlines 167
   exiting 101
   importing outlines from 166

219

INDEX

minimum axis value 67
misspellings. *See* spelling checker
mouse
   clicking 6
   clicking and dragging 6
   double-clicking 6
Move Down button 162, 163, 164
Move Up button 162, 163, 164
movies, inserting 191
moving
   boxes in organization charts 92
   bullet items 34, 162
   data labels on a graph 55
   legends 61
   lines 118
   objects 120
   pie charts 84
   slides between presentations 173
   slides in Outline view 26, 163, 164
   slides in Slide Sorter view 27, 171
   text 34
   text placeholders 33

N

new presentations 18, 158, 165, 173
New Slide
   button 5, 49, 57, 88, 162
   dialog box 19, 20, 21, 30, 49, 88
Next Slide button 5, 23
Notes Master
   defined 199
   editing 207
notes pages
   defined 199
   formatting 207
   printing 208
   typing notes 206
Notes Pages view 199, 206
   button 5
numbers
   formatting 68, 79

O

opening
   outlines 166
   presentations 24
Organization Chart toolbar 87, 90

organization charts 87
   assistants 87
   Box tools 90
   branches 93
   co-managers 93
   co-workers 87
   colors 98
   creating 88
   deleting boxes 90
   entering text 89
   formatting box text 96
   formatting boxes 97
   formatting lines 98
   groups 93
   inserting boxes 90, 91
   managers 87
   moving boxes 92
   revising 100
   selecting boxes 93
   styles 94, 95
   subordinates 87
   zooming in and out 99
Outline view 26, 159
   bulleted lists 162
   button 5
   collapsing 161
   expanding 161
   hiding formatting 26, 160, 204
   importing an outline 166
   inserting slides 162
   moving a slide 26, 163, 164
   showing all text 26, 161, 204
   showing formatting 26
   showing only titles 26, 161, 204
   switching to 159
   toolbar 159
   typing an outline 165
Outlining toolbar 26, 160, 161, 162, 163, 205
output 199
overhead transparencies 199, 202

P

Pack and Go Wizard 196
page numbers 157, 207, 209
palette
   color 42, 62, 122, 148

INDEX

paragraphs
   aligning 43
   spacing 45
      in a table 114
Paste button 164, 171, 172
Paste Link command 52
pasting graphic images 132
patterns
   data series 62, 81
   object fills 122
percents on pie charts 78
periods
   adding and removing 37, 38
perspective of a 3-D chart 70
Pick Up Object Style command 46
pictures. *See* clip art; graphic images
pie charts 75
   3-D effects 83
   adding data labels 78
   coloring the slices 81
   creating 76
   entering data 77
   exploding a slice 80
   formatting slice labels 79
   moving 84
   resizing 84
   rotating 82
placeholders
   clip art 128
   graph 49, 76
   org chart 88
   table 102
   text 30
plot area
   formatting 71
   resizing 61, 84
   selecting 71, 84
polygons
   drawing 126
PostScript 213
PowerPoint Viewer 196, 197
PowerPoint window
   explained 4
presentation designs. *See* templates
presentation graphics
   defined 2
presentations
   closing 24
   creating 18, 158, 165, 173

displaying side-by-side 173, 174
   opening 24
   printing 25
   saving 24
Previous Slide button 5, 23
Print button 202
printers
   selecting 200
printing
   canceling a print job 203
   handouts 210
   notes pages 208
   outlines 204
   slides 25, 202
Promote button 162

R

radar graphs
   formatting data markers 63
rearranging slides. *See* moving: slides
recoloring pictures 141
Rectangle tool 120
rectangles
   adjusting the size 120
   drawing 120
   filling 122
   moving 120
   typing text inside 120
rehearsing slide shows 187
removing gridlines 64
replacing fonts 152
replacing words 36
Report It button 167
resizing
   objects 142
   pie charts 84
   text placeholders 33
revising
   graphs 56, 57
   tables 104
Rotate Left button 145
Rotate Right button 145
Rotate/Flip command 145, 146
rotating
   axis titles 54
   objects 145
   pie charts 82, 83

INDEX

rows
    adjusting heights 108
    deleting in a table 110
    inserting in a table 109
    specifying in a table 102
rulers
    adjusting column widths in a table 106
    adjusting row heights in a table 108
    displaying 40, 134
    displaying in a table 104
    indent markers 40
    indenting text in a table 114
running slide shows
    in PowerPoint 179
    on another computer 196, 197
    without running PowerPoint 198

S

Save As command 24
saving presentation files 24
scaling
    objects 142
    slides 212
scroll bar 5
    moving to other slides 23
Select All button 21, 50
selecting
    all text in a placeholder 45
    boxes in orgranization charts 93
    bullet items 34
    multiple objects 138, 139
    multiple slides 173, 174, 184
    text 31
selection box 33
Send Backward command 144
Send to Back command 144
Series in Columns command 50
service bureau 213
shaded background 150, 151
shading cells in a table 112, 115
shadow
    color 148
    organization chart boxes 97
    text 42
shapes
    drawing. *See* drawing
    filling 122
    flipping 146

resizing 120
rotating 145
typing text inside 120, 121, 127
shortcut menus 7
    for formatting graphs 59
Show Formatting button 160, 169
Show Titles button 204
slice labels
    adding 78
    formatting 79
slices
    coloring 81
    exploding 80
slide icon 159, 163, 164
Slide Master
    defined 147
    editing 153, 155, 156, 157
slide miniatures 137
Slide Navigator 180
slide shows 177
    annotating a slide 182
    branching to other slides 181
    builds for bulleted lists 188, 189
    button 5, 179
    canceling 28, 179
    navigating 179, 180
    rehearsing 187
    self-running 186, 187
    slide order 178
    timing 187
    transition effects 177, 184, 185
        speed 185
    viewing 28, 179, 198
Slide Sorter view 27, 169
    button 5
    copying slides 172
    copying slides between presentations 174, 175
    deleting slides 176
    hiding formatting 169
    moving slides 27, 171
    moving slides between presentations 173
    switching to 169
    toolbar
        169, 177, 183, 184, 185, 186, 187, 189
slide timings 186, 187
Slide Transition
    button 185, 186
Slide Transition Effects field 184

INDEX

Slide view
   button 4, 5
slides
   moving to 23
   setting the size 200, 212
Snap to Grid command 135
sounds, adding 192, 193
spacing
   line 45
   paragraph 45, 114
speaker notes. *See* notes pages
spell checking
   correcting mistakes automatically 36
   using the spelling checker 35
squares. *See* rectangles
stacking objects 144
Standard toolbar
   4, 5, 16, 24, 25, 128, 164, 167, 170, 171, 172, 176, 202, 205, 210
stopping a print job 203
Style Checker 38
styles. *See* organization charts: styles
subordinates. *See* organization charts: subordinates
subscript 42
subtypes. *See also* chart type
   choosing 53
Summary Info dialog box
   filling in 24
superscript 42
symbols
   at data points 63
   bullet 39

T

tables
   adjusting the size 102
   aligning text 114
   autoformatting 115
   borders 112
   cells 103
   column widths 106
      adjusting automatically 106
   creating 101, 102
   default size 102
   deleting rows and columns 110
   entering text into 103
   erasing cells 110
   formatting text 111
   formulas 116
   gridlines 103
   indents 114
   inserting rows and columns 109
   modifying 101
   moving the cursor 103
   paragraph spacing 114
   revising 104
   row heights 108
   rulers 104, 106
   selecting cells 105
   shading 112
   summing columns 116
templates
   applying 18, 158, 173
   button 5
   defined 147
text
   anchoring 44
   changing the default color 148
   changing the default format 155
   changing the font 41
   formatting in a graph 69
   moving 34
Text Import Wizard 51
text placeholders
   copying 33
   creating 32
   deleting 33
   entering text into 20, 31, 49
   moving 33
   moving the cursor within 31
   positioning of text inside 44
   resizing 33
text slides
   creating 29
Text tool 32
tick marks
   defined 48
   formatting 66
timing slide shows 187
Title Masters 154
title placeholders 20, 21, 49
titles
   changing the default color 148
   inserting 54
   rotating 54

223

INDEX

toolbars 16
   Animation Effects 188, 190
   Drawing
      4, 5, 16, 117, 118, 120, 121, 123, 125, 126, 127
   Drawing+ 119, 139, 144, 145, 146
   Formatting 4, 5, 16, 41, 43
   Graph 47, 50, 51, 53, 56, 64, 77
   Organization Chart 87, 90
   Outlining 159, 160, 161, 162, 163, 205
   Slide Sorter
      177, 183, 184, 185, 186, 187, 189, 190
   Standard
      4, 5, 16, 24, 25, 128, 164, 167, 170, 171, 172, 176, 202, 205, 210
   using 16
Tools menu 13
Tools/Animation Settings command 190, 191, 192, 193
Tools/AutoClipArt command 130
Tools/AutoCorrect command 36
Tools/Crop Picture command 143
Tools/Hide Slide command 183
Tools/Interactive Settings command 181
Tools/Meeting Minder command 194
Tools/Recolor command 141
Tools/Replace Fonts command 152
Tools/Style Checker command 38
Tools/Transition command 185
Tools/Write-Up command 211
transition effects 177, 184, 185
   speed 185
transition icon 184
typeface. *See* font
typing text
   bullet items 20
   in a datasheet 21, 50, 77
   in a table 103
   in an outline 162, 165
   in organization chart boxes 89
   inside a rectangle 120
   inside an AutoShape 127
   inside an ellipse 121
   inside text placeholders 20, 31
   on notes pages 206

U

underline 42
ungrouping objects 139
unindenting bullet items 20
user-defined AutoFormats 73

V

value axis
   defined 48
   formatting the numbers 68
   scaling 67
Vertical Gridlines button 64
View Datasheet button 21, 50, 56, 77
View/Black and White command 201
View/Header and Footer command 157, 207
View/Slide Show command 179, 186
View/Toolbars command 188, 190
View/Zoom command 136, 170
Viewer. *See* PowerPoint Viewer
views
   Outline 2, 5, 26, 159
   Slide 5
   Slide Sorter 2, 5, 27, 169

W

Window menu 14
Window/Arrange All command 173, 174
Wizards
   ChartWizard 52
   Pack and Go 196
   Text Import 51
Word for Windows. *See* Microsoft Word
Write-Up dialog box 211

X

x-axis. *See also* category axis
   defined 48
   labels 50
XY graphs
   formatting data markers 63

Y

y-axis. *See also* value axis
  defined 48

Z

z-axis. *See also* value axis
  defined 48
Zoom Control field 27
zooming in and out
  Microsoft Organization Chart 99
  Slide Sorter view 170
  Slide view 136

More from Peachpit Press

Microsoft Office For Windows: Visual QuickStart Guide

Steve Sagman

Microsoft Office for Windows combines the top-flight word processor (Word 6), spreadsheet (Excel 5), presentations package (PowerPoint 4), database (Access 2), and e-mail system (Mail). What's missing from this integrated suite is a quick and easy way to learn how to use each of the component applications, and then how to put them together. *Microsoft Office for Windows: Visual QuickStart Guide* uses simple step-by-step instructions and more than 1,200 screenshots that show you just how to get up and running—fast.
$17.95 *(334 pages)*

The Non-Designer's Design Book

Robin Williams

Robin Williams wrote this one "for all the people who now need to design pages, but who have no background or formal training in design." Follow the basic principles clearly explained in this book and your work is guaranteed to look more professional, organized, unified, and interesting. Full of real-life design examples. Runner-up for "Best Introductory Systems How-to Book" in the 1994 Computer Press Awards. $14.95 *(144 pages)*

Jargon: An Informal Dictionary of Computer Terms

Robin Williams with Steve Cummings

Finally! A book that explains over 1,200 of the most useful computer terms in a way that readers can understand. This book is a straightforward guide that not only defines computer-related terms but also explains how and why they are used. No need to ask embarrassing questions: Just look it up in *Jargon!* $22 *(688 pages)*

The Little PC Book, 2nd Edition: A Gentle Introduction to Personal Computers

Lawrence J. Magid

Wouldn't you love having a knowledgeable, witty, endlessly patient pal to coach you through buying and using a PC? Well, you do. Popular columnist and broadcaster Larry Magid's expertise is yours in *The Little PC Book,* described by *The Wall Street Journal* as "the class of the field." This edition includes the latest on Windows 95, the Internet, CD-ROMs, and more. Includes a handy Windows 95 Cookbook section. $17.95 *(384 pages)*

The Little Windows 95 Book

Kay Yarborough Nelson

Your guide to Windows 95. This easy, informative and entertaining volume spotlights the essentials so you can get to work quickly. Short, fully-illustrated chapters explore the Windows interface in detail, offering numerous tips and tricks. Each chapter includes a handy summary chart of keyboard shortcuts. $12.95 *(144 pages)*

Clip Art Crazy, Windows Edition

Chuck Green

Here's everything you need to incorporate sophisticated clip art into your desktop-created projects. *Clip Art Crazy* offers tips for finding and choosing clip art, along with a vast array of simple designs showing how to incorporate clip art into your documents and presentations. The CD-ROM includes almost 500 reproducible samples, culled from the archives of leading clip-art design firms. $34.95 *(384 pages w/CD-ROM)*

More from Peachpit Press

The PC Bible, 2nd Edition
Edited by Eric Knorr

Sixteen industry experts collaborated on this definitive guide to PCs, now updated to include Windows 95 and Internet access. Whether you're a beginning or advanced PC user, you'll benefit from this book's clear, entertaining coverage of fonts, word processing, spreadsheets, graphics, desktop publishing, databases, communications, utilities, multimedia, games, and more. Winner of 1994 Computer Press Award for "Best Introductory How-to" book. $29.95 *(1,032 pages)*

The Windows 95 Bible
Fred Davis

Here's absolutely everything you need to know about Windows 95, from installation and interface design to telecommunications and multimedia. This fun-to-read, easy-to-use reference is packed with detailed illustrations, plus insider tips and tricks. Reviewing the previous edition, *The New York Times* wrote, "Toss out the other Windows books. This one is the best." (Finalist, Computer Press Awards). $29.95 *(1,200 pages)*
Available Jan. '96

Corel Ventura 5: Visual QuickStart Guide
Jann Tolman

A perfect companion to the most powerful, automated, power-packed Windows publishing software available for projects of all sizes. This book uses the power of pictures to lead you through the software. With succinct, to-the-point instructions and hundreds of illustrations, complex maneuvers are reduced to a series of easy-to-follow steps. $18.95 *(320 pages)*

Windows 95: Visual QuickStart Guide
Steve Sagman

This fast-paced, easy-to-read reference guide uses the same approach that's made other books in the Visual QuickStart series so popular: illustrations dominate, with text playing a supporting role. *Windows 95: Visual QuickStart Guide* provides a thorough tour of Windows 95, from introducing the basics, to managing your computer, to communicating online with Windows 95. $14.95 *(192 pages)*

Zap! How your computer can hurt you— and what you can do about it
Don Sellers

From eyestrain to carpal tunnel syndrome, computer-related injuries are on the rise. This easy-access, well-illustrated guide explains a variety of potential hazards and what you can do to reduce your risk. Includes chapters on backache, headache, tendinitis, radiation, pregnancy, job-related stress, and much more. $12.95 *(160 pages)*

Everyone's Guide To Successful Publications
Elizabeth Adler

This comprehensive reference book pulls together all the information essential to developing and producing printed materials that will get your message across. Packed with ideas, practical advice, concrete examples, and hundreds of photographs and illustrations, it discusses planning, designing, writing, desktop publishing, printing, and distributing. "The perfect companion to almost any computer publishing or design tome." — *PC Magazine* $28 *(416 pages)*

Order Form

USA 800-283-9444 • 510-548-4393 • FAX 510-548-5991
CANADA 800-387-8028 • 416-447-1779 • FAX 800-456-0536 OR 416-443-0948

Qty	Title	Price	Total

SUBTOTAL
ADD APPLICABLE SALES TAX*
SHIPPING
TOTAL

Shipping is by UPS ground: $4 for first item, $1 each add'l.

*We are required to pay sales tax in all states with the exceptions of AK, DE, HI, MT, NH, NV, OK, OR, SC and WY. Please include appropriate sales tax if you live in any state not mentioned above.

Customer Information

NAME

COMPANY

STREET ADDRESS

CITY   STATE   ZIP

PHONE ( )   FAX ( )
[REQUIRED FOR CREDIT CARD ORDERS]

Payment Method

❏ CHECK ENCLOSED   ❏ VISA   ❏ MASTERCARD   ❏ AMEX

CREDIT CARD #   EXP. DATE

COMPANY PURCHASE ORDER #

Tell Us What You Think

PLEASE TELL US WHAT YOU THOUGHT OF THIS BOOK: TITLE:

WHAT OTHER BOOKS WOULD YOU LIKE US TO PUBLISH?

PC   PEACHPIT PRESS • 2414 Sixth Street • Berkeley, CA 94710